Ma
from
mom
12/25/85

Books by Bob Greene

CHEESEBURGERS   (1985)

GOOD MORNING, MERRY SUNSHINE   (1984)

AMERICAN BEAT   (1983)

BAGTIME (WITH PAUL GALLOWAY)   (1977)

JOHNNY DEADLINE, REPORTER   (1976)

BILLION DOLLAR BABY   (1974)

RUNNING: A NIXON-MCGOVERN CAMPAIGN JOURNAL   (1973)

WE DIDN'T HAVE NONE OF THEM FAT FUNKY ANGELS ON THE WALL
OF HEARTBREAK HOTEL, AND OTHER REPORTS FROM AMERICA
                                                    (1971)

Cheeseburgers

Bob Greene

Cheeseburgers

The Best of Bob Greene

ATHENEUM   NEW YORK   1985

Lyrics to "A Dying Cub Fan's Last Request" reprinted by
permission of Big Ears Music, Inc./Red Pajamas Music, Inc.

Library of Congress Cataloging-in-Publication Data

Greene, Bob.
    Cheeseburgers, the best of Bob Greene.

    1. United States—Social life and customs—1971-
Addresses, essays, lectures.   I. Title.
E169.04.G74   1985   973.92   85-47602
ISBN 0-689-11611-X

Published simultaneously in Canada by Collier Macmillan Canada, Inc.
Composition by Yankee Typesetters Inc., Concord, New Hampshire
Manufactured by Fairfield Graphics, Fairfield, Pennsylvania
Designed by Harry Ford
First printing August 1985
Second printing August 1985

For A. S. G.

Introduction

When I first became a newpaperman, there was a city room cliché. The reporter would come back to the office after a day of chasing a story. He would sit down, go over his notes, and craft his piece on deadline. A copyboy would take it to the city editor, who would pass it on to the copy desk, who would send it downstairs to be set in type.

And then the reporter would head for the bar closest to the newspaper building, and his colleagues would begin to come in at the end of their shifts, and they would say to him: "What really happened?" And he would tell them. The story he would relate in the bar often would bear little resemblance to the story he had just written for the newspaper; in almost every case it would be better, truer, livelier.

When I started writing a column, I made one resolution: I would try to tell the same story in the newspaper that I would want to tell my friends later on in the bar. My rule of thumb was that if I succeeded in doing that, I was succeeding as a reporter. That rule still seems to hold up pretty well.

I think of the prototypical national columnist, and I envision six hundred Washington pundits sitting back in six hundred easy chairs, sucking on six hundred pipes and spewing out six hundred great thoughts about the MX missile debate in Congress or the latest Supreme Court decision. It often seems that if a story didn't first appear on the front page of the *New York Times* or the *Washington Post*, then it just doesn't qualify as news.

I'm after something a little different. I like to think of my stories as snapshots of life in America in the Eighties—snapshots taken as I wander around the country seeing what turns up. My guiding principle is that if something interests me viscerally—as a person, not necessarily as a "journalist"—then I'll try to write about it. The nicest compliment I ever get is that my stories sound not so much like someone who is sitting down at a typewriter with something he has been assigned, but like someone who is calling his best friend at the end of the day and saying, "You'll never guess what I saw today. . . . You'll never guess who I met today."

So most of the stories in this book probably don't fit the classic definition of "news." I was curious about what the Alamo was like in the middle of the Eighties, so I went to take a look. I wanted to know what went on at the factory that manufactures Trojans, so I paid a visit. I wondered what it must be like for Frank Gifford to have walked into rooms all of his life and always to have been considered the coolest guy in every one of those rooms, so I sought him out and asked him. Stories like that. The stories come from two places: my monthly "American Beat" column in *Esquire* magazine, and my syndicated newspaper column based in the *Chicago Tribune*.

There is one story in the book that bears some amplification. In my last collection, *American Beat*, there was a story called "Reflections in a Wary Eye"—an essay about a meeting I had with Richard Nixon after he had given up the Presidency. The story consisted mostly of my reactions to spending the time with Nixon. I received many letters from people saying that they would enjoy reading, in detail, exactly what Nixon had said during the meeting. "Reflections in a Wary Eye" had originally been an *Esquire* column; I had also written a five-part newspaper series that was basically the raw transcript of my conversation with Nixon. Because so many people have expressed curiosity about it, I have put those newspaper stories together for this book; the entry is called "Nixon on Nixon." It's not a very stylish writing job, but it provides a view of the man a little different from most.

A word of explanation about the title of this book: Someone once told me that the name of a book like this—a collection—should convey the fact that it's "a bunch of things that you like a lot." That's cheeseburgers.

BOB GREENE

Contents

Contents xiii

Cheeseburgers

Remember the Alamo?

I wanted to see something real. I had had enough of the Eighties; enough of the disposable and the modern. I wanted to go somewhere that felt . . . different.

I thought about it. In all of the United States, where could I go that promised a change? Where could I go that was unspoiled by the rush of time?

It took me several days to figure it out, but when the answer came it was as clear as daybreak. The Alamo. Of course. The Alamo.

I had never been there, but it had to be perfect. I envisioned the big, legendary old mission standing out by itself on the high desert, the wind whistling over the empty miles, sagebrush bouncing along the plains. The Alamo—where for thirteen days in 1836 Jim Bowie, Davy Crockett, Colonel William Travis, and their brave companions fought off the attack of Santa Anna's Mexican troops. The Alamo—that was it. Everything else in America might be geared to let a fellow down, but the Alamo remained. I closed my eyes. I could almost see it, standing lonely sentry in the desolate heat.

4 Remember the Alamo?

. . .

I caught a midday flight to San Antonio. The trip was smooth; riding to my hotel from the airport, I thought about getting into the south Texas mood. Maybe I'd stop somewhere and have a long-neck bottle of Pearl beer. Honest, full-bodied, robust Pearl.

I looked out the window of the cab. The billboard on the right said TASTES GOOD—ONLY 68 CALORIES—PEARL LIGHT.

At the Hyatt my room overlooked the lobby atrium. It occurred to me that I had no idea how to get to the Alamo. I picked up the telephone book to see if it could give me any guidance.

From the San Antonio telephone directory:

Alamo Accessories Filter Division. Alamo Advertising Specialties Company. Alamo Aligning Service. Alamo AMC Jeep Renault Inc. Alamo Answering Service. Alamo Auto Parts. Alamo Awning. Alamo Bail Bonds. Alamo Barber & Beauty Supply. Alamo Belt & Screw Inc. Alamo Bone & Joint Clinic. Alamo Catering. Alamo Childbirth Training Association. Alamo Continuous Guttering. Alamo Dog & Cat Hospital. Alamo Fitness & Leisure Company Inc. Alamo Hearing Aid Service. Alamo Ice Cream & Delicatessen. Alamo Legal Clinic. Alamo Limousine Service Inc. Alamo Maid Service. Alamo Pawn Shop. Alamo Pecan Co. Alamo Ready Mix Concrete Inc. Alamo Rent A Car. Alamo Spring Co. Alamo Toyota. Alamo Uniforms. Alamo Welding & Boiler Works Inc. Alamo Wheel Aligning.

I went downstairs and asked the doorman how I would get out to the Alamo, and if he could arrange transportation for me. I said I'd need a way to get back, too; I didn't want to be stranded out on the desert.

He smiled a curious smile at me.

"Just walk over to the next block," he said. "It's right across from Woolworth's."

"What's right across from Woolworth's?" I said.

"The Alamo," he said.

I walked a block. There, across from Woolworth's, was the Alamo.

It was right downtown. In addition to Woolworth's, the edifices that surrounded the Alamo included the H. L. Green Variety Store, the G/M Steak House, the Big Apple unisex jeans store, Maldonado Jewelers, and Texas State Optical.

In front of the Alamo itself was Vasquez's Snow-Kone stand.

Next to Vasquez's Snow-Kone stand was a vending box for *USA Today.*

I entered the Alamo. It was tiny. It felt like a one-room schoolhouse. It was dwarfed by the rest of downtown San Antonio.

My fellow tourists included young women wearing Walkman headsets, and young men carrying tape players the size of suitcases. Most of the visitors wore T-shirts; the printing on the front of the shirts featured promotional slogans for the Incredible Hulk, for "M*A*S*H," for Nike running shoes, for the Men at Work '83 North American Tour.

A woman from the Daughters of the Republic of Texas handed out Alamo pamphlets. There was a sign advising GENTLEMEN REMOVE HATS, but the sign was widely ignored; males inside the Alamo favored baseball-style caps bearing the trademarks of Caterpillar tractors and International Harvester farm machinery, and the logo of the Johnson Space Center.

There was a courtyard outside the Alamo. I ran into a family in the midst of an argument. The son was blasting a song called "Ride Like the Wind" from his tape box; his mother, carrying a camera with faces of Mickey Mouse on the strap, and wearing a T-shirt bearing Elvis's face and the words THE KING LIVES ON, was telling him that he had to keep the tape turned off.

"Didn't you see the sign that said 'Quiet, please'?" she said.
"That was for the library, dummy," he said.

In the courtyard of the Alamo were two soft-drink machines—one Pepsi, one Coke. I walked toward them, passing on the way three babies in blue canvas Aprica strollers.

Apparently not even the Alamo is safe from jitters about crime. On the Pepsi machine, a red-and-white sign advised: NOTICE—ALL MONEY REMOVED FROM THIS MACHINE DAILY.

Back inside the Alamo I walked over the flagstone floor and stopped in front of a case that held some of Davy Crockett's personal effects. There was Crockett's beaded buckskin vest with onyx buttons; a lock of his hair; his fork; his bear-hunting knife; his razor; his powder case and shot pouch; and his rifle, "Old Betsy."

I heard a mother saying to her son: "Doesn't look like John Wayne, does it?"

I followed her eyes. She was looking up at a portrait of Crockett, painted from life in 1834 by an artist named John C. Chapman. I found it hard to fault the woman standing next to me; if the truth be told, Davy Crockett—at least based on the evidence of the Chapman painting—looked like a cross between Bob Hope and Abbie Hoffman.

I asked Mrs. Boyd (she was wearing a name tag) of the Daughters of the Republic of Texas if I might speak to someone in charge. Mrs. Boyd had sort of a stunned look on her face; I got the impression that she spent many days inside the Alamo. She directed me to a man named Charles Long, who she said was the Alamo's curator.

Charles Long sat in a private office; above his desk was a portrait of Jim Bowie.

There was a digital clock beside Long, and an AM/FM radio. A Radio Shack pocket calculator rested on his desk, as did a Kodak Disc 4000 camera. He leaned against an IBM Selectric typewriter.

I asked him what it felt like, coming to work at the Alamo every day.

Before he could answer, there was the sound of an electronic beeping. "Just a second," Long said.

He picked up a beige-and-brown Freedom Phone 1550—one of those wireless telephones, manufactured in Japan. A metal antenna protruded from the phone.

"Alamo," Long said.

I waited while he completed his conversation. When he had, he told me that it had been a lengthy fight to keep the Alamo as a shrine.

"For a long time, it was used for commercial purposes," he said. "When motion pictures first came along, the first place in San Antonio they were shown was right on the side wall of the Alamo. The promoters sold tickets."

I asked him if that was the most blatant example of the Alamo's commercial use.

"Oh, no," Long said. "Years ago, there used to be a liquor store and a hardware store in the long barracks. And at one time the Alamo was a police station, and then a bank."

I excused myself and walked over to the Alamo's gift shop. A woman in an I'M WITH A STUPID T-shirt asked her husband, wearing a CHARLIE DANIELS BAND T-shirt, to buy her a book of Texas recipes.

A sign said that a movie telling the story of the Alamo would start in five minutes. I followed the directions, and ended up in a long, bench-filled room.

The film was not projected on a movie screen, however. At the front of the room was a 105-channel, cable-ready, large-screen Quasar Compu-Matic television set with a sign that said it featured electronic remote tuning. The set was of the type commonly used by bars and taverns to show sporting events. In the ancient room, the battle of the Alamo was reenacted on the screen all day long; when the videotape was over, it repeated itself.

. . .

If the woman who had seen Davy Crockett's portrait had been disappointed by the way he looked, I hoped she had continued her tour of the Alamo. There were two other exhibits that, judging by the size of the crowds, were the most popular on the grounds—and that probably would have pleased her more than the Crockett painting.

One of these exhibits was a picture of Davy Crockett, Jim Bowie, and Colonel Travis fighting off the Mexican hordes. In this picture, Davy Crockett looked much more like John Wayne. This was because Davy Crockett *was* John Wayne; the painting was of Wayne's 1960 movie *The Alamo.* Jim Bowie looked like Richard Widmark (who he in fact was); Colonel Travis looked like Laurence Harvey (likewise). The painting was far more satisfying to the visitors than the actual portrait of Crockett.

But as a crowd pleaser, the painting was nothing compared to an artifact that was displayed inside a glass case. At first the object was puzzling; it looked like a gold director's chair.

Which, in fact, it was. It was John Wayne's Screen Directors Guild Award, which officials of the Alamo displayed along with the genuine Crockett-Bowie-Travis memorabilia.

I walked out of the Alamo. Downtown was bustling; the street in front of the Alamo was busy. A city transit bus passed by. On the side was a painting of San Antonio's skyline. Superimposed on the buildings were the faces of the Newswatch 12 television news team—male anchor, female anchor, sportscaster, weatherman.

I followed the wall surrounding the Alamo around to the back, to see what I might find if approaching from the rear. But it was more of the same; more downtown buildings and, overlooking Bonham Street, two billboards for RonRico rum and Merit cigarettes.

I decided to take a stroll rather than go directly back to my hotel. I thought I might pick up some more authentic frontier color if I didn't make such a big thing of looking for it.

I passed a restaurant and glanced up at its sign. It was called Lone Star Yogurt.

Back at the Hyatt I went for a drink to the Regency Club, a top-floor hospitality room constructed to give guests the best view of San Antonio. Directly out the window, sixteen floors below, was the Alamo itself; I was surprised the management of the Hyatt hadn't decided to build an enclosed skywalk to it.

Late at night, alone in my hotel room, I couldn't sleep. I got up and got dressed; I walked back over to the Alamo.

Now I was the only person on the grounds. The building itself was locked, but bright lights illuminated its limestone front. In the artificial light, something showed up that hadn't been quite so noticeable in the daylight: names—names carved by visitors on the facade of the Alamo. Lil Garrett, J. D. Thomas, Billy Waters; I stood there and moved slowly from one edge of the Alamo to the other, reading the names.

I looked back the other way. There was the Hyatt; there was Woolworth's; there was Texas State Optical. A chill wind had come up; now it seemed very cold at the Alamo. I had a Pocket Flight Guide in my suitcase in my room; I could be out of town by ten the next morning.

The Goods

Out past the railroad tracks in a crumbling industrial section of Trenton, New Jersey, is a long, low-slung, mustard-yellow building. This is the building where they manufacture Trojans.

They manufacture Trojans twenty-four hours a day. More than 1.1 million Trojans on a good day, 170 million Trojans a year. There are other brands of condoms for sale, but in the United States the word "Trojans" has become almost generic. The Trojans brand—which was launched more than fifty years ago—accounts for 57 percent of the condoms sold in drugstores in the U.S.; all of the other manufacturers split the rest of the market.

Nowhere on the outside of the building is the word "Trojans" apparent. Just the name of the parent company: Youngs Rubber Corporation.

The manager of operations and planning at the Trojans plant is Daryl Kress, thirty-seven, a former lieutenant commander in the navy. A trim, serious man in a dark-blue suit and crisp white shirt, he sits behind a tidy desk; in front of him is a coffee cup painted with the legend LIEUTENANT COMMANDER.

At no time does Kress use the term "condom," or "prophylactic," or "rubber" when mentioning the product that is manufactured in this building. Instead he refers to what is made here as "the goods."

"The goods come in seven different varieties," Kress says. "Regular, nipple-end, nipple-end lubricated, ribbed . . ." Or he says, "When the goods are shipped from our plant . . ."

When he is explaining the tensile strength of the product,

he reaches into a top desk drawer and comes out with a foil-wrapped Trojan. He opens the package and—still unsmiling—lifts the condom to his mouth. He blows into it and inflates it, then hands it to me for inspection.

Kress says he is married, with two sons, ages fourteen and twelve. He says the world in which his boys are growing up is far more relaxed about Trojans than the world in which previous generations of American males grew up.

"With us, we always hoped we'd get the druggist instead of that gal who worked behind the counter," he says. "Now most of the time they aren't sold behind the counter. They're hung up right next to the cash register. Heck, you just pull as many packages as you need off the rack and go right to the check-out counter."

Kress leads me into the manufacturing area of the Trojans plant. The heat is overwhelming; in some parts of the building the temperatures approach 180 degrees. And the smell—the intense, hot, oppressive smell of liquefied latex—is enough to knock you to your knees.

When it first hits us, I stop in my tracks. I have never smelled anything like it before.

"What is that smell?" I say to Kress.

"I don't smell anything," he says.

The interior of the Trojans plant looks like some woodcut used to illustrate the Iron Age in an old encyclopedia. There is absolutely nothing high-tech about what is done here; the four main manufacturing machines, each as long as a city block, creak and groan and rumble as they do their ceaseless task.

Inside the machine we are standing in front of, 3,412 glass forms in the shape of penises move, pointing downward, along a conveyor belt. The forms are dipped into liquefied latex. They are pulled out of the latex, with a thin rubber coating now formed on the glass. They are heat-dried. They are dipped a second time. A ring is mechanically formed around the top of each new condom. Talc is applied to prevent the condoms from sticking to themselves. The condoms are mechanically rolled off the glass forms in preparation for the next step of the process.

Kress raises his voice to be heard above the sound of the machines. "The goods are tumbled dry to remove the excess talc," he says. "Follow me."

"I guess this puts to rest the joke we all used to tell each other," I say to Kress.

"What joke is that?" he says.

"Well, you know," I say. "When a kid buys a rubber, his friends ask him what size he got. But it's obvious from looking at these things being made that they're all the same size."

"Actually, that's not true," Kress says. "There are two standard sizes in the world for these goods. An American size and a Japanese size."

"What's the difference?" I say.

"The Japanese size is smaller," Kress says. "When you lay one of these goods flat and measure its width, it is fifty-two millimeters wide. It is 7.1 inches long. The Japanese standard is forty-nine millimeters wide and 6.3 inches long."

As we walk through the factory, we pass some of the more than two hundred laborers who divide the three daily shifts at the Trojans plant. They are members of the United Rubber, Cork, Linoleum and Plastic Workers of America.

I ask Kress if the workers are allowed to take samples of the project home.

"There's no official policy on it," he says. "But we wouldn't say anything if they did. We make so many each day, it wouldn't make any real difference."

He says that, despite the recent rugged economy, there have been no layoffs in the Trojans plant.

"In a recession, our business actually goes up a little bit," he says. "People tend to stay home instead of going out."

.   .   .

Each of the million-plus Trojans that are manufactured daily is individually tested for holes or other flaws.

Each Trojan that comes off the line goes to the testing rooms. Here, women sitting at long tables slip the Trojans over more forms—called mandrels—that move by on another conveyor belt. These mandrels, also long and erect, are made of metal; they point upward. After the women place Trojans over them, the mandrels are dipped into an electrolytic solution; if any of the charged solution gets through a condom and makes contact with a steel mandrel, a mechanical alarm is tripped and that Trojan is rejected.

The steel mandrels move past the women in rapid, unrelenting succession. In front of each woman is a bin full of new Trojans; all day long she reaches into the bin, comes out with a Trojan, slips it over the top of a mandrel, then reaches back into the bin for another Trojan before the next mandrel moves past her.

Some of the women use their right hands to apply the Trojans to the mandrels. Some use their left hands. Some use both hands. There is no music in the room; there is no visual diversion. Just the mandrels moving by. When you first catch sight of the testers doing their job, you are struck by two immediate impressions: first, this has to be one of the most deadening, monotonous, dreary forms of human endeavor; and second, these women would really make great dates.

As the mandrels pass by the women and the Trojans are slipped over the tops, I approach several of the testers and talk to them. The conveyor belt does not stop; the women continue to work with the Trojans and the mandrels while we speak.

A fifty-three-year-old grandmother named Wilber Holloway tells me she has been doing this for seventeen years. "It took me about six weeks to learn," she says. "The trick is in how you pick them up."

I ask her what she thinks about all day while she is doing this.

"Money and men," Mrs. Holloway says. "I dream of winning the lottery, and I dream of young men."

Cindy Gerner, thirty-three and married, says, "It takes patience at first. You get nervous that you're going to break them when you put them on, and because you're nervous you do break them. You get your system down before long, though."

She says she thinks about different things to get her through the day. "I'm a Baptist," she says. "While I'm doing this I either go over Bible verses in my head, or I think of songs I heard in church."

Terry Scott, twenty-four, says that sometimes at night she dreams of the mandrels moving past her. I ask her what she tells strangers when she meets them and they ask her what she does for a living.

"I tell them, 'Flip rubbers,' " she says.

Daryl Kress leads me through the room where the Trojans are sealed inside foil packets, and then he takes me back to his office.

"The mail is very interesting," he says. "We think we have the best quality-control operation in the business, but when you sell as many goods as we do, you're bound to get some complaints."

He searches through his desk, and finds some correspondence. He flips through the letters and begins to sort them out.

"We had one man write us to complain that his Trojan was all dried out—he said that the lubricant had dried up. He sent us the package, so we took a look at the date on it. The guy had been carrying the thing around for eleven years."

I ask him what the most common complaint is.

"People write us to say that their Trojan won't unroll. Nine out of ten times, they're doing it backwards. They're doing it in the dark, and instead of unrolling it, they're trying to roll it up tighter."

I ask him if people really take the time to write letters about something like that.

"Oh, yes," he says. "They can get pretty eloquent. One man

wrote us to accuse a Trojan of 'complete prophylactic recalcitrance.'"

Kress is busy; he is due in another part of the plant, used to test the strength and resilience of the Trojans. Here the condoms are placed on a machine that inflates them automatically.

"You'd be amazed at how big these things can get," Kress says.

And indeed the machine does blow the Trojans up until they are approximately the size of shopping bags.

We walk through the shipping area. Charles Reed, forty-four, who has been working in the Trojans plant for twenty-two years, is packing the individual cartons of Trojans into big brown boxes; the boxes will be loaded onto trucks and distributed around the nation. Reed hardly looks up as he scoops the small packages from the end of the conveyor belt and arranges them in the larger crates.

"When you first come to work here, I guess you think it's going to be a pretty sexy job," Reed says. "I mean, this is an awfully famous product. But before long you quit telling people where you work.

"The reason is that they're going to react one of two ways. Either they're going to think it's tremendously interesting, and they're going to ask you questions all night about it. Or they're going to think it's funny, and make a lot of jokes.

"Now I just say that I'm a machine operator, or a shipping clerk. It makes things easier."

Like the Trojans factory itself, the large brown crates in which the individual packages of condoms are packed for shipping do not have the word "Trojans" printed anywhere on their exteriors.

"That was a conscious decision," Kress says. "These things sit around a lot of docks on their way to their destinations. We feel that if we were to print the name of the product on the outside of the shipping box, it would become a fairly pilferable item in transit."

As I leave the Trojans factory, I pass through the reception area. A secretary is on the telephone; a security camera is sending a black-and-white picture of the parking lot onto a TV monitor; a copy of *Reader's Digest* is placed on a coffee table.

Behind me, behind a series of doors, are the machines and mandrels and pallets and workers. Ahead of me, the real world waits again. On a table, someone has left a package of Trojans. On its front, the design is soft pastel; a young couple is shown in profile, strolling on a deserted beach. The printed slogan is brief and to the point: FOR FEELING IN LOVE.

Behind Closed Doors

GRAND RAPIDS, Mich.—I finished shaving in the bathroom of my room at the Amway Grand Plaza Hotel, and turned the knob to return to the bedroom. The door stuck. It stuck for only a moment; one good shove opened it up. But in that moment my life flashed before my eyes, and I was transported back through time to a day in the distant past, a day that was one of those breakthrough experiences in a man's walk through this world.

Some people remember when a bullet intended for someone else whizzed past their ear. Some remember when a car on the highway swerved threateningly toward their own. Some remember when a snake on a forest path struck out at them.

My brush with the hereafter was not quite so dramatic. But it has stuck with me all these years.

It was the summer of 1968. I was a college kid from Ohio, assigned by my hometown newspaper to work as a copyboy at the 1968 Democratic National Convention in Chicago, doing errands for the Scripps-Howard newspaper chain.

I was very excited. This was my first out-of-town trip as a newspaperman—all right, a copyboy—and Chicago promised to be a thrilling place.

I received my assignment only a few days before the convention was to begin; much too late to get a room reservation. I was told, though, that a veteran Scripps-Howard reporter named Jim G. Lucas was ill, and that I could have his room. All I had to do was show up at the Palmer House, tell the desk clerk that I was Lucas, and take his room.

This I did. I checked in at the hotel on the afternoon before the convention was to begin. The city was packed; every room in the hotel was taken. In the morning I was supposed to report to press headquarters and meet my Scripps-Howard bosses.

So I had some dinner by myself, and decided to get a good night's sleep. I went back to my room, put the "Do Not Disturb" sign on the outside doorknob, then locked the door and fastened the chain lock.

In the morning I was up early. I wanted to get started on time and impress my bosses. I went into the bathroom, took a shower, shaved, and headed back into the room.

But it was not to be. The door had stuck in the closed position. It was jammed solid. The knob would not even turn.

This struck me as unusual—even as a naive twenty-year-old I realized that hotel doors were supposed to open when you wished them to. Still, I did not see any reason to panic. There would be some way to open the door, and I would be on my way.

Alas, no. The door was stuck and stuck good. I was in that bathroom, like it or not.

As the minutes passed, the situation became progressively

less humorous. I tried the door, I pushed at the knob, I hit my knee against the wood. Not only did it not open—it didn't budge.

That is when the facts of the situation struck me. I was in a jam-packed hotel where all the employees, this particular week, were overworked and harried. I had the "Do Not Disturb" sign on the outside of the room's main door. That door was double-locked and chained. No one from the Scripps-Howard papers realized I had even arrived in Chicago. My family back in Columbus knew I had set out for my trip—but did not realize that Bob Greene was registered not as "Bob Greene," but as "Jim G. Lucas."

No one in Chicago would come looking for me; the hotel staff would be too busy to investigate a "Do Not Disturb" sign that remained on a door for days on end, and the Scripps-Howard people would assume that I had simply never arrived. Anyone back home who phoned the Palmer House would be told that there was no Bob Greene registered.

I sat on the floor of the bathroom and reached a calm, rational conclusion: I was going to slowly starve in this bathroom. This bathroom would be where I died.

I began to scream and shout. I began to bang on the walls. My voice soon grew hoarse, but I heard only echoes. The Palmer House is built as solidly as any great old hotel can be built; no one was going to hear me.

I tried to pace, but there was nowhere to go; this was a small bathroom. I was naked, of course; for some reason my nose had started to bleed, and when I looked in the steamed-up mirror what I saw did not please me: a nude, bedraggled youth from the American heartland, with terror in his eyes and blood running down to his chin, trapped like a hamster.

An hour passed; it seemed like a day. I sat on the edge of the sink. I knew I was a goner. And what a way to die—slowly feeling the life seep out of me while, only a few feet away, in the Palmer House corridor, other men and women walked blithely to the elevators.

I began to use my only weapon—my frail but willing body.

I stood at one end of the bathroom, picked up as much speed as I could in five or six feet, leaped into the air, and slammed myself against the door, like a human battering-ram. Every time I did this I picked myself up from the cold tile and made myself do it again. It hurt, and the vision in the mirror was ridiculous. But it was my sole chance.

For at least nineteen times I flew through the air and hit the floor. On what seemed to be the twentieth try, though, the miracle happened. I hit the door—and went sailing into the bedroom. I had unjammed it. I felt as if I had escaped from Alcatraz.

When I got to work, the Scripps-Howard editor asked why I was so late; I thought about explaining, but then thought better of it. "I got locked in my bathroom" didn't seem like the proper response for a fledgling tough-guy reporter. And now, fifteen years later, here I am in Grand Rapids, still gun-shy at the first hint of a sticky bathroom door. You can be in my nightmare if I can be in yours.

Party Line

On a recent Sunday afternoon, just after lunch, Vic Larson picked up the telephone in his house, which is in Park Ridge, Illinois. Larson's intention was to call a friend. But when he held the receiver to his ear, he did not hear a dial tone.

What he heard instead were voices. Maybe a dozen voices, talking intermittently, sometimes talking all at once. Larson thought about hanging up, but for some reason he did not. He stayed on the line.

It did not take him long to figure out what was going on. Because of some kind of glitch in the telephone company's computer system, people from all over the area were picking up their phones and dialing into this one circuit. They found themselves talking not with the people they had intended to call—but with this random group of strangers.

Vic Larson joined in the conversation. He is twenty-eight years old, a senior medical technologist at Lutheran General Hospital. He recognized almost immediately that most of the people on the telephone circuit were a decade or so younger than he was; older people would find themselves part of the party line and hang up, but teenagers would stay on.

Larson listened, and he talked. "Anyone from Park Ridge?" a voice would say. "Yeah, I'm from Park Ridge," another voice would answer. "Anyone go to Maine South?" "Yeah, I go to Maine South." Larson found himself smiling as he stayed on the phone.

For three hours he held the receiver to his ear. He wasn't sure quite why he was doing it, but he was having a great time. The makeup of the group on the phone kept changing; some people would hang up, but then more would get patched into the circuit. Vic Larson kept talking to the other people.

It was kind of like he was back in high school. That's what appealed to him about it; staying on the phone and talking with these strangers made absolutely no sense at all, but for a few hours on a Sunday afternoon, he wasn't sitting around his suburban house; he was acting like a high school kid.

Around 2:30 P.M.—he had been on the phone for better than two hours—some of the people on the line began shouting out their phone numbers. Larson wrote one of the numbers down on a piece of paper. The boys and girls on the line said they should all get together at four o'clock; they should meet at River Road and Higgins, over in Rosemont. One of the boys said he would be in a red Dodge van; the van would be the place where everyone should congregate. Boys' voices said they would be there; girls' voices said they would be there.

Just after 3:00 P.M. a dial tone came onto Larson's phone line. He clicked the receiver a few times, trying to get the party line back; he couldn't. Apparently whatever had gone wrong in the telephone computer had been fixed; the party line was no more.

Larson sat around the house for a while. He kept thinking about what he had just been a part of. He wasn't sure why he had liked it so much; maybe it was because, last summer, he had gone to his high school graduating class's ten-year reunion and had been so disappointed. He couldn't really put his finger on what it was about the reunion. It had just seemed to him that everyone had . . . averaged out. The jocks were in the same businesses that the nerds were. Everyone had grown up.

On the phone today, though . . . no one had grown up yet. Larson had felt, for a few strange hours, that he wasn't a working man taking his two days off between shifts; this was the *weekend,* just like in high school, and he was like everyone else—looking for action, looking for something to do.

On an impulse, he called the number he had written down— the number someone had shouted out over the party line. A young man answered; when Larson asked if the young man had been a part of the conversation, the young man acted defensive, as if he would get in trouble if he admitted it. But finally he said yes, he had been on the line; Larson asked if the gathering at River Road and Higgins was still on, and the boy said he thought it was.

Just before four o'clock, Larson decided to do it. He thought to himself: I'm going to look foolish. I'm older than these kids, and I've got a receding hairline, and I'm starting to get a spare tire around my middle. But I have to go meet them.

He got in his car. He headed toward Rosemont. His feeling of foolishness was mixed with a twinge of excitement. He wasn't sure what he would do when he got there. Maybe not even get out of the car. But he knew he had to go. He was envisioning something out of a movie. Maybe thirty people or so, all strangers just a few hours before, now having a picnic together next to the red van. He hoped he would have the nerve to join in. He promised himself: If the kids weren't old enough to drink, and they asked him to buy them beer, he wouldn't do it.

He approached the intersection. There was a gas station, and a car wash. He looked for a red van. He didn't see one.

He cruised around the streets bordering the intersection for the next twenty minutes. He looked in the parking lots. No red van. No group of people. He drove until he was certain that no one else would be coming.

So he drove back home and parked his car. He went back into his house and walked around for a while. Then he sat down in front of the television set. He waited for "60 Minutes" to start. It was Sunday night, after all.

The Most Famous Man in the World

It was the voice that was shocking.

"How much you going to pay me?"

The voice was slurry, blurred, almost a whisper. Coming over the long-distance line, the words seemed to be filled with effort.

I said that as far as I knew, *Esquire* did not pay people who were written about in the magazine. In any event, this was a special sort of issue; fifty men and women from the past fifty years had been selected as the most influential of their time. He was one of them. The magazine wanted to include him in the issue.

"You're just using me to sell magazines," Muhammad Ali said. The voice was fading. "You just want to put me on the cover."

No, I said, Ali would not be on the cover. But he would be in very good company.

"I'm the most famous man in the world," the voice said.

I said that there would be other famous people in the issue; people, perhaps, as famous as he.

"Who?" Ali said.

I said that some of the others were John F. Kennedy, Franklin D. Roosevelt, Martin Luther King.

"They're all dead," Ali said.

I waited for American Airlines Flight 184 from Los Angeles to arrive at Chicago's O'Hare International Airport. Ali's manager, Herbert Muhammad, had told me that Ali would be on board, and then would be switching to another flight to Washington, D.C. Ali would be addressing a rally of Muslims in Washington.

Herbert Muhammad had said he could not guarantee that Ali would speak with me; it would be up to him. He said that if I wanted to take a chance I should pack a bag, buy a ticket to Washington, and be at the gate when Ali's plane arrived.

So I sat on a chair directly next to where the jetway opened into the terminal. The plane was a few minutes early. About a dozen passengers disembarked, and then came Ali. He was wearing a gray suit; he wore no belt with the pants. The suit was expensive, but his brown shoes were worn and scuffed.

I walked up to him and introduced myself. He did not look at me, but he said: "Where's Herbert?" The voice was as soft and fuzzy as it had been on the phone.

I said I didn't know; I said the Washington flight would be leaving in forty-five minutes from a gate just down the corridor.

Ali removed his suit jacket. Even though it was a frigid winter day, he was wearing a short-sleeve blue shirt. He began to walk toward the next gate.

The scene in the airport was like one of those brokerage

commercials in which everyone freezes in place. I have traveled with celebrities before; I had never seen anything like this. Everyone—everyone—stopped in their tracks when they caught sight of Ali. He was considerably heavier than in the days when he had been fighting; now he had just turned forty-one, and his hair was flecked with gray. But there was no question about his recognition factor; each pair of eyes stared at him, each mouth silently formed the word "Ali."

"Champ, you're the greatest there ever was," a man cried. Ali walked past him, not looking.

"Where's Herbert?" his voice said again.

I said again that I didn't know. A woman—she was middle-aged, well dressed, not eccentric looking in the least—caught sight of Ali and dropped to her knees in front of him, as if praying. He stepped around her.

I led him to the proper gate. We took seats in the boarding area. He was carrying a briefcase; actually, it was bigger than that, more like a salesman's sample case. He opened it and took out a book called *The Spectre of Death, Including Glimpses of Life Beyond the Grave.*

He opened the book. He leaned over to me and began reading aloud from it, but so softly that I could barely make out the words:

"Life will soon come to an end, and we will part with the comforts. Whenever you see a dead man being led to the grave, remind yourself that one day you will also meet your end. . . ."

I asked him what else he had in the salesman's case. He began to rummage through it; the contents looked like something in a bag lady's sack. Pamphlets, old photographs, receipts, scraps of paper—the case was chock-full. He pulled out a copy of the Bible and opened the cover. There was an autograph I could not quite make out.

"Oral Roberts," he whispered.

A woman was standing in front of us. Her young daughter—she said that the girl's name was Clarice, and that she was six—was with her. The woman shoved the girl gently in Ali's direction. The girl kissed Ali on the cheek.

"She's not real, real friendly," the mother said. Ali, saying nothing, stood up and kissed the mother on the cheek, too.

"See," the mother said to her daughter, "now you met somebody great."

A man named Joseph Loughry, manager of international banking programs for General Electric Information Services in Rockville, Maryland, stopped in front of Ali. "I have a little guy named James," Loughry said. Ali, not looking up, not saying anything, accepted a piece of paper from Loughry, and wrote on it: "To James from Muhammad Ali."

Loughry said some words of thanks to Ali, but Ali neither spoke to him nor looked at him. When he had walked away, Ali said to me: "The least little thing we do, God marks it down. Each little atom, He sees. On the day of judgment, all the good and all the bad will be weighed. Every leaf that falls from a tree, God sees. Think of all the trees."

A man was sitting behind us, in a chair facing the other way. "Watch me do this," Ali said. He rubbed his thumb and first two fingers together in a way that resulted in a cricket sound. He turned around, placed his fingers next to the man's ear, rubbed the fingers together, and made the sound. By the time the man turned around, Ali was looking away, as if nothing had happened. But then he did it to the man again. The man jerked his head to the side. He rubbed his ear. When he had gone back to his newspaper, Ali reached back again, made the cricket sound with his fingers again.

The man stood up and looked around. But Ali was talking to me again, as if nothing had happened. I said something about him being treated as a "super figure."

"Super nigger?" Ali said.

"Figure," I said. "Super figure."

"I know," he said. "I heard you the first time. I was just joking. I don't know about 'super figures.' But I do know that I am the most famous person in the world."

"Are you sure?" I said.

"Who's more famous?" Ali said.

"What about Reagan?" I said.

"Be serious," Ali said. "If Reagan were to go to Morocco or

Persia, he could walk down the street and no one would bother him. If I go there, they have to call out soldiers to guard me. I can't go outside."

"Why?" I said.

"What do you mean 'why'?" Ali said.

"Why you?" I said. "You were a great boxer. But all of this other stuff . . . why you?"

"I don't know," he said. "I'm not smart. I'm dumber than you are. I can't spell as good as you. I can't read as good as you. But people don't care. Because that shows I'm a common person, just like they are."

At that moment a woman named Pam Lontos interrupted us. She handed Ali a business card; the card indicated that she was the president of a sales motivation firm based in Dallas, and that she made motivational speeches.

"Have you ever done any motivational talks about how to believe in yourself?" she said to Ali.

He did not speak, did not look at her.

"I'd like to talk to you about making public speeches," she said. "Are you with any booking agency? I think you'd be amazed at how much money you can make for just forty-five minutes' work. You can make just a ton of money."

Ali still did not look up at her.

"The booking agency I'm with handles David Brinkley and Norman Vincent Peale," she said. "Wouldn't you like to make a lot of money just by getting up and talking?"

"I talk for free," Ali said. "For God."

Just then Herbert Muhammad arrived. Ali's manager was a rotund man wearing a fur cap. "Ali, where have you been?" he said. "I've been looking all over the terminal for you."

The gate agent announced that the flight was boarding; Pam Lontos walked away, and we got in line to get on the plane. There was a businessman in front of us. Ali reached forward, put his fingers next to the man's ears, and made the cricket noise. When the man turned around, Ali was looking in another direction.

.   .   .

We sat in the first row of first class on the right side of the plane. Ali was by the window; I was on the aisle. Other passengers were filing on. Ali didn't seem to be paying any attention to them, but then he said to me, "I have to do something."

He climbed over me. He reached for a man who was heading back into the coach section. He tapped the man on the shoulder.

"*Psst,*" Ali said.

The man turned around. His face froze at the sight of Ali. Ali pointed to the floor of the plane, where a ticket envelope lay.

"You dropped something," Ali said.

"Why . . . why, thank you," the man said.

But Ali had already turned away. He walked up to the cockpit. He bent over slightly and ducked inside. He tapped the pilot on the shoulder.

The pilot and the first officer and the flight engineer looked up in wonder. Ali nodded at them. Then he turned and came back toward his seat by the window. Before he could get there, though, a flight attendant who was struggling to lift a carton onto the overhead rack said to him: "Would you like to put that up there? You have more muscles than me."

Silently Ali put the box away. He slid past me. Another flight attendant leaned over and said: "Would you like a cocktail or a soft drink after we take off?"

"Milk," Ali said, so softly that the woman could not hear.

"I beg your pardon?" she said.

"Milk," Ali said, looking straight forward.

We taxied out onto the runway. As we picked up speed and then lifted off, Ali said to me: "You never know when your time to die will come."

About five minutes into the flight, he turned to me and said, "I'm not going to say anything to you for a while. It's time for me to pray." He held up his wrist; he was wearing a fancy watch with a floating arrow inside.

"This is a Muslim prayer watch," Ali said. "We have to pray at different times during the day. An alarm goes off every time I have to pray. The arrow is always pointing towards Mecca."

"Where'd you get it?" I asked.

"The king of Saudi Arabia gave it to me," he said. "He was wearing it on his arm and he took it off and gave it to me. I was wearing a Timex before." He closed his eyes, as if in prayer.

When he opened his eyes, he said to me: "My desire, my main goal now, is to prepare myself for the hereafter. That should be all men's goal."

"But what about life right now?" I said.

"This life is not real," Ali said. "I conquered the world, and it didn't give me satisfaction. The boxing, the fame, the publicity, the attention—it didn't satisfy my soul.

"Who could be more popular? Who could achieve greater heights? It's all nothing unless you go to heaven. You can have pleasure, but it means nothing unless you please God."

A man who had been sitting across the aisle unbuckled his seat belt and came over to us. He was William Doré, the president of Global Divers & Contractors, Inc., in Lafayette, Louisiana.

"Ali," he said, "I want to shake your hand. I made twelve dollars on you when you fought against Sonny Liston."

"Is that all?" Ali said.

"I only bet three," Doré said.

Ali was looking away by now.

"It's been a pleasure to watch you over the years," Doré said. "You've done a lot for the game."

When Doré had returned to his seat, Ali said to me: "Boxing was nothing. It wasn't important at all. Boxing was just meant as a way to introduce me to the world."

But he was interrupted in mid-thought. Pam Lontos, the motivational speaker, had come up from the coach section; she was kneeling in the aisle, and she was pushing a brochure at Ali. The brochure began: "The basics of broadcast selling help you find your true potential, to turn that potential into profit . . ."

A flight attendant put both hands on Lontos's shoulders. "Ma'am," the flight attendant said, "if you want an autograph, we'll be happy to bring you one back."

"But I don't want an autograph," Lontos said as she was led back into coach.

Ali was sniffling. He seemed to be getting the beginnings of a cold. He took the small pillow from behind my head, tore a piece from its paper casing, and blew his nose. In a moment he was sleeping.

We were approaching Washington. Ali tapped me on the shoulder. He pointed out the window. The lights of the monuments and government buildings were below.

"What do you think of that?" he said.

"It's pretty," I said.

"Look at all those lights on all those houses," he said. "Those are all my fans. Do you know I could walk up to any one of those houses, and knock on the door, and they would know me?

"It's a funny feeling to look down on the world and know that every person knows me. Sometimes I think about hitchhiking around the world, with no money, and just knocking on a different door every time I needed a meal or a place to sleep. I could do it."

We walked into Washington's National Airport. A group of Muslims were waiting in the concourse for Ali; they were sponsoring the rally he had come to address.

We walked toward the baggage claim area. There was an immediate difference in Ali. On the airplane, even though his voice had still been slurred and vague, his mind and his attention had appeared to be fairly sharp. In here, though—with every person calling to him and stopping to gaze at him—he seemed to put himself back into the same sort of trance he had apparently been under back at O'Hare. His eyes glazed over; he looked at no one; his face took on a blank, numb expression. As the voices spoke his name, this grew more marked.

All I could think of was: He's not punch-drunk in the traditional sense. He's not woozy from being hit too many times.

Rather, he is suffering from a different kind of continual beating. For twenty years and more, he has been assaulted with constant attention, constant badgering, constant touching, every time he has ventured out in public. That is what he has had too much of—not the fists, but the nonstop contact from strangers. Clearly it had done something to him; and what it had done was most noticeable when he was in the midst of more onslaughts.

He moved through the crowds. His eyes stayed unfocused. Only once did he speak. A man stepped right in front of him. The man talked not to Ali, but me. He said: "Hey, ask Ali if he can still fly like a butterfly and sting like a bee."

"Float," Ali whispered, not looking at the man. "Float like a butterfly."

There was screaming and shouting as Ali was led to a car waiting outside. We were driven by one of the Muslims to a Holiday Inn downtown. It was not one of Washington's fancier hotels. Ali's suite was on the far end of the seventh floor.

The manager of the hotel, Thomas Buckley, was waiting for Ali in the living room of the suite. "Is there anything I can do for you?" Buckley said.

Ali's cold seemed to be getting worse. "How do you make it hotter in here?" Ali said.

Buckley went to the thermostat and adjusted its lever. "I'm in the service business," Buckley said.

Ali's eyes still seemed to be somewhere else. His voice was barely decipherable.

"Service to others is the rent you pay for your room in heaven," he said.

In the morning, Ali sat in the hotel's coffee shop with Herbert Muhammad and several of the Washington-based Muslims. He wore the same suit he had been wearing the day before. His address at the Muslim rally was not for another day; today he had been scheduled to appear at several inner-city schools.

"Herbert," Ali said, his voice as soft as it had been the day before, "what does Allah give you credit for?"

"What do you mean?" Herbert Muhammad said.

"Well," Ali said, "if you help an old lady across the street, does Allah give you credit for that?"

"I'm sure He does," Herbert said. Ali nodded; Herbert turned to me and said, "Ali has a good heart."

Ali had ordered some wheat toast; it was slow in arriving. He reached across the table and took a piece of toast from one of the Muslims' plates. When Ali's toast came, he took the top piece and handed it back to the Muslim.

The woman at the coffee shop's cash register picked up the ringing telephone. She listened for a second, and then came over. "Mr. Ali," she said, "it's for you."

"Who is it?" Ali said, looking at his wheat toast.

"The person said he was Eddie Cantor," the woman said.

Ali stood up and walked to the phone.

"Ali," Herbert called to him before he got there, "who are you going to talk to?"

"Eddie Cantor," Ali said in an emotionless tone.

"Ali," said Herbert, laughing, "Eddie Cantor's dead. If he's calling you I want to hear about it."

Ali picked up the telephone and started talking. As he did, he used his fingers to make the cricket sound next to the ear of the cashier. She looked around, then rubbed her ear furiously. Ali did it again. She rubbed her ear again.

He came back to the table. I asked him who had been on the phone.

"Eddie Kendricks," he said. "He used to sing with the Temptations."

"How did he know to find you here?" I said.

Ali shrugged. He looked at his Muslim prayer watch, then gave me a signal to be silent. As the others in the coffee shop worked on their breakfasts, he closed his eyes and prayed.

We drove through the streets. At the Sister Clara Muhammad Elementary School, up a flight of stairs in a run-down section of town, Ali stood in front of a class of seventy-five students. He crossed his arms while the children sang to him. Once in a while he motioned back and forth with a finger, as if conducting an orchestra.

"I'm so happy to see all you children," he whispered to them. They were very young; it was obvious that they knew he was an important man, but unclear if they knew precisely who he was.

At Shaw Junior High School, in a modern, low-slung building, faculty members and students ran toward him and pawed at him as he was led to the school auditorium. Lipstick smeared his cheeks from where the female teachers had kissed him.

We were shoved back and forth in a sea of bodies as we tried to get to the stage. The school band was playing; the auditorium was alive with shrieks and shouts.

"This is the whole world," he said to me. "This is what my whole life is like."

He made it to the stage. While the band played the theme from *Rocky*, he took a blue comb from his pocket and ran it through his hair.

"Boys and girls," the principal said into the microphone, "being here on this stage with this man is probably the greatest moment of my life. And it should be the greatest moment of your life."

Ali, whose cold had seemed worse all morning, took out a handkerchief. A cook from the school's kitchen yelled, "Muhammad Ali, I love you." Ali blew his nose.

The principal called Ali to the lectern. He said that he wanted the students to ask questions of Ali, but that he wanted to ask the first one himself.

"Muhammad," he said, "would you say your toughest fight was with Frazier?"

"My toughest fight was with my first wife," Ali said.

He talked with the students for about fifteen minutes. On the way out he stopped in front of a couple of boys. Ali began to shadowbox with them, moving his feet back and forth in the famous "Ali Shuffle." The boys held up their hands and backed off. A woman teacher who had not been at the assembly caught sight of him and began to tremble. "Oh, Lord," she said, her eyes wide.

At Cardozo High School, in one of Washington's toughest neighborhoods, police officers stood guard at the front door. The students were gathered in an assembly, but had not been told that Ali was scheduled to come.

So they were listening to another speaker when, unannounced, Ali walked in a back door of the auditorium. First a few of them caught sight of him, then a few more. A buzz moved through the room as he walked, sniffling, down the aisle toward the stage.

By the time he was halfway there the chants had begun: "Ali! Ali! Ali! Ali!"

When he started to speak, though, his voice was so soft and slurred that no one could hear him. They began to call out for him to speak louder; but he didn't seem to notice, he just kept calling them "boys and girls" in that whispered tone.

He asked if there were any questions. A pretty young woman in the front row, who had been visibly puzzled by his slow, quiet, faltering speech pattern, raised her hand, and he pointed at her.

"Are you really Muhammad Ali?" she said.

Ali stared at her. "I'll see you after school," he said. "And tell your boyfriend that if he don't like it, I'll see him after school, too."

A fellow who apparently was her boyfriend stood up. "Fool," Ali said, "I'll see you after school." But beyond the first five or six rows, no one could hear him.

Ali turned to the principal and, with his fists raised, again went into the boxing routine and the Ali Shuffle. The principal shook his head and backed away.

Ali was coughing badly as we arrived at Dunbar High School. He followed wherever the local Muslims led him; in this case, into an administration office.

Ali stood there coughing and wiping his nose, waiting to be instructed where to go next. A female administrator looked up at him and said, "This man is sick. Has anyone called a doctor for him?"

But he was already being taken to a classroom. In the hallway a young mother who was visiting the school ran up to him and handed her baby to him. Ali reached out for the child, but Herbert Muhammad said, "Ali, you have too bad a cold to be handling that baby." Ali handed the infant back.

We moved through the corridors. Children moved to the doors of their classrooms. Ali leaned close to me and said, "They're all mine. This is what Allah has given me. This is heaven in the world." We moved past an elderly man who for some reason was at the school. Ali made the cricket sound with his fingers next to the old man's ear, but the man, apparently hard of hearing, did not react.

We went into the school library. Everyone in the room stopped what they were doing. One boy, though, had his back to us; he was reading at a table, and was immersed in his book.

Ali approached him. He put his hand on the boy's shoulder. The boy looked up and his mouth fell open. He started to say something, but Ali held a finger up to his own mouth, as if to silence the boy.

On the way out of the room, Ali passed by a tall, muscular young man. Ali stopped.

They looked at each other. Then Ali held up his fists. He went into the Ali Shuffle and began to leap about in front of the young man.

The young man did not back off. He held up his own fists. He did not attempt to strike Ali, but neither did he give an inch. He moved with Ali, making it clear that he was not afraid. Ali began to perspire. The young man moved closer. The young man had a confident smile on his face. He started to push Ali, establishing command of the situation.

No one in the room stirred. Ali coughed. The young man brought his punches closer and closer to Ali's face. Their arms began to make contact. The sound of their forearms slapping against each other echoed off the walls, and suddenly there was a clattering sound, and everything stopped.

There, on the yellow carpeting, was Ali's Muslim prayer watch. Ali slowly leaned over. He picked up the watch and fastened it back onto his wrist.

"Come on, Ali," Herbert Muhammad said. "We're running late." They moved toward the door of the school library. Ali's eyes met the eyes of the tall young man for just a moment. Then they clouded over, and once again he seemed to be somewhere else.

Born Too Late

It had been a lousy week all around, but then I met Mary Jackson and things immediately got better.

Mary Jackson—she has the perfect American name, right?—is sixteen. She wanted to talk to me for a very specific reason.

"You were around when the Beatles were around," she said. "I want to know what it was really like."

I thought she was kidding, but she soon made it clear that she wasn't.

"I wish I had been a kid when you were a kid," she said. "No one my age understands how much I love the Beatles."

She said that any time she sees pictures and movies of the Beatles, or hears their music, her reaction is the same.

"Rebellious, free-spirited, happy, confused," she said. "I just wish I lived during a time when everyone was walking around like that all the time."

She was wearing a Beatles T-shirt with a Beatles button on

it. She reached into her purse and pulled out her Beatles wallet and her Beatles key chain.

"I look like any girl my age and I talk like any girl my age," she said. "But I'm different because of the Beatles. If you believe in the Beatles, you're different."

She said that she worked part time selling jeans at a Gap store.

"These girls come in wearing AC/DC T-shirts," she said. "I hate the music they listen to. AC/DC, Rush . . . those guys sing songs about 'TNT' and 'Dirty Deeds Done Dirt Cheap.' Real deep, huh?

"And if I hear Michael Jackson sing 'Billie Jean' or 'Beat It' one more time, I think I'm going to throw up. If you listen to the Beatles, you get a feeling about life that other people don't have. Even on a song like 'Long Tall Sally,' you can hear them beating it out and you can imagine them smiling and moving around. . . .

"Other kids my age listen to the Beatles once in a while and they dig 'em, but not to the extreme like I do. I'll get up at three o'clock in the morning to see *Yellow Submarine* on TV, and when the movie's over I'll get dressed and go right to school."

She said one of the things she feels especially bad about is her year of birth, which was 1967.

"I've thought about it, and I wish I had been born in 1952," she said. "That way, in 1964, when the Beatles came over to America, I would have been twelve, and I would have been fourteen in 1966, and they still would have been touring."

As it is, she said, she was in the sixth grade when she realized she loved the Beatles.

"There was this physical attraction to doe-eyed, baby-faced Paul McCartney," she said.

Even now, she feels that way.

"Paul makes me melt," she said. "I go to Beatlefest every year, and I see guys who look like Paul, and even that makes me start shakin'."

If she is totally infatuated with McCartney, she feels even more deeply about the late John Lennon.

"Paul McCartney is the perfect male image," she said. "But John Lennon is my hero.

"People say that John was 'slain,' but I never use that word, because John was not defeated.

"All the things the Beatles make me feel, John makes me feel the strongest. If I'm feeling real nervous I'll go into my room and turn up 'Helter Skelter' as loud as I can, and even if my mom is mad at me for doing it I think, 'Yeah, you don't bug me, Mom,' because I'm thinking about John Lennon."

She said that the Beatles are the most important thing in her life.

"The Beatles have been the answer to every misery I have had in my teenage years," she said. "Even in the eighth grade, I'd sit in school during the last hour of the day and think about what Beatles albums I'd play when I got home.

"People say the Beatles hit it big because they came along right after Kennedy died. People say that youth lost a hero in Kennedy, and the Beatles took his place. But that can't be the reason, because I wasn't around when Kennedy died, and I still love the Beatles."

She said she baby-sits for the children of parents in their thirties, and that she envies the parents.

"Right now, nothing's going on in the world," she said. "But when those people were teenagers, they could go to the record store and say, 'When's the new Beatles album coming in?' Or they could drive around and change all the stations on the car radio, trying to find Beatles songs."

Her pleasures, she said, are simple.

"After school I'll go to the 7-Eleven, buy a bag of Taco Doritos and two liters of Pepsi, go home, put on my headphones, play 'A Day in the Life,' turn off my mind and relax and float downstream."

She is ready for the new school year to begin.

"Last year I dated a football player," she said. "But this year I know that God will bring me a Paul McCartney look-alike."

Johnny Appleseed
in the Eighties

Johnny Appleseed roamed the countryside in the early 1800s. Some people think Johnny Appleseed was a myth, but he wasn't. His real name was John Chapman; he was born in Massachusetts in 1774, and he devoted his life to sowing seeds so that there would be fruit for the pioneers as they headed west.

He often traveled barefoot, and sometimes he wore a coffee sack for clothing. He planted his seeds in Pennsylvania, Ohio, and Indiana. He was extremely kind to animals, sometimes purchasing sick livestock from farmers and then nurturing them back to health.

Because of this, the story of Johnny Appleseed was passed down from generation to generation; he became a genuine American folk hero, and he is remembered fondly after all these many years.

But you have to wonder: What would the story of Johnny Appleseed have been like if he had lived in the 1980s?

He might start off in relative anonymity, but a reporter from the "P.M. Magazine" television show in Pittsburgh would hear about him by the time he reached the western border of Pennsylvania. The reporter would videotape a cute feature on Appleseed, including cutaway shots of the reporter, in his blazer and gray pants, strolling and talking to Appleseed, in his coffee sack, as they walked down the road.

Soon enough Charles Kuralt would pick up on the story; Appleseed would appear on the entire CBS network, and by the next day he would be the talk of every office lunchroom in the country.

Within a week, *USA Today* would give Appleseed its ultimate accolade—a small color picture on top of Page One with a teaser headline referring to a story about him in the Life section.

Phil Donahue would invite Appleseed on his show as a representative of a coming trend—men who dress in coffee sacks and walk barefoot dropping seeds on the ground.

By the end of the first month, Appleseed would sign on with the International Creative Management talent agency in New York. From that point on, all decisions about his career would go through the agency. The first thing that the agents would demand is that anyone wishing to deal with Appleseed would have to fly him first class and provide him with a chauffeured limousine for ground transportation.

After the initial flurry of stories in the press, Appleseed's new managers would hire the bicoastal Rogers and Cowan public relations agency to handle all future media inquiries. Reporters wishing to speak with Appleseed would now have to get prepared statements from his publicist.

Appleseed would sign a book contract to tell the story of his life. The book would be ghostwritten by a former newspaperman, who would be paid a straight fee; all royalties would go directly to Appleseed.

When the book was in galley proofs, it would be sold to NBC for a miniseries.

Appleseed's managers would license designer versions of his coffee-sack clothing, complete with his signature across the front. They would fret over a way to license the rights to his bare feet, but would give up in frustration.

A chain of "Johnny's Apple Shops" would be franchised in malls nationwide. The stores would sell apples, apple pies, apple turnovers, apple candy, apple cake, etc. The visual trademark would be an apple tree planted next to the front door of each store; the apple trees would be made out of plastic, for longer wear. Appleseed himself, accompanied by managers, publicists, and security guards, would make a national promotional tour, visiting the stores and signing autographs. This effort would be buttressed by a series of television commercials, in which Appleseed would smile and say, "Hi! I'm Johnny Appleseed, and I'd like to invite you to my Apple Shops. . . ."

Appleseed would retain a team of investment counselors to advise him on his growing wealth. He would move to Beverly Hills, California, and buy a house with a pool, a sauna, a hot tub, a Jacuzzi, and a tennis court. He would be spotted at a disco in the company of Cathy Lee Crosby; within a week their picture would appear on the "Star Tracks" page of *People* magazine.

Appleseed would appear as the featured guest on "Lifestyles of the Rich and Famous," offering host Robin Leach a tour of his home, and granting an interview about the pleasures and headaches of being a worldwide celebrity.

In the fall, Westinghouse Broadcasting would offer Appleseed his own talk show. The company would cite surveys showing that Appleseed was the most trustworthy celebrity in the country, in the eyes of the American people. For his hosting duties Appleseed would give up the coffee sack, instead wearing clothes made especially for him by Ralph Lauren. On the wall directly behind the talk-show chairs, though, a logo showing Appleseed in his old coffee-sack garb would be prominently displayed, to act as a nostalgic reminder for viewers.

The book, the miniseries, the designer coffee sacks, the Johnny's Apple Shops, and the talk show would be enormous hits for two years.

In the third year, all of them would begin to decline in popularity.

By the fifth year the book would be out of print, the miniseries would be off the air, the designer coffee sacks would be out of production, the Johnny's Apple Shops would be in Chapter 11 bankruptcy, and the talk show would be canceled.

In the sixth year Johnny Appleseed would be arrested for possession of cocaine. His picture would appear in the paper; his head would be hanging, his posture would be slumped. His managers would issue a statement saying that he was "struggling with personal problems." A judge would release him on probation, with the stipulation that he seek counseling.

Cut

I remember vividly the last time I cried. I was twelve years old, in the seventh grade, and I had tried out for the junior high school basketball team. I walked into the gymnasium; there was a piece of paper tacked to the bulletin board.

It was a cut list. The seventh-grade coach had put it up on the board. The boys whose names were on the list were still on the team; they were welcome to keep coming to practices. The boys whose names were not on the list had been cut; their presence was no longer desired. My name was not on the list.

I had not known the cut was coming that day. I stood and I stared at the list. The coach had not composed it with a great deal of subtlety; the names of the very best athletes were at the top of the sheet of paper, and the other members of the squad were listed in what appeared to be a descending order of talent. I kept looking at the bottom of the list, hoping against hope that my name would miraculously appear there if I looked hard enough.

I held myself together as I walked out of the gym and out of the school, but when I got home I began to sob. I couldn't stop. For the first time in my life, I had been told officially that I wasn't good enough. Athletics meant everything to boys that age; if you were on the team, even as a substitute, it put you in the desirable group. If you weren't on the team, you might as well not be alive.

I had tried desperately in practice, but the coach never seemed to notice. It didn't matter how hard I was willing to work; he didn't want me there. I knew that when I went to school the next morning I would have to face the boys who had not been cut—the boys whose names were on the list, who were still on the team, who had been judged worthy while I had been judged unworthy.

All these years later, I remember it as if I were still standing right there in the gym. And a curious thing has happened: in traveling around the country, I have found that an inordinately large proportion of successful men share that same memory— the memory of being cut from a sports team as a boy.

I don't know how the mind works in matters like this; I don't know what went on in my head following that day when I was cut. But I know that my ambition has been enormous ever since then; I know that for all of my life since that day, I have done more work than I had to be doing, taken more assignments than I had to be taking, put in more hours than I had to be spending. I don't know if all of that came from a determination never to allow myself to be cut again—never to allow someone to tell me that I'm not good enough again—but I know it's there. And apparently it's there in a lot of other men, too.

Bob Graham, thirty-six, is a partner with the Jenner & Block law firm in Chicago. "When I was sixteen, baseball was my whole life," he said. "I had gone to a relatively small high school, and I had been on the team. But then my family moved, and I was going to a much bigger high shcool. All during the winter months I told everyone that I was a ball-player. When spring came, of course I went out for the team.

"The cut list went up. I did not make the team. Reading that cut list is one of the clearest things I have in my memory. I wanted not to believe it, but there it was.

"I went home and told my father about it. He suggested that maybe I should talk to the coach. So I did. I pleaded to be put back on the team. He said there was nothing he could do; he said he didn't have enough room.

"I know for a fact that it altered my perception of myself. My view of myself was knocked down; my self-esteem was lowered. I felt so embarrassed; my whole life up to that point had revolved around sports, and particularly around playing baseball. That was the group I wanted to be in—the guys on the baseball team. And I was told that I wasn't good enough to be one of them.

"I know now that it changed me. I found out, even though I couldn't articulate it at the time, that there would be times in my life when certain people would be in a position to say 'You're not good enough' to me. I did not want that to happen ever again.

"It seems obvious to me now that being cut was what started me in determining that my success would always be based on my own abilities, and not on someone else's perceptions. Since then I've always been something of an overachiever; when I came to the law firm I was very aggressive in trying to run my own cases right away, to be the lead lawyer in the cases with which I was involved. I made partner at thirty-one; I never wanted to be left behind.

"Looking back, maybe it shouldn't have been that important. It was only baseball. You pass that by. Here I am. That coach is probably still there, still a high school baseball coach, still cutting boys off the baseball team every year. I wonder how many hundreds of boys he's cut in his life?"

Maurice McGrath is senior vice-president of Genstar Mortgage Corporation, a mortgage banking firm in Glendale, California. "I'm forty-seven years old, and I was fourteen when it happened to me, and I still feel something when I think about it," he said.

"I was in the eighth grade. I went to St. Philip's School in Pasadena. I went out for the baseball team, and one day at practice the coach came over to me. He was an Occidental College student who had been hired as the eighth-grade coach.

"He said, 'You're no good.' Those were his words. I asked him why he was saying that. He said, 'You can't hit the ball. I don't want you here.' I didn't know what to do, so I went over and sat off to the side, watching the others practice. The coach said I should leave the practice field. He said that I wasn't on the team, and that I didn't belong there anymore.

"I was outwardly stoic about it. I didn't want anyone to see how I felt. I didn't want to show that it hurt. But oh, did it hurt. All my friends played baseball after school every day. My best friend was the pitcher on the team. After I got whittled down by the coach, I would hear the other boys talking in class about what they were going to do at practice after school. I knew that I'd just have to go home.

"I guess you make your mind up never to allow yourself to be hurt like that again. In some way I must have been saying to myself, 'I'll play the game better.' Not the sports game, but anything I tried. I must have been saying, 'If I have to, I'll sit on the bench, but I'll be part of the team.'

"I try to make my own kids believe that, too. I try to tell them that they should show that they're a little bit better than the rest. I tell them to think of themselves as better. Who cares what anyone else thinks? You know, I can almost hear that coach saying the words. 'You're no good.' "

Author Malcolm MacPherson (*The Blood of His Servants*), forty, lives in New York. "It happened to me in the ninth grade, at the Yalesville School in Yalesville, Connecticut," he said. "Both of my parents had just been killed in a car crash, and as you can imagine, it was a very difficult time in my life. I went out for the baseball team, and I did pretty well in practice.

"But in the first game I clutched. I was playing second base; the batter hit a popup, and I moved back to catch it. I can see it now. I felt dizzy as I looked up at the ball. It was like I was moving in slow motion, but the ball was going at regular speed. I couldn't get out of the way of my own feet. The ball dropped to the ground. I didn't catch it.

"The next day at practice, the coach read off the lineup. I wasn't on it. I was off the squad.

"I remember what I did: I walked. It was a cold spring afternoon, and the ground was wet, and I just walked. I was living with an aunt and uncle, and I didn't want to go home. I just wanted to walk forever.

"It drove my opinion of myself right into a tunnel. Right

into a cave. And when I came out of that cave, something inside of me wanted to make sure in one manner or another that I would never again be told I wasn't good enough.

"I will confess that my ambition, to this day, is out of control. It's like a fire. I think the fire would have pretty much stayed in control if I hadn't been cut from that team. But that got it going. You don't slice ambition two ways; it's either there or it isn't. Those of us who went through something like that always know that we have to catch the ball. We'd rather die than have the ball fall at our feet.

"Once that fire is started in us, it never gets extinguished, until we die or have heart attacks or something. Sometimes I wonder about the home-run hitters; the guys who never even had to worry about being cut. They may have gotten the applause and the attention back then, but I wonder if they ever got the fire. I doubt it. I think maybe you have to get kicked in the teeth to get the fire started.

"You can tell the effect of something like that by examining the trail you've left in your life, and tracing it backward. It's almost like being a junkie with a need for success. You get attention and applause and you like it, but you never quite trust it. Because you know that back then you were good enough if only they would have given you a chance. You don't trust what you achieve, because you're afraid that someone will take it away from you. You know that it can happen; it already did.

"So you try to show people how good you are. Maybe you don't go out and become Dan Rather; maybe you just end up owning the Pontiac dealership in your town. But it's your dealership, and you're the top man, and every day you're showing people that you're good enough."

Dan Rather, fifty-two, is anchor of the "CBS Evening News." "When I was thirteen, I had rheumatic fever," he said. "I became extremely skinny and extremely weak, but I still went out for the seventh-grade baseball team at Alexander Hamilton Junior High School in Houston.

"The school was small enough that there was no cut as such;

you were supposed to figure out that you weren't good enough, and quit. Game after game I sat at the end of the bench, hoping that maybe this was the time I would get in. The coach never even looked at me; I might as well have been invisible.

"I told my mother about it. Her advice was not to quit. So I went to practice every day, and I tried to do well so that the coach would be impressed. He never even knew I was there. At home in my room I would fantasize that there was a big game, and the three guys in front of me would all get hurt, and the coach would turn to me and put me in, and I would make the winning hit. But then there'd be another game, and the late innings would come, and if we were way ahead I'd keep hoping that this was the game when the coach would put me in. He never did.

"When you're that age, you're looking for someone to tell you you're okay. Your sense of self-esteem is just being formed. And what that experience that baseball season did was make me think that perhaps I wasn't okay.

"In the last game of the season something terrible happened. It was the last of the ninth inning, there were two outs, and there were two strikes on the batter. And the coach turned to me and told me to go out to right field.

"It was a totally humiliating thing for him to do. For him to put me in for one pitch, the last pitch of the season, in front of all the other guys on the team . . . I stood out there for that one pitch, and I just wanted to sink into the ground and disappear. Looking back on it, it was an extremely unkind thing for him to have done. That was nearly forty years ago, and I don't know why the memory should be so vivid now; I've never known if the coach was purposely making fun of me—and if he was, why a grown man would do that to a thirteen-year-old boy.

"I'm not a psychologist. I don't know if a man can point to one event in his life and say that that's the thing that made him the way he is. But when you're that age, and you're searching for your own identity, and all you want is to be told that you're all right . . . I wish I understood it better, but I know the feeling is still there."

The Mugging of
Howdy Doody

It's not the major headline stories that tell us the most about what is happening to our world; sometimes the smaller news items speak much more eloquently of what is going on.

And so it is that the most telling and symbolic story of the year is the mugging of Howdy Doody.

If you saw the story at all, it was probably in one of those "people" columns that boil news of "personalities" down to one paragraph. The news was that the original Howdy Doody marionette had been assaulted and damaged in a New York suburb.

It seemed to me that there was more there than could be reported in a brief item. So I got in touch with Howdy Doody's owner—E. Roger Muir, the former executive producer of the old Howdy Doody television show.

"It happened, all right," Muir said. "It's enough to make you sick."

Muir oversaw the production of "The Howdy Doody Show" during its legendary years on NBC television from 1947 to 1960. During those years, Howdy—the grinning, freckle-faced marionette—became beloved to a generation of American children, and an unwitting symbol of what this country was like during simpler and perhaps happier times.

Muir now is a partner in a video production firm in Larchmont, N.Y. When he came to work one morning, he saw immediately that burglars had broken into his offices.

"Whoever did it completely ransacked the place," he said. "They came in during the night, and they uprooted potted plants, they destroyed three television sets, they threw everything around."

On the floor, amid the debris, Muir found Howdy Doody.

"They had assaulted him and torn him apart," Muir said. "Howdy's head was in one room. They had ripped his right arm off, and that was in another room. And the rest of his body was thrown in a third room. His clothes were all torn."

Muir picked up Howdy Doody's smiling head, and all he could think about was how twisted things had become in our modern society. He knew that the crime rate was high; he even knew that some criminals routinely vandalized and destroyed the homes and offices that they burglarized. But casually destroying Howdy Doody?

"Howdy had been displayed in a trophy case in my office," Muir said. "He was one of the three original Howdys that still remain. The children who watched the show thought there was only one, but we used three Howdys for different purposes at different times.

"Seeing Howdy torn into pieces . . . it made me just sick to my stomach. He had this big gash on his face; it looked like they had stomped on him. I don't know why it affected me so strongly, but it did. There was just no reason for anyone to do this.

"Some witnesses saw three men running away from the office. They appeared to be between eighteen and twenty-two; they probably didn't even know who Howdy Doody was. In a way, that's fortunate; if they had known how valuable Howdy was, they would have taken him instead of ripping him apart, and then we'd never have seen him again."

One of the first things that Muir did after notifying the police was to call Buffalo Bob Smith, the genial human host who appeared on TV with Howdy for all those years.

"Buffalo Bob was just sick about it, too," Muir said. "He was almost in a state of shock. He kept saying, 'Why would anyone do such a thing?'"

Muir got in touch with Pady Blackwood, a New York puppet master who specializes in the repair of dolls and marionettes. Blackwood said he would attempt to repair Howdy.

"When Howdy was brought to me, I couldn't believe what I was seeing," Blackwood said. "It was as if he was the victim of an ax-murderer.

"They brought me a suitcase full of parts, basically. Luckily, Howdy's body is made of wood, so it was pretty sturdy. But his face is more brittle; there was a lot of damage."

Blackwood worked for more than a week putting Howdy back together. "I felt very emotional when I was doing it," he said. "I grew up in Kansas City; our family didn't have a television in the late Forties and early Fifties, and I would go down to the local furniture store after school every day. There was a TV set there, and I would watch 'Howdy Doody.' It was the thing that first got me interested in puppets and marionettes. And now . . . this."

The surgery was a qualified success. Howdy's arm was sewn back on, and so was his head. There are suture marks where the neck and head are joined, but Howdy's famous bandanna covers the scars.

E. Roger Muir has tightened security precautions in his offices; there are new locks, and Howdy has been stored in a new case. But Muir realizes that all the precautions in the world can't change the basic message of what has happened.

"We now live in a world where someone would do something like this to Howdy Doody," he said. "There's no getting around that."

All Stars

One of the great side benefits of the reporting business is that you get to meet people you'd otherwise never have a chance to be near. But you get spoiled; you meet those folks on such a regular basis that before long they become just sources of quotes for you—you lose sight of the fact that most people would kill for the opportunity to spend time with them.

It's too bad. I've had a chance to sit down with a couple of men who were President of the United States, and I met Prince Charles once; after each of those encounters I felt like kicking myself for not feeling more like a little kid about it.

Last week, though, I felt like a little kid.

As part of the festivities surrounding the All-Star game, dozens of members of baseball's Hall of Fame came to Chicago for an old-timers' game the day before the main event. I went out to Comiskey Park; by the time I got home I had stars in my eyes, and I was calling friends all over the country to tell them what had happened.

It was simple; in the space of one hour, I talked with Joe DiMaggio, Stan Musial, Willie Mays, Duke Snider, Roger Maris, Bob Feller, Bobby Thomson, and Pee Wee Reese.

I suppose I had forgotten how much I had idolized them. We go nuts over baseball stars when we are little boys; by the time we are teenagers our allegiance has switched to other folks—rock stars and the like—and we forget how much the baseball players meant to us. When I say "we" and "us," I'm referring to my own generation; I really don't know if little boys today feel quite the same way about the millionaire ballplayers with agents and financial advisers as we did about the men whose faces appeared on our Topps baseball cards.

That's what it was like last week—like being a wide-eyed boy again, collecting baseball cards that had suddenly, in a fantasy, come true, sprung to life. It was sort of like having someone say, "Come with me," and then walking with that person into a private room and finding out that all of the Beatles were waiting to say hello.

Except this was even better. Of all the good things that have happened to me, I don't think any will surpass the moment last week when I realized Duke Snider was being nice to me.

Duke Snider. I had sat in my bedroom as an eight-year-old, writing letters to him in care of the Dodgers in far-off Brooklyn, begging for an autographed picture. He was more glamorous to me than any movie star—because he wasn't acting; he was a real-life hero whose luster didn't fade when the film ended. If someone had told me back then that one day Duke Snider would actually sit down and speak with me as if we both lived in the same universe, I would have thought that person was engaging in a cruel taunt.

And yet here we were, on a summer afternoon in the 1980s, and as the other old-timers took batting practice and Duke Snider and I sat watching, he gently tried to give me some perspective on what was real and what was myth.

"I went to the car wash last year," Snider said. I had just blathered some embarrassing version of the emotions contained two paragraphs above this one.

"I went to the car wash last year," Snider said. "And when my car came out, the fellow said that I owed him $2.50. And I said, 'I thought it cost $4.' And the fellow said, 'Yes, sir, but we give a discount to senior citizens.'"

I knew the anecdote wasn't an apocryphal one; Snider isn't the firm-jawed stud of those 1955 baseball cards now, he is a white-haired man who might, indeed, pass you unnoticed on the street. But the great thing about this gathering was that it didn't matter; it was so marvelous to be able to spend time with these men who had meant so much to so many of us that nothing else counted.

So Pee Wee Reese told me that his leg was bad, and that in

the old-timers' dressing room Snider and Willie Mays had helped him put his uniform on. The Comiskey Park organist played "When I'm Sixty-four" as we talked, and when I told Reese the name of the song, he said, "Do they have one called 'When I'm Sixty-five'?"—and said that he would, indeed, turn sixty-five later this year.

Joe DiMaggio said that he wants to look the truth "right in the eye—I am an old-timer now, and I know it." Roger Maris said that although he remains unhappy that he never got what he felt was the proper recognition for hitting sixty-one home runs in a single season and breaking Babe Ruth's record, "baseball basically meant everything to me"—and that holding a bat during warm-ups on this day, he had been surprised and a little saddened to realize how awkward it felt. Willie Mays was unexpectedly unpleasant—combative and defensive and sensitive to slights that just weren't there. But even that was interesting; who ever thought that the chance would come to find out anything at all about Willie Mays, except batting averages and historical anecdotes?

And it was fine to discover that some legends and stereotypes are based on truth. At the beginning of this day, while the rest of the old-timers waited leisurely in the locker room, getting dressed and renewing old friendships, one man hurried onto the field alone and, in full uniform, paced back and forth, impatiently waiting for the others to come out and play baseball with him. Ernie Banks.

When I headed home from Comiskey Park, I realized that those men could never understand what meeting them had meant. I am one of millions of American males who grew up almost dizzy with reverence for them. We were the dreamers; they were the dreams. And it was gloriously good news on a hot July afternoon to discover that, after all these years, the dreams are still there.

Bathroom Humor

The village of Schaumburg, Illinois, is buzzing over a controversy involving bathroom humor.

At the Hyatt Regency Woodfield hotel, there is a disco called the Playground. Several weeks ago, workmen installed video screens above each of the three urinals in the Playground's men's room.

When a man walks up to a urinal, he trips an electronic eye that causes a film to be projected onto the video screen above that urinal. The films feature attractive, scantily clad young women saying naughty things.

"The idea was for it to be funny," said Larry Sode, technical director for the Playground. "It was supposed to make people laugh; it was supposed to be one more reason for them to come to the Playground."

Each film lasts between ten and thirty seconds. The women are dressed in negligees, in bikinis, in low-cut gowns, in leotards. The screens are positioned so that the women seem to be looking into the eyes of the men in front of them.

There are about twenty-five different things they say. Some of the milder samples:

"Aren't you the Lincoln Park flasher?"

"Nice try."

"Do you know what a woman says when she's sexually satisfied? [Pause] I didn't think so."

Larry Sode said that response from the Playground's customers has been overwhelmingly enthusiastic.

"They love it," he said. "Everyone out here is talking about it. People are lined up trying to get into the men's room. We haven't advertised it or anything, but people are coming to the Playground just to go to the men's room.

"We've even caught women trying to sneak in so they can see the films."

Unfortunately, some other Schaumburg residents have also dropped by to see the films—Mayor Herb Aigner and police officers dispatched by him. They are not amused.

"Look, I like a good joke as well as anyone else," Mayor Aigner said. "But a lot of this stuff isn't funny. It's just dirty.

"Yes, I paid an inspection call on the Playground's men's room last week. Frankly, I find the whole thing sleazy. A lot of this isn't good-natured humor; it's sleazy humor. I asked our police chief to have a look, too.

"I must confess, I do not find this kind of thing in keeping with the image of a Hyatt hotel. We look for certain institutions to maintain a level of taste above the average, and Hyatt hotels are one of those institutions.

"We in Schaumburg have worked very hard to keep certain elements out of our village. You won't find pinball machines or video parlors out here. You won't find adult bookstores out here. And now we have the Playground doing this kind of thing. I find it upsetting."

The mayor said that he has determined there is nothing legally he can do to make the Playground stop featuring the risqué jokes on the video screens above the urinals.

"It's not a case of forcing them to stop," he said. "There's nothing we can do. This is America, and in America we have something called freedom of speech. There is no Schaumburg ordinance they are violating.

"But are you asking me if I would prefer that they took those screens down? Yes, I would. I wish they would get the message and stop doing it. I would feel better if those screens weren't there.

"It lowers the prestige of the hotel, and more importantly, it lowers the prestige of Schaumburg. If a man goes into the men's room and sees a woman on a screen above the urinal saying sleazy things, what does he do next? Maybe he goes back out into the bar and starts looking around to see if he can find any hookers."

At the Hyatt Regency Woodfield, general manager Helmut Brenzinger said the purpose of the video screens was not to offend anyone.

"There is no nudity on the part of the women in the films," he said. "And there is no profanity. It is more double meanings, not profane words.

"I was born in Germany, so I probably do not understand all of the phrases. But the customers seem to like it very much. They realize it is strictly fun. Maybe they're a little shocked at first, but they end up realizing it is all in good fun."

Brenzinger said he did not mind if the Village of Schaumburg wanted to keep sending police officers to monitor the video screens.

"I have no problem with that," he said. "I like having the police here. It helps to keep the rowdies out.

"I know that Schaumburg is a very conservative city; the city administration is very strict about what can happen here and what cannot happen. Believe me, I support them one hundred percent. I want what they want. But this is just good fun."

In the meantime, Larry Sode—as technical director of the disco—is responsible for the maintenance and operation of the video screens in the bathroom. He has no interest in the political ramifications of the controversy.

"That's between the village and the hotel," he said. "I just happen to be very proud of the job we've done in setting this up. Do you realize that we have a JBL speaker over each urinal? When the women on the films speak, the sound quality is excellent. This is a very high-class operation."

A Testing Time

For a couple of years, I had been having a nagging feeling. The feeling was that I was dumber than I had been in high school.

This feeling hit me at all kinds of times, but usually when I was trying to add up a column of figures without using a calculator, or attempting to do some elementary long division or multiplication in my head. Something had definitely happened to me, and I suspected that it had happened to a lot of men and women like me who had been out of the high school classroom for twenty years. The mental exercises that used to be so simple now loomed as almost impossible; there were plenty of social moves that I had learned in the real world, but a lot of cerebral skills that I had owned as a high school junior seemed to have gone with the wind.

Rather than brood on this, I decided to do the only logical thing:

I would take the SATs again.

The SATs—it stands for Scholastic Aptitude Test, but the shortened version is always used in the plural—are administered by the Educational Testing Service and, of course, are the most intimidating thing that happens to a boy or girl during his or her high school career. The SATs measure verbal and mathematical abilities; the results of the tests, figured against a scale of eight hundred points, are sent to university admissions offices, and play a significant role in determining whether a high school student will get into a particular college.

I was a pretty smart kid in high school; I did well on my SATs, scoring a 724 on the verbal part and a 706 on the math part. That, though, was in 1964; as I have mentioned, I was convinced that I had become considerably dumber during the ensuing years.

So I decided that I would be one of the 1.6 million people a year—virtually all of them high school juniors and seniors—to take the SATs. I had only vague memories of the test; the memories involved pain, clocks, and lead-point pencils. I was not especially looking forward to going through with it again, but it seemed like something that had to be done.

I applied for the SATs. It turned out that there wasn't any age limit; as long as I sent in my eleven dollars, I could take the test.

I filled out my application form. There were spaces to list the colleges to which I wished my test results sent. I thought about it for a minute, then wrote in Harvard, Princeton, Yale, and Ohio State.

I received my admission ticket in the mail, along with an orientation booklet. The ticket informed me that I would be taking the test at Evanston Township High School in Evanston, Illinois, on a Saturday morning.

The orientation booklet was sixty-two pages long, and I didn't open it until the night before the test. Just trying to read it made me dizzy. I got only to page 6; there was a section headed "The Day Before the Tests," and it said, "You'll accomplish little by worrying about the next day. Read a book, watch a television program you enjoy, or do anything you find relaxing."

I took the booklet to a bar that I like and laid it on the wood surface in front of me. I halfheartedly attempted to read the section called "Test-Taking Tips," but the music and the conversation around me were too loud and soon enough I gave up.

Shortly after 8:00 on a crisp Saturday morning, I walked into the lobby of Evanston Township High School. There is something about a high school on a Saturday morning that feels the same after all these years. I went to the school office and was directed to a study hall on the first floor. About twenty boys and girls were already there, lined up. They were not being allowed inside yet. I joined the line.

The two girls in front of me were showing each other snapshots from the previous spring's prom. One of the girls displayed her two pencils—the orientation booklet had instructed each of us to bring "Two No. 2 pencils with erasers." The girl said, "My mother is so bogus. She told me, 'You'd better bring more than two. What if one of them breaks?' I said, 'Mom, did you ever hear of pencil sharpeners?' "

I sheepishly looked down at the front pocket of my shirt, where I had stashed six sharpened pencils, just in case five of them broke.

We were allowed into the room. There were three adult proctors there, all women. One of them sat at a desk and made each of us present ID cards with photos on them; the cards had to verify that we were the same people whose names were on our admission tickets. This was new; I did not recall having to do it twenty years ago. Apparently it was to discourage students from taking the tests for their friends.

We were instructed to sit in vertical rows, leaving an empty row between each row of us. I found a seat; it was one of those desks that are attached to the chair, and as I slipped into it my mind flooded with high school memories.

I looked around the room. There were approximately fifty-five of us taking the test. I had expected to be the object of curiosity—after all, these kids were seventeen, and I was thirty-seven—but no one was paying a bit of attention to me. These boys and girls were scared to death. I could have been Kareem Abdul-Jabbar and they wouldn't have noticed.

The chief proctor said something else that was new: "Calculators or wristwatches with calculator functions may not be used."

Then, reading from a manual, she said a series of sentences that began with the phrase "Do not worry": "Do not worry if

you do not complete a section by the end of the allotted time."
"Do not worry if you do not know the answer to every question."

Ha. Easy for her to say.

Another one of the proctors began handing out the answer
forms. I looked around the room.

There was total silence. Whatever wise-guy poses these students might affect during the school week were gone; these
were the SATs that were heading their way, and nothing in
the world was more serious than that.

The boy sitting closest to me had on a white jersey that said
LAS VEGAS on the front and featured colorful drawings of playing cards and dice on the back. Another boy, sitting a couple
of aisles to my left, made a steering-wheel motion to a friend
of his over by the window; the friend nodded yes. He had
driven to school; he would give the other boy a ride home.

The tests were handed to us. They were in booklet form.
The chief proctor said that there were six sections; we were
to have thirty minutes to complete each of them. If we completed a section early, we were to sit quietly at our desks with
the test booklets closed.

It was just after 9:00. The proctor looked at her watch. Apparently she was waiting for the second hand to hit the twelve.
After what seemed to be an interminable wait, she said:

"You may begin."

The covers of fifty-five booklets were pulled open; fifty-five
of us leaned over our answer sheets.

It became evident right away that, for me, the verbal part
was going to be pretty easy. I had assumed that I would have
to identify sentence structures that I had long forgotten the
terms for; but the test wasn't like that at all. Most of the verbal
questions were commonsense things; I have been writing every day for a lot of years now, talking to copy editors as a
matter of course, and I wasn't having any problems with the
verbal stuff.

The math was another story. With the math, much of the time I didn't even understand the questions. There was a long line drawn; the farthest point to the left was marked P, the midpoint was marked Q, the farthest point to the right was marked R. The space between P and Q was marked $x + y$. The space between Q and R was marked $2x - y$. The question was, "Segment PR is divided into two segments with lengths as shown above. If Q is the midpoint of PR, which of the following statements must be true?" We were asked to choose any one of five: "$x = 0$," "$x = \frac{1}{2}y$," "$x = \frac{2}{3}y$," "$x = y$," "$x = 2y$."

I developed a terrible headache doing the math questions. There was some pretty simple stuff that you could figure out using basic logic; but a lot of it was truly impossible for me to deal with. I kept thinking that, twenty years ago, I had come very close to totally mastering questions just like these; now I was stumped. I forged on, with very little enthusiasm, and even less hope.

At the end of the first two test sections—one hour into the morning—the chief proctor said that we would have precisely five minutes to go out into the hallway and relax. We marched out there. All of us looked dazed, unhappy, and disoriented, although I believe that I was the only student to go to the water fountain and take an Inderal for his blood pressure.

We went back into the room. There was something vaguely comforting about being there. Maybe it was the clear, definite tone of the instructions in the test booklet. In the real, grown-up world, so much is left up to individual interpretation. Here, at the end of every page, there was a bold arrow marked with the words GO ON TO THE NEXT PAGE. And at the end of every test section, a spaced-out, capitalized S T O P. And the flat-out message: IF YOU FINISH BEFORE TIME IS CALLED, YOU MAY CHECK YOUR WORK ON THIS SECTION ONLY. DO NOT WORK ON ANY OTHER SECTION OF THE TEST.

The chief proctor was just as definite about what she was doing. At the end of the fourth section of the test—the second hour—she said, "We will now have a one-minute stretching period. You may stand and stretch by your desks." When one boy started out into the hallway, the proctor said, "The stretching period is to be conducted by your desk only. You may not leave the room."

The rules, the feeling of sitting in that combination desk-chair, the sounds I was hearing—the girl behind me popping her gum, the fluorescent lights above me humming softly, the hiss from the pipes—I don't know why, but I liked it a lot.

We finished the test a little after noon. Many of the boys and girls knew each other from school; they talked about the questions on the way out of the building. As I left, the chief proctor said to me, "Do you mind if I ask you a question?" I thought she was going to ask the obvious one: What was I doing there? But she said, "Why did you choose to wear a tie this morning?" I was so startled that I could only answer, "If you don't look sharp, you're not going to feel sharp."

Weeks went by. I was aware of a vague sense of apprehension; occasionally I lost sight of what it might be about, and then I remembered: my SAT scores were going to be coming.

One day there the envelope was, in the morning mail. The return address said it was from the College Board. I knew it was ridiculous to feel nervous; these results weren't going to have any effect on my life. I was already a college graduate; these scores weren't going to get me in or keep me out of anywhere.

But my hands were undeniably shaking as I ripped open the envelope. And there they were: my scores. Verbal—780. Math—500.

My instincts while I had been taking the test had been correct. In the verbal sections, I had actually gone up more than fifty points since high school. But in the math sections, I had dropped more than two hundred points.

That was sort of depressing to me—being two hundred points

dumber in math than when I was seventeen years old. I kept it to myself, though. How could I burden people with my problem? My contemporaries were walking around worried about making partner at their law firms, about getting a mortgage for a new house, about deciding whether to accept a transfer that would move their families halfway across the country. When they asked me why I was so down in the mouth, I just couldn't say it:

"I screwed up on my SATs."

Scene of the Crime

You walk into the small, neat, neighborhood clothing store at 5408 West North Avenue, Chicago, and you realize that this is the awful news that never makes the paper. The news of what happens afterward.

You walk into the clothing store—it is called The Spot—and you see the owner standing near the cash register. His name is Kwang Nam Kim; he is forty-four years old, a true believer in the American dream. He came to the United States from Korea ten years ago, accompanied by his wife and two sons. Kim had been a tailor in Korea. But he wanted more for his family.

So he brought them to Chicago. He got a job at Hart Schaffner & Marx; his wife, Kyung Soon Kim, worked there too, as a seamstress. When he had saved enough money, he opened up The Spot in this West Side neighborhood, and he and his wife went into business for themselves.

On January 18, 1982, Mr. and Mrs. Kim were working alone

in The Spot right after the store had opened for the morning. Two young men came into the store. They casually tried on some jeans and jackets. Then they announced that they were going to rob the Kims.

Mr. and Mrs. Kim did exactly what the men told them to do. They did not resist, they did not try to call the police. The men ordered them into a back room and told them to lie on the floor, face down. They did. The men went back out front to steal whatever they wanted.

Before the men left the store, they went to the back room again. The Kims were still face down, still following orders. One of the men pointed a gun at the back of Mrs. Kim's head. He pulled the trigger. The bullet bored through her head and exited through her mouth. Then the men left the store with $100 and some clothing.

The murder of Mrs. Kim was handled in crisp, professional style by all the police and law agencies involved. Chicago police arrested two men—LeRoy Carter, Jr., nineteen, the gunman, and Earvin Newsome, twenty-one, his accomplice. Carter pleaded guilty and was sentenced to forty years in prison; Newsome was vigorously prosecuted by assistant state's attorneys Michael Spivack and Joan Corboy. He was found guilty and sentenced to thirty-three years in prison.

This time the criminal justice system worked precisely the way it is supposed to.

And on a summer night a year and a half later, Kwang Nam Kim stands alone in his store, his wife dead for no reason. A handsome, immaculately dressed man, he waits for seven P.M., closing time.

You enter the store and introduce yourself. Kim is polite and quiet. He locks up the store; he invites you to visit with him in his apartment above the store. You walk up a flight of wooden stairs.

You sit with him in his living room. Kim speaks halting English; he is more comfortable speaking Korean. His son John, fifteen, a student at Weber High School, joins you to act as translator. The other son, Sam, nineteen, is away at summer school at Harvard—paid for by the work his father and mother put in downstairs.

There is a classical music album—*Swan Lake*—resting next to the stereo. The apartment is small but well tended. Kwang Nam Kim sits on the edge of a chair and tries to tell you what it is like to live, after having lain next to his wife in their store while she was casually executed.

"We came to America to have a better life," he says. John translates. "I wanted to live better, so I would be able to send my sons to college. I never knew this would happen, of course."

You ask him if he is satisfied with the results of the court cases against the two men. He seems not very interested. The court cases seem to have nothing to do with him.

"It's a little hard on me, yes," he says. "But at least I can hope to see my sons grow up."

He says that his life is simple now. He opens the store each morning, he stays until early evening, he goes out to dinner, he goes to bed. He has not been out with a woman since the death of his wife, and has not even thought of the prospect of marrying again.

He says the worst time of day for him is in the morning. "I go down to open the store," he says. "I play some Korean music on a tape player. It is the music my wife and I used to listen to. When I hear that music, I think of being with her in the store, and I miss her very much."

John, listening to the words about his mother, continues to translate for his father.

Kim says that he tries not to think of the past, but of the future. But he says that sometimes he cannot help thinking about his wife, and what his life might have been like had the men not chosen to come into his store that morning.

"She was the best wife a man could ever have," he says. "She was the best . . ." He has to stop, because all this time later his eyes are welling over with tears, and he is crying.

"She took care of us," he says, and the tears roll down his face.

You sit with him and you wonder what you can possibly

say. You think of what you had asked Michael Spivack, the assistant state's attorney who successfully prosecuted the case. Forty years for one defendant, thirty-three years for the other. Relatively stiff sentences. You had asked Spivack if he felt justice had been done.

"I don't know," Spivack had said quietly. "What's justice?"

Teen Idol

Several odd things have happened to me in my life, but perhaps none was ever as odd as the one I never talk about—the time I appeared in *Dig* magazine.

Dig magazine is long dead. But when it was around, in the late 1950s, it had a loyal audience of young boys and girls who were hooked on the movie stars, TV actors, and rock singers of the day. It was basically a fan magazine; it's probably safe to say that the same youngsters who read *Dig* went on to read *Rolling Stone* a decade or so later.

Dig had a section—it was a two-page center spread—that featured pictures and brief comments from readers. They printed thirty or forty of the pictures every month; the readers signed their names and addresses, and other readers, if they so chose, could write letters to them.

One day in 1959, without telling anyone in my family or any of my friends, I wrote a letter to *Dig*. It was brief:

> My name is Bobby Greene. I am only 12, but I dig *Dig*. I dig Elvis, Kookie, and Ricky. My address is 2722 Bryden Rd., Columbus 9, Ohio.

I enclosed a sixth-grade school photograph in which I let my eyes half-close in what I hoped resembled a come-hither bedroom look, and in which I attempted a sultry Presley sneer.

I never expected anything to happen. The school year ended, and I went off to Camp Arrowhead, in Jackson, Ohio. I spent the summer hunting frogs and playing baseball and doing other boylike things; on the last day of camp my father drove down to pick up my friend Allen Schulman and me and take us home.

When my father arrived, he didn't say anything. He merely handed me a large box that had been in the back seat of the car.

In the box were approximately four hundred letters. All were addressed to "Bobby Greene."

For a second, I didn't know what had happened. But I only had to open the first letter to find out.

It went something like:

> Dear Bobby—
> I loved the way you looked in *Dig*, and I just had to write you. I live in Louisville, Kentucky. . . .

The letters were all from young girls. *Dig* had printed my picture and note. Some of the girls had enclosed the clipping from *Dig;* the editors, for some reason, had added a year to my age, so the text under my picture said, "I am only 13, but I dig *Dig*."

Apparently the motivation of the editors was to make me seem like an older man. It had worked; the whole ride back to Columbus I opened the letters, and I was shocked by what I read.

There was no getting around it. At twelve, I was a national sex symbol for young girls. They couldn't have Elvis or Kookie or Ricky—if you need to be told who Ricky was, by the way, you are of the wrong generation to be reading this—but they had my home address and my sneering, leering picture right in front of them.

Most of the letters were pretty tame; the girls said that they wanted to "meet" me, and let it go at that. But the message was clear; because I had been in *Dig*, I had become a celebrity to them. The only specific letter I remember came from a girl who said, "My father drives a dumptruck and my measurements are 33-23-33."

This all presented a dilemma for me. Yes, I had sent the letter; and yes, I had sent the now-notorious photograph. But basically I was a pretty sheltered, innocent, suburban kid; what was I supposed to *do* with all these girls?

When I got home I asked my parents what they thought. "You wrote to the magazine, so you have the obligation to answer each of those girls," my mother said. I went to my room with the box of four hundred letters and I started to try to answer them.

Within a day, though, I knew it was going to be impossible. The mailman showed up, and he had dozens of more letters. The onslaught had just begun. Every day I would get a bundle of letters. I became jaded by them, inured to them; I would go out into the back yard and sit under a tree and casually open the letters up. Always the contents would be the same: a letter from a girl who also dug Elvis, Kookie, and Ricky; a photograph of the girl; and an invitation to write or visit her.

This went on for months, every single day. I answered some of the letters; most I just kept under my bed in my room. I didn't know what I was supposed to do with them once I had finished reading them, but I knew it would be wrong to throw them away.

Even after the letters stopped arriving regularly, they continued to trickle in once in a while. Two or three years later, at least once a month, I would get a letter that began: "I don't know if you still live at this address, but I found an old copy of *Dig* magazine . . ." One letter came five years later; it began, "I figure you must be 18 by now . . ." [They were still operating under the assumption that I had been thirteen, not twelve, when *Dig* had ordained me.]

I grew up and moved away, and went to college and got on

with my life. But the experience of being in *Dig* had affected me in ways I was not quite able to define; I always knew that other boys might have certain advantages over me—but that they had never been made a teen idol by *Dig*. Somehow it had changed my life.

Even now, when each day's mail arrives at my newspaper office, I flip through it, half-expecting a letter to begin:

Dear Bobby—

I just came across an old copy of *Dig* magazine. You must be 37 by now. . . .

And I always know I can answer: "Thirty-six. The editors of *Dig* added a year."

Dog Days on Publishers Row

So you say you want to be a published author. You're looking for advice.

You've sat under a bare sixty-watt light bulb for years. You've cranked reams of white bond paper into your ancient manual typewriter. You've poured your heart, your soul, and your very guts onto those pages. You've come up with your idea of a masterwork.

But you can't get anyone interested. Publishers send your book back with form rejection notices. Agents tell you they can't help. You're confused. You know your stuff is good; why won't anyone print it? What can you do?

All right, you asked for a straight answer, and a straight answer you'll get. You want to get your book published? You want to see your work in the stores? You want enthusiasm from the Manhattan literary community?

Be a dog.

One of the major titles on the spring list of Doubleday and Company, one of New York's oldest and most respected publishers, is *C. Fred's Story*. The byline on the book belongs to C. Fred Bush.

C. Fred Bush is a dog. Specifically, he is a golden cocker spaniel; he is owned by Vice-President George Bush. Although the words in the book were actually written by Bush's wife, Barbara, the narrative is told from the dog's point of view, purportedly in the dog's own voice.

Doubleday is not taking C. Fred Bush's book as a joke. Interest in the book reaches to the very top of the Doubleday corporation, and that interest has filtered down to employees all through the publishing house. Doubleday is poised to commit its full resources to the literary debut of George Bush's dog.

The editor at Doubleday assigned to handle *C. Fred's Story* is Lisa Drew, who has been with the house for twenty-two years.

"The idea came to me directly from Nelson Doubleday, the president of the corporation," Drew said. "It's very unusual for Mr. Doubleday to get directly involved with bringing a book into the house, but Mr. Doubleday is a friend of the Bushes', and a neighbor, I think, of the Vice-President's mother in Florida. Mr. Doubleday asked me if I was aware of the Bushes' dog. He told me that the dog was really kind of a character, and that he thought there was a book there."

Drew wrote a letter to Mrs. Bush. "Mrs. Bush told me that C. Fred got a lot of fan mail," Drew said. "Apparently whenever there was a picture in the paper of the Bushes and the dog, people would write to the dog. Mrs. Bush would write letters of reply over the dog's name. One day Mrs. Bush's chief of staff said, "Why waste it in a letter? Why not put it in a book?"

Drew conferred with Mrs. Bush; they decided that the book should contain both text and photos and should describe the dog's life in Washington and on his travels around the world.

"As far as point of view goes, we decided early on that it had to be by the dog," Drew said. "He talks about his views of the world and how proud he is to be the Bushes' dog. This is a dog who has taken trips to China, New York, Maine, back to Texas. It wouldn't have worked in the third person. It had to be first person, in the dog's voice."

Drew said that Mrs. Bush's manuscript went through the editing processes largely unchanged.

"The major suggestion I made was for Mrs. Bush to get rid of all the exclamation points," Drew said. "She had a tendency to include four or five exclamation points after each sentence. And I asked her to use another typewriter. The one she was using was the kind used for typing speeches, with the big letters."

At any publishing house, one of the key executives who will determine the financial success of a book is the subsidiary rights director. The subsidiary rights director is in charge of selling a book to paperback houses, to magazines that will excerpt it, to book clubs.

"At our first meeting, when this book by the Bushes' dog was presented to us, our first reaction was, 'Gee, is Lisa serious?'" said Jackie Everly, Doubleday's director of subsidiary rights. "When we found out that she was, we got right into it. We're not exactly a bunch of pushovers. We have to be hard-nosed. We have to consider what the book will mean to us in the sense of business."

The ground rule was that Mrs. Bush would donate the dog's personal royalties to two charities. Doubleday's revenues from sales of the book, though, would remain with the publishing house; Everly was to handle subsidiary arrangements as she would with any other Doubleday title.

Everly said she thought she could help make *C. Fred's Story* a winner for Doubleday. "We lunch with people from the magazines, the book clubs, and the reprinters," she said. "This is a perfect kind of book to talk about at lunch. We like to whet these people's appetites for the book, and this dog's book is very upbeat. We have more than five hundred books a year on our list, and frankly, we just don't have the time to have a separate lunch for each book. But this is a book that is coming up all the time at lunch."

Everly said that, based on her experience, "I think rights-wise it will be a very successful book. I don't see how it can miss, to tell you the truth. Especially if it goes on the best-seller list in hardcover, the reprinters are really going to stand up and take notice. The fact that the book is written by a dog will not hurt us at all. I think this is something we can run with."

Alex Gotfryd is Doubleday's art director. To him fell the task of supervising the design of the Bushes' dog's book's jacket. "A book jacket is a tool of promotion and advertising," Gotfryd said. "When a person carries a book on a bus or on the subway, or walks down the street carrying it in his hand, that's free advertising. A jacket can be thought of as a little poster. And the poster should emphasize the content of the book."

In this case, Gotfryd said, "I knew right away that the main element on the front of the jacket had to be C. Fred Bush himself. After all, it's his book. So when people look at the jacket we've come up with, they'll see a dog. Actually, they'll see a dog and Mrs. Bush; she's holding him."

He said he had attempted to make the jacket "attractive and appropriate"; the color scheme he accepted was red, ivory, and dark blue. "A great deal of thought and effort and logic and intelligence go into these decisions," he said. "The whole idea is to come up with a jacket that is imprinted in the memory. If a potential customer does not buy it the first time he sees it, perhaps he will remember it and buy it the second time."

His goal with the jacket for *C. Fred's Story*, he said, was "to capsulize the essence of the book, but not to give away the book entirely. There should be a little mystery in the cover, a little drama—we should make the reader discover something special about the book, but not make him work too hard.

"I'm an artist, but I'm also a businessman. I'm hired to produce a very fine commercial package. I try to seduce the customer to pick that book up in a bookstore and to purchase it. I think that in the case of this dog's book, we should do very well in those terms."

For Dick Heffernan, Doubleday's sales manager for trade books, the problem is always the same. Doubleday's thirty-two trade sales representatives present the house's list of books to booksellers twice a year. That means that on each client call, a sales representative has approximately 250 books to pitch.

"We don't require our salespeople to actually read any of the books they are selling," Heffernan said. "A good reader is not necessarily a good salesman, and vice versa."

Instead, Doubleday prepares a "T.I. (title information) sheet" for each book, summarizing what the book is about. Included on the T.I. sheet is a "keynote"—a phrase that describes the book in twenty-five words or less.

That way, even if a sales representative has never seen a particular book, he can describe it to a bookstore owner in precisely the way Doubleday's executives would like to have it described.

"You have to understand, on some books we have only five to eight seconds to talk about it with a bookstore owner," Heffernan said. "On a major title, we might take up to a minute."

C. Fred's Story, Heffernan said, will probably fall somewhere in between. "It won't be a one-minute presentation, because it's not the biggest book on our list," he said. "But it won't be an eight-second presentation either, because we consider it to be an important book.

"The keynote we give the sales reps will probably be something like: 'A cute little story told by the Bushes' dog and all about the dog's travels around the country and the world.'"

When a sales representative is presenting the book titles to a bookstore owner, Heffernan said, it is not difficult to tell how the bookseller is reacting to each pitch. "You get a pretty good feeling for it," he said.

"You can see the response in the other person's face. He usually places his order right there, before you go on to the next title, so it's important that you make your sale the first time around."

Heffernan said that, compared with other books on the Doubleday list, *C. Fred's Story* should be a relatively simple sell. "No questions about it. No matter how good a first novel might be, for example, this dog's book is much easier for us to sell. You've got the fact that the author is a dog, you've got the fact that in addition to being a dog he's the Vice-President's dog, you've got guaranteed advertising and promotion and publicity, you've got a possible Phil Donahue . . . this book has all the elements."

Elizabeth St. John, Doubleday's publicity manager, said she has seldom encountered a title that promised to make her job easier than *C. Fred's Story*.

"Barbara Bush has promised us to help as much as she can in the promotion of the book," St. John said. "She is an enormously well-known political figure, the wife of the Vice-President—and, at least in Washington and New York, the dog will be made available to the media, also. We can't really ask the dog to make the entire tour—a publicity tour is grueling enough as it is for a human being."

Mrs. Bush is scheduled to make appearances on behalf of the book in New York, Chicago, Washington, Los Angeles, and San Francisco, St. John said. "With someone like her, who has been on all the shows, we'll ask her what her preference is. Normally it can be hard to book someone on a show—the network morning shows in particular. But of course in this case, that will be no problem. Mrs. Bush can talk about this book on virtually any show she chooses."

The publicity drive has begun even before the release of the book. "We sent out a release about C. Fred Bush," St. John said. "We showed a picture of him riding aboard—what is it called, the plane where the Vice-President rides? Air Force One? Air Force Two? In any event, we sent out a very nice photo of the dog on board that plane. The book has everything going for it. It's brief. It has sixty-two photographs of C. Fred. It has a message, and the message is that celebrities are just like us. They have dogs that they spoil and they love just like we do. In that sense, *C. Fred's Story* is a very intimate book."

Although St. John was uncertain whether George Bush would take part in the publicity campaign, "the important thing is not so much Vice-President Bush's participation, or even Mrs. Bush's participation. The important thing is that we get the word out that the Bushes' dog has written a book, and that the book is in the stores. I think we can do that. And I think we have one of the big books of the spring."

And for you who still say you want to be a published author; for you who say you're still slaving away under that light bulb, still cranking that paper into your typewriter; for you who say that you've become discouraged by reading this, and that you want to know what the moral is:

Quit whining. Just shut up and eat your Alpo.

Underpass

The first few times, I didn't realize why I was feeling that way.

I had arrived in Dallas the week before for the Republican National Convention; each morning I would get in a cab and

head for the convention center, where our temporary newsroom was set up. All the way down the freeway nothing would
seem amiss. Then we would ride through an underpass, and I
would get this uncomfortable sensation. Thirty or forty seconds later it would go away.

This happened for three or four days, and then I figured it
out. It wasn't just any underpass we were riding through; it
was the triple underpass from November 22, 1963. And the
parks and buildings around it; they weren't just any landmarks
in any city. There they were: Dealey Plaza. The grassy knoll.
The Texas School Book Depository.

There is a syndrome; maybe you share it with me. Whenever I see something that's supposed to be dramatic and historic and important, it never quite feels that way. We are fed
so much instant history these days, I always fail to feel the
impact of the places I have been taught are historic.

But it was so curious: every time another cab would drive
through that underpass, and I would look over at the red brick
building, I experienced a wave of nausea. To tell the truth, I
felt a little as if I wanted to cry. I'm a little embarrassed to
admit something like that; but the fact is, I don't think I've
ever been as affected by being in a particular place.

My generation has been accused of acting as if history did
not exist before we came along; we have been accused of being shortsighted and naive when it comes to events that truly
matter. And I know that there are events that must be just as
affecting to older Americans: the start of the Great Depression,
the bombing of Pearl Harbor, the death of Franklin Delano
Roosevelt.

For millions of us, though, there was one day that divided
the hemispheres of our lives. The world seemed innocent and
tranquil and full of trust, and then on that November 22, it
didn't seem that way any longer. We couldn't have told you
that at the time. Only as the years passed did we realize what
had happened.

There is a tendency to overanalyze the legacy of that November 22. Historians and political scientists and sociologists

have debated the subject for more than twenty years. In the end, though, it has less to do with history, less to do with politics, less to do with sociology, than it has to do with real life. I know that when I think of that day, it is not in broad, monumental terms. My thoughts are quite basic; quite simple.

Sixth-period English class, Bexley High School. A bright fall day in Ohio. Mrs. Amos is at the blackboard, and then the loudspeaker on the east wall of the room crackles to life. An unusual occurrence; announcements from the principal's office were generally made in the morning.

A disc jockey's voice over the loudspeaker: "This is your country music station . . ." Laughter in the classroom; someone must be fooling around down in Jones's office.

Then the sound of other stations blipping in and out, as an unseen hand twists the radio's knob, moves the tuner. And finally the words from Dallas—words of the gunshots. In a few minutes we will know that the President is dead; now we are merely told that shots have been fired at him, and that he is presumed to be injured. None of us could have told you that he was even taking a trip that day.

I remember walking home. I sat on the front stoop until the paperboy arrived with the evening *Columbus Dispatch*. I had never seen a headline that big; a newspaper had never seemed so important. When my parents had finished reading it, I took it and put it on the top shelf of my closet. For some reason it seemed important that I not throw it away.

I remember going out that night and walking the streets. I had never felt any interest in politics; I had not been one of the young Americans who were fanatical followers of the man who had been President. But inside it seemed that something had been cut out of me; nothing that had happened in my life had ever made me feel this way, and I was scared about it. It was cold that night; later I would meet up with my friends and we would drive around and the radio—WCOL—would tell us that a man had been arrested in Dallas. But what I recall most clearly is walking all by myself, and never having felt so alone.

In later years we would learn things about that President and that administration that would have surprised all of us on that November night; as a matter of fact, a recent nonfiction best-seller was a family history of that President and his parents and his brothers and sisters and their children, and the information in that book was of a nature that we weren't reading about in 1963. But that doesn't really matter; what matters is that there was a time when things felt different, and that that time ended in an instant, and that a lot of us still haven't been able to shake it. When we try to figure out when everything changed in the world, we always come back to that day.

Which is why, riding through that underpass, seeing that red brick building and those plots of grass, I didn't feel like a grown man on his way to work. I felt like a sixteen-year-old kid sitting out on a cement stoop, reading a front-page story that somehow didn't seem real. It was cold in Ohio that November afternoon; in Dallas last week, with the temperatures exceeding one hundred degrees, I rode through that underpass each morning and the chill came back from over all the years.

The ABC's of Courage

It is nearing dusk. The man has finished his day's labor; he is a plumber, and today he was working at a construction site, and his shift has ended.

Now he is sitting in the dining room of Mrs. Patricia Lord, in Cicero, Illinois. Mrs. Lord and the man are bending over a list of words.

"Can you try these now?" Mrs. Lord says.

"Yes," the man says.

He looks at the top word on the list. The word is *is*.

"Is," the man says.

"Yes," Mrs. Lord says.

The next word on the list is *brown*.

The man looks at it for a moment. Then he says: "Brown."

"Yes," Mrs. Lord says.

The next word is *the*.

"The," the man says, touching the word with his hand.

"Yes," Mrs. Lord says.

The next word is *sleep*.

The man hesitates. Seconds pass. He is having trouble with this one.

Finally he says: "Play?"

"No," Mrs. Lord says. "Look at it again."

The man stares. He says nothing. Then he says, "I don't know what it is."

"All right," Mrs. Lord says softly. "Skip it and come back to it later."

The man is fifty-five years old. He is trying to learn how to read. He is a large man, balding and wearing thick glasses; he bears a resemblance to the actor Ernest Borgnine. His plumber's work clothes—denim overalls, a flannel shirt—are still on. Today, as he does twice a week, he has driven straight from work to Mrs. Lord's house. His hands are dirty from his day's labor; as he points to the words on the spelling list you can see that he has not had time to stop and clean up. He has been coming to Mrs. Lord's house for just over a year.

The next word on the list is *down*.

"Down," the man says with confidence in his voice.

"That's right," Mrs. Lord says. "Very good."

The man—we will not name him here, because he has asked us not to—never learned to read as a child. His mother was sick and his father was an alcoholic; the boy did not do well in school, and at the age of twelve he dropped out and began to work. Sometimes his mother would try to teach him something; his father, if he had been drinking, would say, "What the hell are you bothering to teach him for? He don't know nothing."

The man went through most of his life hiding his secret. He learned to be a plumber; he married and started a family. He concealed his inability to read even from his wife and children; his wife did all the paperwork around the house, read all the mail, handled all the correspondence.

A year and a half ago, the man lost a job because he could not read. The company he was working for required each employee to take a written test about safety procedures. The man knew the rules, but could not read the questions. The company allowed him to take the test over, but he didn't have a chance. He couldn't admit the real problem.

Out of work, he felt panic. He heard that a local community college was offering a nighttime course in reading improvement. He enrolled. But as early as the first evening he realized that the course was meant for people who at least knew the basics of reading. After a few sessions he approached the teacher after class.

"I know you can't read," the teacher said to him. "If you'd like to keep coming just to see what you can pick up, it's all right."

Instead, the man went to a dime store and bought a book called *Reading Fun* for ninety-three cents. The book was designed for pre-school-aged children. On the pages of the book were simple, colorful pictures of ambulances and taxis and trucks, followed by the proper word for each picture. He looked at the pages and tried to teach himself. He couldn't.

Finally, he sat down with his wife. "You know when I lost my job?" he said. And he told her he couldn't read.

Time went by. On television, he heard a public service announcement about private tutoring offered by the Literacy Volunteers of Chicago. He called up and explained about himself. The person on the other end of the line said that there were no suitable volunteers available at the moment. The man left his name.

Four months later, while he was out of the house, the literacy organization called. When the man arrived back at home, his wife said she had some news for him.

"There's a teacher for you," his wife said. "Her name is Pat."

Patricia Lord, fifty-nine, remembers the first time he showed up at her door.

"He was such a nice man," she said. "At first I didn't realize how deep his problem was. But it soon became clear—he didn't even know the alphabet."

So, twice a week, they started to work together. "He was so grateful," Mrs. Lord said. "I do this for free, but he kept saying that if I ever needed any plumbing done, even if it was an emergency in the middle of the night, he would do it for nothing."

She taught him the alphabet. She taught him how to print letters. She taught him the first words other than his own name that he had ever known how to read or write.

"We work with reading cards," she said. "He picks out words that look interesting to him, and I'll teach him. One of the words he wanted to learn, for instance, was *chocolate*. He was fascinated by it because it was longer than most of the other words on the cards. So we learned it."

There are books scattered all over Mrs. Lord's home—*The Fate of the Earth,* by Jonathan Schell; *Findings,* by Leonard Bernstein; *Schindler's List,* by Thomas Keneally.

"I tried to explain to him about the pleasures of reading," she said. "It's something he's never known. I've always gotten so much information and so much joy from reading, but when I try to explain that to him, it's almost beyond what he can imagine. When I was young I had a friend, and we'd go sit together in the park and just read for hours, and talk about what we were reading. The idea of something like that seems to intrigue him.

"I tell him that one of these days he'll be able to read a book," Mrs. Lord said. "That's far off in the future, though. I have a second-grade spelling puzzle book, and even that's way too advanced for him right now.

"But he's making progress. There's a list of about forty words that he knows now. When a lesson goes well, he is definitely elated. He'll smile at the end of the session, and he'll get more talkative than usual, and he'll just seem . . . lighter. I can tell that he's feeling good about it."

In the time since he started studying with Mrs. Lord, the man has found a new job. His employers do not know that he cannot read; he is deathly afraid that they will find out and that he will be fired again.

"I never liked to hear anyone called a dummy," he said. "Even when I was a kid, I didn't like it. In fact I once beat up another kid for calling a boy a dummy.

"Let's face it, though, when you work construction, the others would be embarrassed to work with you if they knew you couldn't read—wouldn't they? If they found out about me, I think they'd make it hard on me. Some people get their kicks like that."

He said it was losing the other job that convinced him he had to learn how to read. That, and something else.

"I've got a little granddaughter," he said. "I never want her to come up to me and say, 'Grandpa, read this,' and I can't do it. I already went through life not being able to read to my own children. I want to be able to read to my granddaughter."

He said he was proud of how far he had come in his life without knowing how to read. "I can take a blueprint and figure out how a whole building works," he said. "I built my own house. I think that's a pretty good accomplishment for a man who can't read. That, and going this far in my trade."

Still, he has always known how large the gap in his life was.

"All my life, I've wanted so badly to be able to read something," he said. "I've had to pretend, all my life. When I would go into a restaurant with people from the job, I would hold the menu up and pretend to be reading it. But I didn't understand a word. I'd always ask the waitress what the specials were, and when she'd say them I'd choose one of them. Or I'd order something that I knew every restaurant had.

"It was something I thought about all the time, but who

could you go talk to? Many's the time that I wished I could read something. But I knew there couldn't be too many people willing to help a person like me, so I just did my best to keep it a secret.

"I've never written a letter in my life. When the holidays came, it was very hard for me to pick out a card for my wife. I'd look at the cards, but I'd have no idea what they said. So I'd buy her a flower instead."

Now that he is studying with Mrs. Lord, he said, he can at least hope that things will change.

"I dream that before long I can really read something," he said. "It doesn't have to be a lot, but just to be able to read something from start to finish would be enough. Mrs. Lord tells me that once you start to read, it comes easier all the time.

"It scares me that there's a possibility I can't do it. I'm fifty-five years old, after all. I get disgusted with myself if I have a bad day here, and I miss a lot of words.

"But when there's been a good day I'll feel great at the end of our lesson. I'll go home and tell my wife, 'I learned this word.' Or I'll say, 'Teacher says I have good handwriting.' And then my wife and I will work on the spelling cards."

He said that, because he is working again, sometimes he will have to skip tutoring sessions. "It kills me when that happens," he said. "But the construction business is pretty good right now, and sometimes in the afternoon the boss will tell me that he needs me to work overtime. I can't tell him why I have to be here. So I'll go off to a pay phone and call Mrs. Lord and give her the bad news.

"I think about reading even when I'm at work, though. I'll be working, but I'll be reciting the alphabet in my head. I keep the spelling cards in my truck, and if it's time for a coffee break I'll go out there and work on my words."

He said that, before he started trying to learn to read, he never picked up a newspaper or a magazine. "Now I like to pick them up and look at them," he said. "I think to myself that maybe someday I can read them.

"And I'll go into a store now and pick up books. I'll pick up the ones that have covers that look interesting. And then I'll flip through them until I see some words that I know. Most of the pages are filled with words that I don't know. But then I'll see some words that Mrs. Lord taught me—*an* or *is* or *the*—and I'll stare at them. It feels so good to know them."

It is getting darker outside. The man has been up since before dawn. His truck is parked outside Mrs. Lord's house; motorists pass by on their way home.

At the dining room table, Mrs. Lord is helping him to write a sentence. "Let's try 'The cow is brown,'" she says. "First word *the.*"

The man checks his list of words. Then, on a clean sheet of paper, he writes: *The.*

"Good," Mrs. Lord says. "Next word, *cow.*"

He checks his list and writes the word.

"Very good," Mrs. Lord says. "Now *is.*"

That word he knows easily. He writes it.

"Now *brown,*" Mrs. Lord says.

He thinks for a second, then writes *brown* at the end of the sentence he has built.

"Right!" Mrs. Lord says. "End of sentence!"

The man looks up. There is something very close to pride in his eyes.

"I can't wait until I can write a letter," he says. "The first letter I write is going to be to my wife. I'm going to tell her how much I love her."

On the cover of *Esquire* every month there is a slogan: "Man At His Best." Once in a while, when you really aren't expecting it, you find out what that means.

One Night with You

The only socialite I know in Chicago, Sugar Rautbord, was in the newspaper building where I work, having her photograph taken for a fashion layout. She stopped by my office.

She asked me what I was up to, and I said that I was about to embark on a trip to various cities. I said that I wasn't especially looking forward to the trip; in many of the cities where I'd be stopping, I didn't know anyone.

"What cities?" she said.

"Oh, Houston . . ." I began.

"Houston?" she said, her eyes brightening. She reached for my telephone. "May I?" she said.

She dialed a long-distance number. "Carolyn?" she said. "I'm sending you a man." They had a brief conversation. Sugar handed me the telephone; across the miles I spoke with Carolyn, whoever she was. She invited me to call her when I got to Houston.

After I had hung up, I asked Sugar who it was that I had been talking to.

"Her name is Carolyn Farb," Sugar said.

"And who's that?" I said.

"You may have read about her," Sugar said. "She's the woman who got the twenty-million-dollar divorce settlement in Houston."

I thought about that for a moment.

"Not the woman with the closet?" I said.

"Well . . . yes," Sugar said.

"My God," I said.

There are very few magazine stories I remember precisely, but there was no forgetting the story in *People* magazine about

Carolyn Farb's closet. Actually, the *People* story was about rich people's closets in general; but the story had referred to Carolyn Farb as the "queen of closets."

The story had said that Mrs. Farb's closet took up two thousand square feet—"more than some three-bedroom homes," according to *People*. Her closet consisted of six rooms, including one equipped with a sofa, a telephone, and a table, presumably to give Mrs. Farb a chance to stop and rest should she become tired while walking through the closet's other rooms. The closet, according to the story, accommodated fifty evening bags, ninety pairs of shoes, sixty hats, twenty pairs of boots, seventy-five gowns—"easily over one thousand pieces," by Mrs. Farb's own estimate.

The really stunning thing about the *People* article, though, was the picture. The picture showed Mrs. Farb, in a beautiful black outfit, smiling and sitting on the couch in her six-room closet, with her clothes arrayed in the background.

After the article appeared, Mrs. Farb was divorced from her husband, Houston developer Harold Farb. They had been married six years; the twenty-million-dollar figure for the settlement was widely publicized. Commenting on the size of the settlement to a Texas reporter, Mrs. Farb said: "Even though we had a house full of servants, I always looked after him myself. I saw to it that he was very pampered. I banished chicken from the house because he hates chicken. I personally went to the bakery and bought his favorite pineapple pies. And when he went on trips, I always packed his bags myself."

My plane arrived in Houston early in the evening. I always feel lonely when I walk into a strange airport.

I walked over to the bank of pay phones. I dialed the number that Sugar Rautbord had given me.

"Mrs. Farb, this is Bob Greene," I said. "We talked on the phone when Sugar called you."

I asked her if she would like to have a drink. She said that might be all right.

"Maybe you could swing by my hotel after I check in, and

we could just go down to the lobby and have a drink in the hotel bar," I said.

"Where are you staying?" she said.

I told her the name of the hotel. There was a pause.

"That is definitely not a place for me," she said. "And I would hope it is not a place for you."

I told her I'd call her when I arrived at the hotel and checked in, and she said that would be fine.

I arrived at the hotel. It was lovely and modern. I got to my room and I dialed Carolyn Farb's number again. I planned on telling her that the hotel was clean and in a nice neighborhood and really quite acceptable for a quick drink.

But before I could tell her anything, she said, "I've sent my security man to pick you up."

"Your security man?" I said.

"Yes," she said. "He should be pulling up to the hotel any minute. But I didn't know what to tell him to look for. I have no idea what you look like."

"I'm just kind of average," I said.

"Well, his name is Warren," she said. "He'll be driving either a Jeep Wagoneer or a Silver Shadow Rolls-Royce."

"Okay," I said.

Warren Hill was a rangy-looking Texan in his early sixties. He wore a blue police-style uniform and a large gun in a black holster. He was waiting for me in the Wagoneer.

"I prefer to drive this over the Rolls," he said.

We pulled into traffic. A thunderstorm was on its way; the sky was black, and bolts of lightning cracked across the towering Houston skyline.

I asked him how he happened to be Mrs. Farb's private security detail.

"Well, I used to work for a security firm that Mr. Farb owned," he said. "I was assigned to the house. But when Mr. and Mrs. Farb separated, he pulled all security from the house. Mrs. Farb asked me to stay on and work for her, and I have ever since."

We were on a side street in a decidedly unprosperous area of Houston. Hill stopped the car.

"Mr. Smith, I think we're lost," he said to me.

We drove around the block a few times, and he regained his bearings. Within fifteen minutes we were entering the exclusive River Oaks section of Houston.

"Have you ever met Mrs. Farb, Mr. Smith?" Hill said.

"Not yet," I said. "What's she like?"

"Just like Cinderella," he said.

"How do you mean?" I said.

"She expects people to treat her like a princess," he said. "And in return, she treats you like a real gentleman. She really does."

We drove along River Oaks Boulevard. As we approached the country club, we swung into a driveway that curved up to a house fronted by white columns.

"We're here," Warren Hill said.

I climbed out of the car and headed for the front door. Down by my feet, a creature leaped out of the grass. I halted in my tracks.

"What was that?" I asked.

"Just a frog," Hill said. "Mrs. Farb keeps frogs. She thinks they're good luck."

He took a key from his pocket and unlocked the front door. We walked into the black-and-white foyer.

"Mrs. Farb," Hill called out. "Mrs. Farb. Mrs. Farb."

There was no answer.

"Mrs. Farb," he called again.

"Warren?" came a female voice. "Is that you?"

"Your guest has arrived, Mrs. Farb," he called.

"I'm in here," the voice said.

I walked into a den. Sitting on a couch, holding a TV channel changer, was Carolyn Farb, in a perfectly tailored jacket and pants.

"Hi, I'm Bob Greene," I said.

She was staring at the television set. "The Burning Bed," starring Farrah Fawcett, was on.

"This is really quite good," Mrs. Farb said. "Do you mind if we have a drink here so we can see the show?"

"That would be fine," I said. She stood up and led the way to a small room that contained her bar.

"What would you like?" she said.

"Well, if you have any lime juice, I'd like a vodka gimlet," I said.

She poured herself a glass of white wine. She reached into a refrigerator and pulled out a bottle of chilled Stolichnaya vodka. "Now what was it you said you needed to make a gimlet?" she said.

"Just some Rose's lime juice, if you've got any around," I said.

She rummaged through a low cabinet and came out with a bottle of Rose's. As I poured it into my vodka, though, I noticed that apparently the lime juice had been sitting around for years. It had turned deep red in color. My gimlet was approximately the color of a beet.

"I think we have a problem with the lime juice," I said.

"Why?" Mrs. Farb said. "What's the trouble?"

"Well, I think it died," I said. "Look at the color."

"What color is lime juice supposed to be?" she said.

"Well, sort of the color of a lime," I said.

She sighed. "That Ricky," she said.

"Who's Ricky?" I said.

"My houseman," she said. "He's supposed to be in charge of stocking the bar. Ricky is a little light in the loafers."

I poured myself a whiskey and Coke, and we went back to the den. Mrs. Farb kept one eye on Farrah Fawcett and did her best to make conversation while still keeping track of the movie.

"Right now I'm making preparations for the Noche de las Américas Ball," she said. "I'm going as Queen Isabella, and I'll be escorted by Jon Lindsay, who is a county judge here. He's going as King Ferdinand."

I tried to make idle chitchat, but I felt like a high school boy who had finally gotten a date with the most buxom girl in the class, and who was doing his best to look anywhere but at the girl's sweater. Only it wasn't Carolyn Farb's chest I was preoccupied with. It was her closet. All I wanted to do was get one look at the famous closet. But how to ask? I couldn't just come out and say it. Should I say, "Would you give me a tour of the house?" Should I say, "So . . . where do you keep all your clothes?" I didn't have a clue.

We talked of minor matters, and finally she said, "Are you getting hungry?"

"Sure," I said. "Where's your icebox? I'll just make myself a sandwich."

"Don't be silly," she said. "We'll go to the River Oaks Grille."

We walked out to the Wagoneer. "Will Warren be driving us?" I asked.

"No," she said. "I will drive."

We sat in the front seat. She searched for something. She seemed to be annoyed. Finally she called out: "Warren!"

Warren Hill, still in full police uniform, appeared. He walked to the driver's side of the car.

"Help me find the headlights," Mrs. Farb said.

Hill reached in and pulled the headlights on. He returned to the house. It was oppressively hot in Houston; I reached for the car's air-conditioning unit to try to turn it on.

"What are you doing?" Mrs. Farb said.

"Trying to start the air conditioner," I said.

"Don't fool with it," she said. "I can tell you're not very mechanical."

We rolled forward, but before we had gone five feet Warren Hill came running in front of the car. Mrs. Farb slammed on the brakes.

"What is it, Warren?" she said.

"It looks like rain, Mrs. Farb," he said. "I wanted to show you where the windshield wipers are. And I brought you this." He handed her a black umbrella.

"Thank you, Warren," she said. "When you get back inside,

will you leave a note for Ricky? Tell him we need some new lime juice."

The River Oaks Grille is a popular gathering spot for residents of the neighborhood. Detracting from its high-toned name and clientele, though, is the fact that it is located in a shopping center.

Mrs. Farb and I pulled up in the Wagoneer. There were dozens of spaces all over the parking lot—the shopping center looked like any small shopping strip in Ohio or Kansas or Missouri—but the River Oaks Grille had a parking attendant stationed outside the front door. Rather than just pull into a vacant space, Mrs. Farb left the car with the attendant.

We walked into the restaurant. "Carolyn!" a voice called out. "Hello, Carolyn!" came another voice. "Wonderful luncheon today, Carolyn," came another.

"We had a luncheon for Jack Lousma, the former astronaut who's running for the Senate in Michigan," Mrs. Farb explained to me. "It was a lovely affair; I think people enjoyed it. There were a lot of astronauts there. Walt Cunningham. Alan Shepard. Alan Bean."

We were led to a table for two. Bob Mosbacher, a Houston oilman, came by and said hello to Mrs. Farb. So did several other patrons.

She looked over at me. "You have a rather abstract expression on your face," she said. "Are you all right?"

"I'm fine," I said.

I asked her what the most important thing in her life was.

"Being constructive," she said. "Doing something with my life. When I was growing up, people took me as a pretty girl. But it was more important to me to be intelligent and constructive. That's why I don't like to be known only as a socialite. I am social, but the term is so frivolous, don't you think?"

I asked her if people treated her differently than they had before her divorce; had all of the publicity about the financial terms affected their attitudes?

"I was a person before my twenty-million-dollar settlement

and I'm a person now," she said. "But to answer your question—yes. Sometimes when you're in my financial position things are difficult. I'd like to be the host of a television talk show, for instance. But I sense some resistance to that, and I really can't put it into words, but I think it has something to do with the divorce publicity. You can be discussed for a job like that, but because you're a wealthy person, some people can't believe that the desire for the American Dream is still there."

I said that in spite of that, she seemed to lead a fairly jam-packed life.

"I think it's fun," she said. "I'm an Aquarian, and we're energetic. I like to have a good time, but there are many times when I just like to stay home. I like my house. It's like a flower. When I first walked into the entrance hall of that house, I felt its spirit."

It was warm in the restaurant. "Do you mind if I take my jacket off?" I said.

"Go right ahead," she said. "I can't take mine off. I'm not wearing anything underneath."

After dinner we returned to the almost empty parking lot. The Wagoneer was approximately twelve feet from the front door.

"It's that one over there," Mrs. Farb said to the attendant, who walked the eight steps to the car and drove it up to us.

We drove through River Oaks and pulled into the driveway of Mrs. Farb's house. Warren Hill was marching back and forth across the front lawn, on patrol.

Mrs. Farb shut off the motor. We walked to the front door.

"I'm getting a little tired," she said. "I think I'm going to turn in. Would you like Warren to drive you back to your hotel?"

What could I say? The same thing was on my mind that had been consuming me all night, but how could I put it? That if she didn't mind, I'd prefer to just borrow a pillow and sleep in her closet? I extended my hand and she shook it.

She disappeared into the house. I opened the passenger door of the Wagoneer.

"Ready?" Warren Hill said.

"Ready," I said.

ABCDJ

It was one of those things that wasn't supposed to happen, but did. I was on the road, and I passed through my hometown; I was staying not with my family, but in a Hyatt Hotel.

In the lobby I heard a voice call my name. I looked over.

"Allen," I said when I saw him. I said the name calmly, as if seeing him was the most natural thing in the world.

He was staying in the hotel, too. He said he was in town on business; like me, he had long ago moved away.

In high school there were five of us; best friends. We were known as ABCDJ—Allen, Bob, Chuck, Dan, and Jack. ABCDJ is what it said in our senior sketches in the high school yearbook; ABCDJ is what had been engraved on the pewter beer mugs we gave each other when we went off to college. I don't know if they kept theirs; mine is still on top of my dresser. It's where I keep old pennies.

We couldn't believe it. Back in the old town, here we were staying at the Hyatt, purely by chance. The other three— Chuck, Dan, and Jack—had not moved away. Allen and I found ourselves talking about them, and before we knew it we were making phone calls.

Within an hour and a half, a miraculous thing—at least miraculous in the context of our personal universe—had happened. The five of us were sitting around a table in the barroom of the Hyatt. For the first time in eighteen years, ABCDJ were together again.

You'd think it might be difficult at first, or awkward. But it wasn't; it was as if no time at all had passed, and within moments we were telling stories and finishing each others' sentences and laughing as if high school had been yesterday, not two decades distant. Our stories probably would have been boring to anyone else; probably they were boring to anyone in the bar who was overhearing us. But I cannot recall the last time I was so excited about something. I have met so many people in the years since ABCDJ disbanded, and still I feel more comfortable with these people than with anyone else in the world.

We were talking about first girlfriends and first fights and first beers; it was true—the five of us had had our first beers in each others' company. If someone had come into the bar and looked at us, he would have seen five men who are not young anymore; we are each thirty-six, and there's no getting around the fact that much time—half our lives—has passed since the stories we were telling had been present-day reality. That's what people coming into the bar were seeing—five guys who are pretty old, and getting older.

But we sure didn't feel that way, at least not this night. We have been through the same personal crises and social changes that have affected much of our generation; things have not always turned out the way we had in mind. Among the five of us there have been eight marriages, eight children. Someone at the table said that his own child had just had Miss Barbara as a substitute kindergarten teacher; Miss Barbara, the woman who had taught us in kindergarten in 1952.

The hour grew later, and the other people in the bar were leaving, but we stayed on. No one was saying it out loud, but this piece of happenstance—this surprise coming together of ABCDJ—was the best thing that had happened to us in years. We kept looking at each others' faces; we kept remembering what those faces had looked like when we were teenagers.

I said something stupid, and the others laughed. Dan shook his head and said: "String . . ."

It was what I had been called in high school. I was a skinny kid; "String" was short for "stringbean," and here in the Hyatt, Dan kept laughing and saying "String," and none of us thought it was remarkable at all.

Just before two A.M. the bartender said that last call was coming up. The reactions among us to the closing of the bar were so interesting; we fit right back into the late-night patterns that we had fit into in 1964. One of us said he had to get home to his wife. One of us said he wanted to get a bottle and go to Allen's room or my room and stay up talking until dawn. One of us said he was hungry; was that all-night rib place out on the east side still open twenty-four hours? One of us quietly tried to get the telephone number of the cocktail waitress. One of us looked dreamily off into space.

But it was time to go. We didn't take our leave dramatically; we were all thinking about how special these hours had been, but none of us tried to put it into words. Someone said something about doing it again the next night, but we knew that would not happen; this was magic, it had happened because it had been destined to, and there would be no repeating it. If we had not been awkward when we had come together earlier in the evening, now we were, at least a little bit; we simply didn't know how to say what we were thinking.

So we stood in the bar of the Hyatt and we said goodbye. We shook hands, like businessmen cementing a deal. We walked out, Allen and I on the way to our hotel rooms, Chuck, Dan, and Jack on the way to their homes. There was something in the air; something fragile and precious. I know that men aren't supposed to confess that they love each other, but I don't know what else you'd call it.

R.I.P. Blinky

Jeffrey Vallance, a twenty-eight-year-old artist who lives in Canoga Park, California, was vaguely troubled about society's attitude toward animals.

"We categorize animals," Vallance said. "We call some animals 'pets,' and we keep them around the house. We call other animals 'food,' and we eat them."

Vallance thought this was odd: "In other cultures, the animals we call 'pets' are regarded as food. In Indochina, for example, people eat dogs all the time. I consider all animals to be the same. I don't think in terms of 'pets' and 'food.'"

Vallance tried to think of a way to dramatize his theory. After a while, the right idea hit him.

He went to a Ralph's Supermarket in his area, and headed for the meat section. His intention had been to take a piece of meat home and make it his pet. But when he saw all the portions of beef, they just didn't seem like pets to him.

So he went to the poultry section. There he found an array of frozen chickens in plastic bags. This was more like it. Although the chickens did not have heads or feet, they still seemed like chickens to him.

He carefully sifted through the chickens. He found one with good coloration. He picked it up. He knew he liked it.

"I named it Blinky," he said. "I decided on its name right then and there."

He took Blinky to the checkout counter and paid for it. He gave the checkout clerk a ten-dollar bill and got change back.

"I didn't get any other groceries," Vallance said. "If I had bought a box of cereal, for example, at the same time I bought Blinky, it would not have been as pure an experience."

Vallance took Blinky home. He took it out of the plastic wrapper. He looked at it for a while. Soon, though, it began to thaw.

"I knew I'd have to do something," he said.

He drove to the Los Angeles Pet Cemetery, which is located in Calabasas. He left Blinky inside a shoebox in his car. He went inside and said to the clerk, "I have a dead bird I'd like to bury."

"What kind of bird is it?" the clerk said.

"A hen," Vallance said.

Vallance filled out a number of forms and paid the fee for pet burial. He went out to his car and brought the shoebox inside. Some attendants took the shoebox into a back room to prepare Blinky for burial.

After a few minutes, one of the attendants came back out.

"Exactly how did your pet die?" the attendant said.

"I don't know exactly how it died," Vallance said. "It just died one day." [He chose those words because he wanted to tell the truth.]

Vallance picked out a headstone. On it he ordered inscribed: "Blinky. The Friendly Hen."

Soon Vallance was informed that Blinky was laid out in the viewing room. Blinky was resting in a small, satin-lined casket. Blinky was thawing quite severely by this time, so the pet cemetery attendants had placed a paper towel beneath it. A spotlight was shining on Blinky; taped organ music played in the background.

Vallance went out to the gravesite. Pet cemetery workers lowered Blinky's casket into the ground by using ropes. Then they filled in the dirt.

The next week the headstone arrived. The pet cemetery called Vallance; he returned to see the headstone installed in place.

Vallance had taken photographs of Blinky at the grocery store, at his home, and in the casket. He is a conceptual artist— his idea of art is more wide-ranging than the traditional idea of art—so he combined the photographs and a little text into a booklet he titled "Blinky." The booklet was included with his other artwork, as a sort of project.

But an interesting thing happened. Vallance could not think of Blinky as an art project. Blinky was his pet who was gone.

"I found myself going back to the pet cemetery to visit Blinky's gravesite quite often," he said. "I still go regularly. I keep the area around Blinky's grave neat and well tended. I leave flowers."

Vallance's friends who know the story inquire about the dead chicken. "How's Blinky?" they will ask, and Vallance will say that he has just visited the gravesite over the weekend, or whatever.

Vallance says that he does not consider this whole story to be a joke.

"My feelings about Blinky are quite complicated, and quite serious," he said. "I have a very sentimental attitude toward Blinky. I think of Blinky as being my pet. Blinky is much more than a frozen chicken to me. Blinky is very special.

"I feel as if I rescued Blinky from all the millions of chickens who are slaughtered and sold as food. In a sense, Blinky is sort of the Unknown Chicken. Maybe Blinky was supposed to end up as food on somebody's table, but as long as that chicken is buried beneath the headstone I bought, Blinky's soul lives on."

Ford Under Glass

I looked at Gerald Ford's christening gown and booties, which were protected inside a glass case.

On this blustery Wednesday I was one of 527 visitors to the Gerald Ford Presidential Museum, located on the banks of the Grand River in Grand Rapids, Michigan. On some days there are more visitors than that; on some less.

The museum is a starkly modern, three-sided, forty-thousand-square-foot structure that was built with private funds and is maintained at U.S. Government expense. There are other museums in the world that feature more extensive collections of artwork, photography, or historical artifacts; but this is the only place inside whose walls you will find in excess of ten thousand individual pieces of Gerald Ford memorabilia.

The curator of the Gerald Ford Presidential Museum is Will Jones, forty-two. His office is on the second floor of the museum, just off a private elevator; standing on the carpet by his door is a small stone statue of Gerald Ford, made of Pennsylvania rock. The stone has been painted so that Ford appears to be wearing a black suit.

"Our goal here is to commemorate the life and career of Gerald Ford and the period of American life in which he lived and operated," Jones said.

He said that the museum staff is always on the lookout for potential new Gerald Ford exhibits.

"Let me give you a recent example," he said. "Back when he was a congressman, Mr. Ford presided over the 1960 Republican National Convention. He used two gavels at the convention—one to open it, one to close it.

"Now, we had the gavel he used to close the convention. The

one he used to open the convention, we did not. But we've located it, and now we have both gavels at the museum."

I asked him how he could be sure the gavel was genuine.

"I'm afraid I don't understand," Jones said.

I asked if there wasn't a chance this was not the authentic gavel that Ford had used to open the convention.

"Oh, no, we're sure," Jones said. "This is the one."

I asked if people from across the country planned their vacations around coming to Grand Rapids and touring the Gerald Ford museum.

"I don't honestly believe that we're many people's final destination," Jones said. "I have no illusions about that.

"People tend to come here if they're on their way to somewhere else. A lot of people come through western Michigan in the course of a year, and once they hear that we're here, they come on over. We get a lot of bus tours."

I asked him if it was a wearying job: thinking full-time about the political career of Gerald Ford.

"I love this job," he said. "It's a great job. I was curator for ten years at the Eisenhower museum in Abilene, Kansas, and I didn't get Eisenhowered out. So I'm certainly not Jerry Forded out."

The exhibit hall, arranged over two levels of the Gerald Ford museum, is a sprawling, well-lighted place. Its purview of life in the White House is somewhat limited, because Ford served only two years and was never elected to the Presidency by the general population. But what it lacks in scope, it makes up for in detail; it is perhaps the only location in North America, for example, where you can get a minute-by-minute account of the *Mayaguez* crisis. ("On May 12, 1975, Gerald Ford's customary workday began with a jolt," a wall plaque reads.)

The exhibit hall is divided into subject areas, each featuring a particular motif. In "The Navy Years," for example, Ford's actual sea uniform can be viewed, as well as his footlocker. In most display cases there are relevant quotations from Ford concerning that time in his life; in "The Navy Years" display case, Ford is quoted as recalling: "My wartime experiences had given me an entirely new perspective. The U.S., I was convinced, could no longer stick its head in the sand like an ostrich."

For those who do not wish merely to read Ford's words, however, his tape-recorded voice can be heard all over the exhibit hall. There are various videotape and film presentations, each of these also centering on specific moments from Ford's life ("Congressional Leadership"; "A New Vice President"; "'76 Campaign"). Sometimes, as you walk from display case to display case, you are beset by a confusing and overlapping cacophony of Ford voices.

All is not politics at the museum, though; one display case features three dresses worn by Betty Ford, with a plaque noting that Mrs. Ford had been awarded an honorary citation from the Parsons School of Design for her "high standard of taste and excellence." But most exhibits are more somber; at "The Pardon of Nixon" area, there is a letter that had been sent to Ford by Walter Hoving, chairman of Tiffany & Co.: "Dear Mr. President: You did the right thing. Let the hyenas howl."

I was perusing an exhibit titled "Romance and Marriage." The plaque informed me that in 1947 the future Mrs. Ford had given Ford a Christmas stocking filled with gifts, including a pair of knitted argyle socks and a pipe lighter engraved "To the Light of My Life."

Standing next to me was Anna DeGraaf, eighty-one, of Denver; she told me that she was in Grand Rapids visiting her grandson, Ken Terpstra, who was with her at the museum.

"President Ford was always a favorite of mine," Mrs. De-Graaf said. "So this is something I was anxious to see. Of course, I doubt if I would have made a special trip."

Ken Terpstra said, "I live in Grand Rapids, and until Grandma came to visit, I had never even come over to the museum. Isn't that something?"

"Well, I'm glad you're with me now," Mrs. DeGraaf said to him. "This is a grand opportunity."

The other tourists with whom I spoke were in a similarly up-beat mood.

Harold Christy, a retired schoolteacher from Indianapolis, said he had learned of the Gerald Ford museum only when he had gone to his local auto club to pick up a map for his vacation.

"At the Triple-A they give you a magazine, and there was a story about the museum," he said. "I've been a member of the auto club for twenty-six years, and I've learned that you can get some pretty good ideas through that magazine.

"My wife and I looked at the map, and we noticed that this was right on the highway. So we decided, 'Why not?' We stayed over an extra night; we're in a motel out on Route Eleven.

"I'm a lifelong Republican; Ford was a Navy man, and I was an Air Force man; we're of the same generation; so this seemed like an ideal place for us to spend a day."

Over by the red, white, and blue "Jerry Ford for Congress" Quonset hut, Ernestine Allen and Bev Janeway, of Jasper, Indiana, said that they had come to the museum as part of a bus tour.

"This was a package deal," Mrs. Allen said. "The museum was on the itinerary for the tour, so here we are."

"Yesterday we went to the tulip farms and the wooden-shoe factory over in Holland," Miss Janeway said. "The shoe factory was okay, but the tulip farm was spectacular."

"Next we're going to the 'fish ladder,' but I don't know what that is," Mrs. Allen said.

The centerpiece of the museum is a full-scale reproduction of the Oval Office. The office is decorated exactly as it was during the Ford years in the White House; the furniture is precisely in place, and there are more plaques explaining various tidbits and sidelights. (The plaque for the replica of the antique Presidential desk reads, "In August, 1974, embedded microphones were removed on Ford's instructions.")

Although visitors are kept off the carpeting by ropes, you

can stand and look at the Oval Office for as long as you want; more tape recordings of Ford play intermittently as you watch the room. There is a pen-and-pencil set with a football in the middle; there is a set of pipes that were actually smoked by Ford; there is the ship's wheel from the S.S. *Mayaguez;* there is the AMVETS Golden Helmet Award.

At the gift shop of the Ford museum, an array of souvenirs is offered for sale to visitors.

"Our little seventy-five-cent Gerald Ford commemorative coins are probably our most popular items," said Judy Lovejoy, a cashier at the shop. "But we just started getting Gerald Ford pencils in stock; they're only thirty-five cents, and we can't get enough of them. People seem to want anything that says 'Gerald Ford' on it."

Indeed, the variety of items available for purchase is impressive. There is a Gerald Ford museum booklet ($5); a Gerald Ford museum poster ($10); a Gerald Ford commemorative envelope ($3); a Gerald Ford bronze medal ($12); Gerald Ford campaign buttons (50 cents to $2); a Gerald Ford portrait folder ($3); Gerald Ford photos ($2 to $2.50); a postcard featuring a color photograph of Gerald Ford's golden retriever, Liberty, posing on the White House lawn (15 cents); a cookbook containing recipes submitted by Betty Ford ($9.95); matchbooks embossed with the Presidential seal (six for $2); a Gerald Ford glass mug ($2); a Gerald Ford napkin ($2); and a Gerald Ford crystal candy dish ($20).

"People really want to buy," Mrs. Lovejoy said. "It's not uncommon for one person to spend forty, fifty, or sixty dollars. That happens at least a couple of times a week."

I took a break from my tour, and went back to my hotel for lunch. Sitting in my room, I decided to call Gerald Ford at his home in Rancho Mirage, California. He was not in when I phoned. But later he returned my call.

"I am very, very proud of the job that was done in the presentation of my life," Ford said. I asked him what pleased him most about the museum.

"I would have to say the full reproduction of the Oval Office," he said. "We made a decision to make it full size. At the Truman museum, the Oval Office is only three-quarter size. At the Johnson museum, the Oval Office is only seven-eighths size. But when you walk into the Oval Office at our museum, it's the exact same size of the Oval Office where I worked. My attitude was: If you're going to do it, do it right."

A female voice came onto the line: "Hello?"

"I'm on this line," Ford said.

"Hello?" the voice said. "Hello?"

"I said, I'm on this line," Ford said, and there was a clicking.

"That was Betty," Ford said.

I asked Ford how often he got to visit the museum.

"We get back to western Michigan several times a year," he said. "We were just there, as a matter of fact, for the Tulip Time Parade. I've never gone in for being romantic about things, but when I walk through the museum I get goose bumps.

"Naturally I'm proud. I feel damn lucky for myself to have a museum like that. But more than for myself, it's an illustration of what can happen to a person in this country. It can happen to anybody."

I walked back over to the Gerald Ford museum. Lines of schoolchildren were waiting to go through the front door.

Off on the far side of the museum, unmarked by plaques or signs, were two cement crypts built into a grassy slope. These crypts, I had been told, will be the final resting places for Gerald and Betty Ford; they have informed the museum staff that they wish to be buried right here, in Grand Rapids, on the museum grounds.

I stood next to the crypts and looked around. Off to one side was the museum building, rising into the gray, cloudy afternoon. Directly in front was the Grand River, rolling gently by. And off to the other side was Sullivan's Riverview Furniture store, and beyond that Interstate Highway 96, heading ever eastward, toward Lansing.

Mrs. Hybl and the International Loveline

Mrs. Charlotte Hybl, a sixty-year-old grandmother who lives in Berwyn, Illinois, answered her ringing telephone one day. Whoever was on the other end seemed to be in great pain.

"He was breathing heavily, taking very deep breaths," she said. "He seemed to be seriously ill.

"I said, 'May I help you?' But he just kept breathing hard, and then he hung up."

Mrs. Hybl was perplexed, but she put the call out of her mind. She couldn't keep it out of her mind for long, though. Because that phone call was the first of many. Men started calling the Hybl home at all hours of the day and night. Usually the men moaned, groaned, or simply breathed in and out.

"I was very puzzled," Mrs. Hybl said. "But then a man called, and he said, 'I'm calling about the ad.' My husband and I had placed several ads in the *Tradin' Times* newspaper, trying to get rid of some old furniture. So I said, 'Which ad?'

"And the man said, 'The ad for telephone sex.'"

Mrs. Hybl asked the man what he was talking about. He said he had seen an advertisement for something called International Loveline in a men's magazine. International Loveline was a telephone sex company. Men were supposed to call a certain number, give their credit card number, and then a woman would get on the line and talk filthy to them.

"I asked him to read to me the phone number from the ad," Mrs. Hybl said. "He did—it was my phone number, but it had the 213 area code in front of it. He had dialed the 312 area code by mistake, and got my home. Apparently all of the other men had made the same mistake."

Mrs. Hybl asked the man what magazines carried the International Loveline ads. He said the ads appeared in the scuzzy, hard-core magazines; he had seen this one in *Hustler*. Mrs. Hybl and the man said goodbye to one another.

The next day Mrs. Hybl drove down to the nearest newsstand to check out the ads.

"I went in, and there were *Oui* and *Penthouse* and *Hustler*," she said. "I opened them up, but I had to close them. As much as I wanted to know what the ad said, I couldn't stand to look at the pictures. So one of the men who owned the newsstand said he would find the ad, and would call me at home.

"He called that same day. He'd found the ad in *Hustler*. It was for the International Loveline, all right, and it had my phone number, except with a 213 area code in front of it. He told me that ad was for 'phone sex . . . the ultimate in phone fantasy.'"

During the ensuing weeks, the calls did not let up. Mrs. Hybl and her husband—Charles Hybl, also sixty, a vending-machine serviceman—got used to picking up their telephone and hearing men in the throes of passion.

"One Spanish-speaking man called seven times the same night," Mrs. Hybl said. "I couldn't make him understand that he should have been calling 213, not 312. Another man called and asked me to talk sexy to him. I said, 'I'm a sixty-year-old grandmother.' He said, 'Could you talk sexy to me anyway?'

"Another man called and said, 'Let's get hot.' I told him that if he wanted to get hot, he should take a hot shower."

Mrs. Hybl was losing her patience. She tried to call the 213 number, but got nowhere with the people on the other end. She did determine that the International Loveline was headquartered in Los Angeles, which did not surprise her.

"I don't know what I should do," she said. "Apparently these men are so worked up that they can't tell the difference between 213 and 312. But I've had this phone number for thirty years. I can't just change it."

At this point I volunteered to call the International Loveline for Mrs. Hybl. I dialed the number. A sultry-sounding woman answered by saying: "International Loveline, do you have a major credit card?"

I said that I certainly did, but that I did not want to talk just then. I identified myself, and asked to speak to the manager.

Several seconds later, a man's voice came onto the line. The man declined to identify himself, but said he was the owner of International Loveline.

I explained Mrs. Hybl's problem to him. He listened.

"That's too bad, but I don't know what I can do about it," he said. He said that when men from around the country called International Loveline, they gave the Loveline operator their credit card numbers. After the numbers were verified, the operator contacted the dirty-talking Loveline women at their homes—and those women called the men back, and said nasty things to them.

"It's like having sex on the phone," the owner said. "The women who work for me are college students and housewives. The college girls can do the phone calls during study breaks, and the housewives can do the calls while they're working around the house. It's easy work for them, it's a good way to make a little extra money, and they can do it without leaving home."

I asked him if he would consider changing his number, so that Mrs. Hybl would not be bothered anymore.

"I can't do it," he said. "I have nine telephone lines, and my advertisements are running in magazines all over the country. It would cost me thousands of dollars to change the number. Tell her to change her number."

I called Mrs. Hybl back and gave her the bad news. She said that she didn't want to change her number. She asked me if I had any other ideas.

"Well, have you considered talking dirty to the men when they phone?" I said.

"I called one of them an S.O.B.," Mrs. Hybl said. "But that's about as dirty as I'm willing to get."

Permanent Record

There are thousands of theories about what's gone wrong with the world, but I think it comes down to one simple thing: The death of the Permanent Record.

You remember the Permanent Record. When you were in elementary school, junior high school, and high school, you were constantly being told that if you screwed up, news of that screw-up would be sent down to the principal's office, and would be placed in your Permanent Record.

Nothing more needed to be said. No one had ever seen a Permanent Record; that didn't matter. We knew they were there. We all imagined a steel filing cabinet, crammed full of Permanent Records—one for each kid in the school. I think we always assumed that when we graduated our Permanent Record was sent on to college with us, and then when we got out of college our Permanent Record was sent to our employer—probably with a duplicate copy sent to the U.S. Government.

I don't know if students are still threatened with the promise of unpleasant things included in their Permanent Record, but I doubt it. I have a terrible feeling that mine was the last generation to know what a Permanent Record was—and that not only has it disappeared from the schools of the land, but it has disappeared as a concept in society as a whole.

There once was a time when people really stopped before they did something they knew was deceitful, immoral, or unethical—no matter how much fun it might sound. They didn't stop because they were such holy folks. They stopped because—no matter how old they were—they had a nagging fear that if they did it, it would end up on their Permanent Record.

At some point in the last few decades, I'm afraid, people wised up to something that amazed them: There is no Permanent Record. There probably never was.

They discovered that regardless of how badly you fouled up your life or the lives of others, there was nothing permanent about it on your record. You would always be forgiven, no matter what; no matter what you did, other people would shrug it off.

So pretty soon men and women—instead of fearing the Permanent Record—started laughing at the idea of the Permanent Record. The kinds of things that they used to be ashamed of—the kinds of things that they used to secretly cringe at when they thought about them—now became "interesting" aspects of their personalities.

If those "interesting" aspects were weird enough—if they were the kinds of things that would have really jazzed up the Permanent Record—the people sometimes wrote books confessing those things, and the books became best-sellers. And the people found out that other people—far from scorning them—would line up in the bookstores to get their autographs on the inside covers of the books.

The people started going on talk shows to discuss the things that, in decades past, would have been included in their Permanent Records. The talk-show hosts would say, "Thank you for being so honest with us; I'm sure the people in our audience can understand how much guts it must take for you to tell us these things." The Permanent Records were being opened up for the whole world to see—and the sky did not fall in.

If celebrities had dips in their careers, all they had to do to guarantee a new injection of fame was to admit the worst things about themselves—the Permanent Record things—and the celebrity magazines would print those things, and the celebrities would be applauded for their candor and courage. And they would become even bigger celebrities.

As Americans began to realize that there was no Permanent Record, and probably never had been, they deduced for themselves that any kind of behavior was permissible. After all, it wasn't as if anyone was keeping track; all you would have to do—just like the men and women with best-sellers and on the talk shows and in the celebrity magazines—was to say, "That was a real crazy period in my life." All would be forgiven; all would be erased from the Permanent Record, which, of course, was no longer permanent.

And that is where we are today. Without really thinking about it, we have accepted the notion that no one is, indeed, keeping track. No one is even *allowed* to keep track. I doubt that you can scare a school kid today by telling him the principal is going to inscribe something on his Permanent Record; the kid would probably file a suit under the Freedom of Information Act, and gain possession of his Permanent Record by recess. Either that, or the kid would call up his Permanent Record on his computer terminal, and purge any information he didn't want to be there.

As for us adults—it has been so long since we have believed in the Permanent Record that the very mention of it today probably brings a nostalgic smile to our faces. We feel naive for ever having believed that a Permanent Record was really down there in the principal's office, anyway.

And who really knows if our smiles may freeze on some distant day—the day it is our turn to check out of this earthly world, and we are confronted with a heavenly presence greeting us at the gates of our new eternal home—a heavenly presence sitting there casually leafing through a dusty, battered volume of our Permanent Record as we come jauntily into view.

Wimp's Funeral

By now there can't be too many people in Chicago who haven't heard about the funeral of Willie M. ("Wimp") Stokes, Jr., the South Side professional gambler who was buried in a casket that had been custom-designed to look like a Cadillac Seville automobile.

Stokes, twenty-eight, appeared at his own visitation propped up in the coffin, his hands on its steering wheel. The casket was equipped with blinking headlights and taillights, a windshield, whitewall tires, a Cadillac grille, and a vanity license plate featuring his "Wimp" nickname.

Stokes was dressed for the occasion in a flaming red suit, a rakish gray hat, and diamond rings. During the visitation he had several thousand-dollar bills sticking out from between his fingers.

More than five thousand people came to the A. R. Leak Funeral Home to pay their respects and view the casket. The *Chicago Defender,* a newspaper serving the black community, covered the proceedings for two days, on the second day devoting a full page of pictures to the funeral; the *Defender,* which referred to the coffin as a "casketmobile," completely sold out copies of the editions featuring the funeral coverage. The newspaper, which normally sells for twenty-five cents, reportedly was going for up to five dollars in the Loop.

Stokes passed away after being shot in the head by gunmen as he stood on the steps of Roberts Motel, 79th Street and Vincennes Avenue. At the funeral he was praised as a "master party-giver"; his father told the *Defender,* "Little Willie did a few bad things. But all in all, he was a loving and caring son, husband, father, brother, and friend to people around the nation."

I had heard so much about the Stokes funeral that I wanted to talk with the people most closely involved—Stokes's parents and the funeral director.

Stokes's mother, Jean, said, "I wouldn't have traded that funeral for anything. I really liked the way it went."

She said that the family had decided on the Cadillac coffin after shopping around for caskets. "We were looking in the showroom, and there was just nothing that we liked," she said. "You know how it is, when the merchandise just doesn't appeal to you.

"That's when we thought it would be nice if Willie could be buried in a Cadillac, because he was so crazy about his car. My only disappointment is that the casket looked like a Seville. Willie drove an Eldorado."

She said that the design of the casket was a joint venture: "The wheels were made out of flowers, put together by Maxine's Florist on 47th Street. It was my husband who said that we should have a windshield put on the casket so it looked like a convertible."

She said that she appreciated the large number of mourners, although "personally, I generally don't like a crowd." She said she thought her son "left like he lived—in a lively manner."

The funeral director, Spencer Leak, said, "Mr. Stokes had let it be known that in the event of his demise, he would prefer a funeral that reflected his lifestyle. I called all around the country trying to find a casket company that could provide me with a casket that looked like a Cadillac. In Indianapolis, I found one. They said, 'How about a Seville?' I said, 'Perfect.'"

Leak said, "The family was elated. They said it was exactly what they wanted. This is a flashy family."

He said he had no problem with the question of tastefulness. "This was not a rowdy thing," he said. "It was very subdued and respectful. It was done with class. As a funeral director, my job is to honor the family's requests, reflect the lifestyle of the deceased, and relate to everyone's bereavement. This I did."

Stokes's father, Willie M. ("Flukie") Stokes, Sr., said that his own occupation, like his son's, was "professional gambler," although Chicago police have characterized him as one of the city's leading drug dealers. Stokes said that his son had been "a fine young man; he was very well liked and did a lot of gambling."

He said the funeral pleased him greatly. "Anyone who wants to criticize it can criticize it," he said. "But my son would have liked it. He liked anything I did for him."

He said he assumed it was the most unusual funeral in anyone's memory, but that he had no real way of knowing. "I don't go to funerals," he said. "Funerals aren't my thing. There's no dice at funerals."

He said that he personally put the thousand-dollar bills between his son's fingers in the casket because "he gambled for that kind of money."

I asked Stokes if there was any particular reason he had opted for such a flashy funeral.

"It's not flashy," he said. "It's just everyday living."

I asked why he thought other families didn't choose to have funerals like this one.

"I don't know," he said. "Maybe not everyone cares about their son the way I did."

The Coolest Guy
in the Room

There are men in this world who, since they were little boys, have had life beaten. There's one in every junior high school—the kid who's a natural on the playground, who's irresistible to the girls, who makes the other boys jealous.

Most of those boys lose it somewhere along the way; the high school heroes discover, twenty years later, that the best days of their lives were left behind in the cement-block football stadium of their teens. Some don't lose it, though. And among all those who didn't lose it, Frank Gifford stands out.

If all you know about Gifford is what you've seen on "Monday Night Football," you might be smirking a little by now. Gifford is clearly not the star of that show. Next to Howard Cosell and Don Meredith, Gifford's electronic image comes off a little bland, a little bloodless; he is just the play-by-play guy, and the casual television viewer might regard him as sort of vanilla.

There's a difference, though. Television makes celebrities out of virtually everyone who appears regularly on it. If you've been on television and people see you on the street, they stop. Some men who were the biggest jerks in their high school classes are sought after now merely because they are frequently televised.

Gifford, quite simply, would command attention if a television camera had never been trained on him. He is one of the few men on national TV who don't need TV for their self-esteem. Every step of his life, he has found himself doing the most glamorous thing a man can do. In the late Forties and early Fifties, when the desired thing was to be a big man on campus, Gifford was an all-American tailback at the University of Southern California. In the Fifties and early Sixties, when the desired thing was to play in the National Football League, Gifford was an all-pro left halfback for the New York Giants. In the Seventies and Eighties, when the desired thing is to be a network television personality, Gifford is a first-string announcer with ABC Sports.

I do some work for ABC News; I have been on the road in the same city with Gifford, and when he walks into a room something remarkable happens. People stop what they are doing and involuntarily focus their eyes on him—and it has virtually nothing to do with his video familiarity. There is something about his stunning looks, something about the absolute self-confidence with which he carries himself; there is something about him that gives off the message that this is no mere television star—this is that kid who ruled the playground, now grown older, but still having whatever it is the playground heroes used to have. Women look at Gifford and covet his company; men look at him and suddenly feel too fat or too bald or too short or too pale.

He apparently has had this effect on people all his life. Author Frederick Exley, in his book *A Fan's Notes,* recalled seeing Gifford in a campus coffee shop when they were both students at Southern Cal. The two had never met, but of course Exley knew who Gifford was. The two did not speak, but Exley recalled thinking: "Listen, you son of a bitch. Life isn't always a goddamned football game! You won't always get the girl! Life is rejection and pain and loss." Alex Karras, who worked in the announcing booth with Gifford briefly on "Monday Night Football," at the time said of Gifford: "Yesterday he had on a pair of Levi's and a T-shirt with MAMA written on it. I had on a five-hundred-dollar suit. I looked like Emmett Kelly and he looked like a guy in a tuxedo."

It's a fairly simple concept: for his whole life, whenever Gifford has walked into a room, he has been the coolest guy in the room. Most of us don't know what that's like. I always wondered about it; I had never had the opportunity to ask him, and I wasn't sure how he'd react to the question if I did.

Gifford greeted me at the door of his Manhattan apartment. He lives with his second wife and stepchildren in Connecticut, but keeps the New York apartment for nights when he is working late or has to be in the ABC studios early. He motioned me inside; we sat at a dining room table. Gifford smoked Larks.

I tried to explain what I wanted to talk about. He showed no reaction to the request. He began to give me a brief autobiography: how his father had worked in the oil fields, and how the family had had to move often—sometimes fifteen times in a single year. The only way he and his brother were able to make friends with new schoolmates was to excel on the athletic field. "That's a way to fit in right away, when you move so often," he said.

I said that there must be thousands of other young boys who have to move a lot, but who aren't Frank Gifford on the playground.

"I can't help that," Gifford said. "You're talking about physical ability. I was born with that. I had nothing to do with it."

He ran through his life as a high school quarterback, a college tailback, a pro halfback. I brought up the Frederick Exley quote; I mentioned the section of *A Fan's Notes* in which Exley mused on his envy of Gifford.

"I think he was stuck on my girlfriend," Gifford said. "He'd seen her around campus."

But surely Gifford was accustomed to people reacting that way to who he was, and what he had.

"I suppose," he said. "People have always looked for things in me that they'd like to see in themselves. I've experienced a lifetime of it. I have never known what to think of it. It wasn't my fault that I was a good athlete. It was just genetic structure." He went to the kitchen and came back with some Oreo cookies and a cup of coffee.

I asked if he had ever had the moment, as an adolescent,

that all adolescent boys have—the moment they look in the bathroom mirror and see all nose or all chin or all acne. That moment in every young boy's life when he realizes he looks awful, and there's nothing he can do about it.

"I guess not, because I don't recall it," he said.

I asked if he had always been so remarkably good-looking.

"I've been attractive all my life, and my looks have helped me all my life," he said. "Attractive, I guess, both to men and to women. Because men don't seem to be threatened by me. Guys will push their wives at me and say, 'Oh, my wife thinks you're adorable,' and I'll just say, 'Thank you very much.'"

And there was never a time, no matter how brief, when he was worried about the way he looked?

"I don't think I ever thought about it."

What about the other boys—the ones who were awkward, who were clumsy on the athletic field, who looked ugly in their bathroom mirrors? When Gifford was growing up, what did he think about those boys?

"Not a hell of a lot, because they weren't in my life," he said. "It's a matter of economy of time. Everyone associates with the people who were in their life. The people who were in my life were the guys who were playing football."

I said that a lot of men who didn't become famous via television until they had reached their forties or fifties seemed to make excuses to go out in public, just so they could reaffirm their fame every day. Was it different for someone who had always known the feel of admiring looks?

"Absolutely," Gifford said. "There are people who hire press agents, who run and try to get their pictures in the paper and to be written about. When you've had that on an ongoing basis all your life, you tend to find it less important. You don't go out frantically seeking love and attention and affection from strangers.

"When I'm on the road for 'Monday Night Football,' I'll get into town on a Sunday and just stay in my room. I'll order all my meals from room service, and study my notes for the game. Maybe I'll go out for a run, or if it's in a warm-weather city I'll go down to the pool and lie in the sun. But do I ever get a sudden flash of insecurity and feel I have to go down to the lobby to make sure everyone knows who the hell I am? No."

Gifford said that he was fifty-two now. "I just had a little grandson," he said. "I thought it might bother me—becoming a grandfather. I didn't know what it would be like. People would kid me and say, 'Here comes granddaddy.' I wondered if it would make me feel old. They said 'granddaddy' as if it were a terrible disease. And people these days are so concerned about age; when you turn thirty or thirty-five you're regarded as an animal that's ready to be terminated.

"So I didn't know how I'd react to being a grandfather. But it's . . . really an interesting rush. My grandson is absolutely adorable. Seeing my daughter, who I held in my own arms, holding that baby in her arms . . . it's an interesting little life-step. And I have no complaints about being fifty-two. A lot of guys didn't make it."

I said that fifty-two might mean one thing for most men; it meant something completely different in the context of Frank Gifford. When people saw him, they did not think "fifty-two-year-old man"; age seemed almost immaterial, and that fact undoubtedly unleashed the same flow of emotions in people that his being an all-American tailback did thirty years ago. I asked him if he had always been aware of the envy he aroused in others.

"There's really nothing I can do about that," he said. "I know what you mean. People thinking, 'You lucky son of a bitch.' If they want to think that, fine. But nobody works harder. I've found that the more you put into it, the luckier you are. Maybe they were lying on their ass drinking a can of beer, when I was getting done with football practice and then putting on a suit and tie so I could meet someone who might be able to help me in the off-season."

I asked him about the thought that had brought me to see him: the idea of walking into rooms his whole life and knowing the effect he would have on the people already in the room. Surely that must do something to a man.

"I enjoy walking into a room," Gifford said. "Most of the rooms I walk into, either I'm working, in which case I don't give a shit what the people think about me, or they're my friends, in which case I know what they think of me. So yeah, I'm comfortable. I've never had a problem walking into any room, if that's what you're asking."

We talked some more, and before I left I found out something that amazed me. I asked Gifford if there was ever anything in his life that he had wanted, and that he had not gotten.

And there was. It seems that he had once asked the New York Giants to let him switch from halfback to quarterback. The Giants had allowed him to try it in practice, but never in a game. All these years later, it turned out, Gifford still resented that.

"There wasn't a whole lot of doubt in my mind that I could have been an all-pro quarterback," he said. "I really felt I could have played the position."

I said that surely the slight couldn't have made much of a difference to him, even back then. After all, he was one of the most famous and successful players in the National Football League.

"Some people thought I wanted to do it for the publicity," he said. "Or for the glamour. But I was already the leading rusher, the leading scorer, the leading receiver. How could it have been more glamorous for me?"

Then why had he wanted to become a quarterback?

"I didn't want to *become* a quarterback," he said. "I *was* a quarterback. I was a quarterback in high school. USC recruited me to play quarterback. Halfback was forced on me."

But could it have made any real difference in his life? Considering the way things had turned out?

Thirty-seven floors below, the Manhattan traffic edged slowly along. Gifford ate another Oreo.

"Look, I don't want you to get the idea that I dwell on this," he said. "But always, in my own mind, I was a quarterback. I was never a halfback. I didn't *want* to be a quarterback. I *was* a quarterback. Nobody ever seemed to understand that."

Strangers on a Plane

On board United Airlines' Flight 1118, I waited for the jet to pull away from the gate. We were parked at Los Angeles International Airport; we were getting ready to take off for San Francisco.

The seat next to me was unoccupied. I was looking forward to stretching out during the flight. But just as the door at the front of the plane was closing, she rushed on. She excused herself and slipped into the seat directly to my left.

She was tall, in a tan dress. She wore diamond earrings. She appeared to be in her early thirties. It was clear that she had been in a big hurry; she was perspiring and breathing more rapidly than is normal, the way people breathe when they've been running down the airport concourse, trying to make a flight they can't afford to miss.

I didn't say anything. We taxied onto the runway, paused briefly, then picked up speed; in a few moments we were in the air.

She was the first to speak. "Are you a nervous flier?" she said.

"I am," I said. "How can you tell?"

She nodded toward my legs. "Your foot's going crazy," she said. I followed her stare. My left foot was indeed tapping away.

"How long has that been going on?" she said.

"Awhile," I said.

"Do you have to fly a lot?" she said.

"I do," I said.

The flight attendant came around and took drink orders. The woman said she'd have a Jack Daniel's and Seven-Up.

She was working on her drink, several minutes later, when she said, "Are you flying for business or pleasure?"

"Business," I said.

She seemed to be expecting me to pursue the line of questioning, so I said, "What about you? Are you flying for business or pleasure?"

"Neither," she said. "I'm just flying."

I didn't understand, of course. So I thought I'd ask it another way.

"How long were you in Los Angeles?" I said.

"About fifteen minutes," she said, and went back to her drink.

Before long she withdrew some pieces of paper from her purse and laid them on the tray table in front of her. I sneaked a look; they were United Airlines write-your-own-ticket passes, the kind that flight attendants carry with them so that they can board any plane they want.

"You fly for United, then?" I said.

"No," she said.

"Then what are the passes?" I said.

"They're spouse passes," she said. "I get them because of my husband."

"What does your husband do for United?" I said.

"He's dead," she said.

She kept ordering drinks, and she gradually told me her story. She lived in Colorado; her husband, she said, had been a baggage handler for United for fifteen years. He had died last December.

"Was it a long illness?" I said. "Did you know it was coming?"

"He killed himself," she said.

She said that since her husband's death, she had been flying. Not flying anywhere in particular; just flying.

"Today I got on the plane in Denver," she said. "What I usually do is walk into the terminal at the next airport, look around for the United flight board, and get onto the next flight, wherever it's going. This afternoon the next flight was going to San Francisco."

She said that, because of the spouse passes, the cost to her

was minimal: maybe four dollars for a short flight, eight dollars for a longer one.

"You mean you just go anywhere the airplanes go?" I said.

"That's right," she said.

"How many flights in a row do you usually take?" I said.

She shrugged. "There's no plan to it, really," she said. "I just
fly until I know it's time to stop flying. Then I go home."

She looked out the window and down at the Pacific Ocean.
"It's so peaceful up here," she said. "Look at that boat in the
water." I leaned over toward the window; the boat was barely
visible far below, but you could, indeed, make it out if you
looked hard enough.

I asked her when she had started her aimless flying.

"My husband and I used to travel together all the time," she
said. "I got used to it then, and now that I'm alone I still
do it."

I looked at her left hand, and she saw what I was doing.
"Putting my wedding ring away was the hardest thing," she
said. "That was like officially admitting it to myself, 'He's
dead.' Until I put the ring away, it didn't seem final."

I asked her if the flying was a way to avoid thinking about
her husband.

"That's not it at all," she said. "I don't want to avoid thinking about him. Actually, it's easier to think up here. You have
more time."

The flight attendant came around again to see if we needed
anything. She ordered another drink, handing the flight attendant her empty glass as she did so; I asked her if she was purposely trying to get drunk.

"I can get drunk on one drink," she said. "Getting drunk has
nothing to do with it."

I said that there might be better ways to sort out her feelings than just getting onto airplanes at random.

"I like it this way," she said.

"But why?" I said.

"Just because," she said.

.   .   .

The seat-belt sign flashed on, and a voice on the plane's loudspeaker system announced that we were beginning our descent into San Francisco. It was nearing dinnertime; I asked the woman if she knew where she was going to sleep.

"I guess on a plane," she said. "I'll probably get an all-night flight, and I'll sleep on that."

"Is that what you always do when you're flying like this?" I said. "Sleep on all-night flights?"

"Sometimes," she said. "If I go to Hawaii, I might stay over for the night, just to say I've been there. But the plane's just as good. I prefer the plane."

I didn't know what to say to her. The runway of San Francisco International was within sight, and the landing gear locked into place, and I found myself for some reason saying, "Do you think one of these days you'll wake up and you'll be able to care about another person again?"

She smiled. "I'm really not into caring these days," she said.

We hit the ground and taxied toward the gate.

"You're nice to talk to," she said. "You're not a grumpo. I end up sitting next to so many grumpos."

A flight attendant, on the PA system, said, "Thank you for flying with us, and for choosing United Airlines. We hope that the next time your plans call for air travel, you'll think of the friendly skies."

The woman smiled again. "Little do they know," she said.

In the ensuing days I found myself thinking about her. I wondered . . . she had been drinking so much, and her story had been so unlikely; could the whole thing have been a put-on, a little airborne fantasy designed to break the boredom and get her through the afternoon? Could she have been just another businesswoman on her way to an appointment in San Francisco, or a housewife on her way to meet her husband?

I had asked her her name, and the name of her late husband; I had written them down on a paper napkin from the flight. I called a man I knew at United's executive offices in Chicago; his name was Joe Hopkins, and I asked him if he could see if United had ever had an employee with the same name as the man whose name was scrawled on my napkin.

He called me back within an hour. "Our records show that the man worked for us for about fifteen years," Hopkins said. "But he died last December."

I asked Hopkins if the records showed whether the death was a suicide. He said he was not at liberty to give out that kind of information. So I got in touch with the United operations center in Denver, where the man had supposedly worked. I asked around and eventually found a baggage handler named Dave Bellavance; Bellavance, forty-one, had been a colleague of the man.

"Yes, he killed himself last December," Bellavance said in a soft voice. "I had really enjoyed working with him. He was a guy who liked to have a good time. It was good knowing him. When I heard what had happened, I was sad and disappointed and even a little angry. I guess I was angry that he had decided to take himself away from the world."

Bellavance asked why I was bringing up these questions, so I told him about the woman on the plane. He didn't respond for a few seconds; I asked him if her story made any sense.

"Yeah," he said. "It makes sense. They were the kind of people who were always flying around. It's so cheap when you work for the airlines, some people do it all the time. They were the kind of people who would fly to Arizona just to pick up a T-shirt."

I asked him if he had seen his co-worker's wife since the suicide.

"No," he said. "But I'm not surprised to hear what she's doing."

Whenever I see a plane unloading into an airport concourse now, I take a look. Whenever I board a United flight, I can't help glancing around the cabin at my fellow passengers.

We all have our own ways of running away, I suppose; we all have our own ways of escaping the parts of our lives we'd rather not acknowledge.

I walk down the street and I hear the sound of a plane up

above, and I stare at the sky and I think about her. She's up there somewhere; I don't know how long she'll keep running, or whether she'll ever stop. But I know she's up there, and I find myself wondering where she's sleeping tonight.

Western Reunion

It was a meeting without fanfare. This year's gathering was smaller than last year's; next year's, no doubt, will be smaller still.

The thirty men were gathered in a small room off the eighth-floor cafeteria in the Carson Pirie Scott & Co. department store in Chicago's Loop. They had all been telegraphers; each of them had operated telegraph keys back in the days when sending dots and dashes over the wires was the fastest, most efficient way of communication. They had worked for railroads, for brokerage houses, for Western Union, for the Postal Telegraph Company.

Now they are not needed. Computers and television and inexpensive long-distance phone lines have erased the requirement for telegraphers. There are no young men coming up to replace the men who had come to lunch in this room.

"You feel like an orphan," said Carl Sostak, eighty, who had gone to work for Western Union in 1923. "In the time it took us to send one character, an IBM computer screen can print pages. You don't feel as if you're a part of this generation. You're out of step. We just don't belong anymore."

Sostak, like his companions at lunch, had dressed in a nice business suit. The men in the room call themselves the Morse

Telegraph Club. There are approximately fifty chapters across the United States—and on this day all of the chapters were holding meetings simultaneously. Here in Chicago it was on the eighth floor of Carson's; in Aberdeen, South Dakota, it was at the Flame Restaurant; in Portland, Oregon, it was at the Mallory Hotel; in Terre Haute, Indiana, it was at Joy's Restaurant.

Western Union had set up a special wire connecting each of the chapter meetings for a few hours. On a table in this room there were a telegraph key and its sounder; by hitting the key, the men could communicate with their brethren around the nation. As the men filed in, the key and its sounder were alive; messages were arriving from Minneapolis, from Oklahoma City, from Cincinnati.

"We all have rabbit ears," said Bill Dunbar, and it seemed to be true; even as the old telegraphers were greeting one another, they were listening to the sounder, and silently translating the messages as they came across the wire. A red metal Prince Albert tobacco can had been attached to the key-and-sounder; the men explained that this was a telegraphers' tradition—the can made the messages louder, made their sound carry more distinctly.

"Someone's calling Seattle," said A. J. Long, sixty-nine, as the sounder clicked.

"We're a proud breed because there's nobody learning it today," he said. "We took a lot of care in the messages we sent out. I remember once, Harry Truman was passing through Salem, Illinois, on a train on his way to Washington. He had just heard that MacArthur was not going to run for President. The train was full of newsmen, and they had all written stories that had to be wired to their papers.

"I got a call at midnight. I was to be down at the station when the train rolled through. They tossed the stories off the train, and I transmitted them to newspapers all over the country until seven A.M. When I finally got home, that day's St. Louis *Globe-Democrat* had arrived at my house. And there was the story I had sent—perfect, right down to the letter."

The men in the room said they have trouble explaining to younger people just what it is they used to do. "It's a skill no one today would ever want to learn," said Glenn Keeney, seventy-nine, a railroad telegrapher. "There's no field for them to get into. We were proud, though; we were doing something that somebody else couldn't do. We felt like we were part of a profession."

Helner Ahlborg, seventy-nine, who worked for Western Union and Postal Telegraph, said, "There was a lot of brag-gadocio among telegraphers about the speed you could attain. Some of the fellows never did develop any speed, while others got to be terrific.

"The important thing was to know the capabilities of the fellow on the other end while you were sending. If he wasn't a speed demon at receiving, you knew to hold back a bit. You got to know the other fellow's way of sending. It was just like listening to his voice. Every man had a certain swing to his transmitting."

At ten minutes before noon, the sounder at the front of the room clicked again. The men, now sitting at tables, turned to it. Out in Lincoln, Nebraska, a retired telegrapher named Cecil Combs was saying grace on the wire. His prayer was clicking into all the chapters around the nation.

The metal arm on the sounder tapped against the Prince Albert can, and suddenly, in unison, every man in the room rose. They listened together; the sounder clicked some more, and they all closed their eyes and reached out to the men on either side of them. They held hands. The only noise in the room was the steady clicking. From Nebraska, Cecil Combs was telling them that it was time to give thanks; time to thank God that, despite all the changes in the world, they were all here again, together.

Alley Girls

The day had been a long one, and darkness had come early. It was enough to depress a fellow.

I was just getting ready to go home when I happened to glance at the calendar. It was Wednesday. Ah, Wednesday. I smiled at the very thought of it. If it's Wednesday, everything's all right.

On Wednesday the Greenettes bowl. I hailed a cab and headed for the lanes.

Most of us can never even dream of owning a professional sports franchise; being a big league owner is the province of multimillionaires, and we have as little chance of identifying with them as of identifying with the king of Saudi Arabia.

But I have discovered that you don't have to be a millionaire to feel like George Steinbrenner. All you really need is twenty-five bucks; for that paltry sum you can own a team that will make you happier than ten years of New York Yankees, with none of the headaches.

Twenty-five dollars is the sponsor's fee for the Wednesday Night Ladies' League at the Mont Clare Lanes bowling alley on the northwest side of Chicago. If you pay the twenty-five, a team is yours. Five frisky females who are as grateful and indebted to you as if you were keeping them in minks, champagne, and duplex condominiums.

The Greenettes are my team. I sponsor them; they wear my name on their bowling shirts. They mean the world to me, especially on dreary Wednesday nights when life is looking dismal. Tonight I needed to check out my girls.

When I arrived at Mont Clare Lanes, the Greenettes were just starting their match. They were pitted against a fivesome called Up Your Alley; the Greenettes and Up Your Alley were seated on a salmon-and-white bench that spanned two lanes.

Spectators are supposed to sit in chairs behind the alleys, but as owner of the team I am permitted to sit on the bench with the Greenettes themselves. When they saw me they let out a chorus of welcoming cheers; as I joined them they gathered around me.

I was wearing a coat and tie, as is my custom when visiting the Greenettes. I walked over to peruse the league standings; the girls, alas, were in eighth place in a fourteen-team division.

No matter. The season was young. I leaned back and took an appreciative gaze at my squad.

The Pindel sisters were looking fine. The Pindels are the heart of the Greenettes; there are three of them on the team. Angela Pindel, twenty-six, a telephone console operator for a newspaper publishing company, had a league average of 117 as of tonight. Helen Pindel-Costa, twenty-four, a secretary for a Loop manufacturing firm, was averaging 153. Jo-Ann Pindel Jasiak, twenty-eight, an employee of the cosmetics department of J. C. Penney, was averaging 135.

Corky Barnash, thirty-two, a bookkeeper for restaurants and bars, was averaging 128. The kid of the team, Sandy McCowan, twenty, a nursing student, was averaging 93.

Angela converted a spare, and pranced back to give a high-five handslap to each of the Greenettes, and to me. It is a custom on the team; when any member gets a strike or a spare, we smack palms. Some of the other teams think it's bush, but we like it.

As Jo-Ann got set to roll her ball I mused on how the fates deal us curious hands. Just one day before I found these five women, they had almost decided that they would not be able to recruit a sponsor. The Pindels' Uncle Norbert, sensing desperation in the girls, had agreed to underwrite the team if no one else could be found. They were going to be called Norb's Nieces.

But why dwell on what might have been? I had found them in time. They were the Greenettes, and they were mine.

All around us, other sponsors' teams were rolling away. Ogden and Carroll Service Station, Willoughby's Two bar, Sam's Finer Foods. As far as I could tell, no other sponsors were there in person—in the owner's box, as it were. This did not surprise me. I had learned that many sponsors are shockingly lackadaisical about providing on-site support. That burns me. They pop for the money, and they think that's their only obligation.

Helen was holding a vodka and orange juice as she waited her turn to bowl. One thing about the Wednesday Night Ladies' League: these women drink and they smoke. You have to accept that if you want to be a good owner. You're not likely to mistake your athletes for potential Olympians in training; if that's what you're looking for, you're best advised to find another sport.

So up and down the thirty-two lanes a haze of smoke hovered over the scoring consoles, and empty beer bottles were discarded in anticipation of a waitress who would pick them up and bring refills.

Jo-Ann was fuming. "If I had known that was the beer frame, I would have tried harder," she said. "I only got a nine. You really want to get a mark in the beer frame. You don't want to be the one who has the low score and who has to put the fifty cents into the pot."

On the Mont Clare's loudspeaker system, the recorded voice of Bobby Vinton could be heard singing "Mr. Lonely."

"Hey!" Angela said. "I saw a Bobby Vinton special on TV last night! Did you know that he wrote this song in three minutes? That's what he said on TV. He said he was in the Army when he wrote it and the words came to him just like that."

Sandy was standing off to the side. She is the quiet Greenette; I have a hunch it's because of her tender years. Whatever the reason, she doesn't say much. I asked her if she wouldn't rather be out chasing boys than bowling.

"Nah," she said. "Not on a weeknight." She lives at home with her mother; she said that her mom, if the truth be told, would prefer that she stay home and study rather than bowl with the Greenettes. She wandered toward the ball-return rack, ever the enigma.

Corky had overheard our brief conversation. She laughed. "Come hell or high water, I'm here," she said. "I have a two-year-old, and Wednesday night is my only night out. I bowl Wednesdays, my husband bowls Thursdays."

I glanced up at the scorecard, which was projected on a screen above the lanes. The Greenettes were ahead in the first game.

There had been a dramatic personal event in the life of one of the Greenettes just four weeks earlier. On the Thursday following a Wednesday night match, Helen had flown to Las Vegas with her boyfriend, Steve Costa, a filling-station employee and part-time rock musician, and had gotten married. The ceremony was still the major topic of the squad's between-frames chatter.

"Look at the pictures she brought back," said Angela, showing me some color snapshots. "She got married in the Silver Bell Wedding Chapel, right on the Strip."

I looked at the photos.

"Stars get married in this chapel," Angela said. "It's the chapel of the stars. Helen, who are the stars who got married there?"

"I don't know," Helen said. "It's on the card. I think I've got it in my purse." She rummaged through the purse, but did not find it. "I must have left the card on my dresser at home," she said.

"I think it said Diana Ross got married there," Angela said.

"Don't go saying that," Helen said. "I don't think it said that Diana Ross actually got married there. I think it might have said that Diana Ross just visited there once."

Sandy rolled her ball down the lane; the pins smacked off one another, and two were left standing.

"Man in your bedroom!" Corky yelled.

"That's just Corky's phrase," Angela explained to me. "It's what she calls it when one pin is hidden behind another. I don't know where she got that. Technically, it's called a sleeper."

I was noticing that, although my team was in fierce competition with Up Your Alley, the members of the two squads were not talking to one another. They were sitting on the same bench, but not more than a dozen words had been exchanged between the two aggregations all night.

I decided to try to find out why. I scooted over next to the other team and started to ask them about it.

"What do you think of the Greenettes?" I said to Marge Wanat, one of their members.

"I don't know," she said. "This is the first time we ever played them."

"I'm their sponsor," I said.

"Yeah," she said. "We know."

"How come you're not talking to them?" I said. "Is there something you don't like about them?"

"No, they seem all right," she said. "Sometimes you play a team that's real crabby. Your team's not crabby."

Another member of Up Your Alley, Pat Grimes, said, "We don't really come here to socialize with the other teams. We come here to socialize with ourselves. This is the only chance we get to see each other all week long."

"They're like every other team here," said Colleen Mahoney. She avoided making eye contact with the Greenettes.

I had a sneaking suspicion that I knew what the problem was. "Who's your sponsor?" I said.

"We don't have a sponsor," Marge Wanat said, a little too quickly. "We sponsor ourselves."

Aha. It must be tough. Here they were—Up Your Alley, a team without an owner—and in walks the owner of the Greenettes himself, in person, on the scene, actually sitting on the bench, giving his girls encouragement. I couldn't say I really blamed Up Your Alley. I dropped the line of questioning and moved back down with my squad.

On the lane to our right, a team called Killer Bees Two was bowling. On top of their console was a stuffed toy bee.

"That's their mascot," Angela told me. "Both Killer Bees Two and Killer Bees One always bring their bees with them. Look down at lane thirty. See? That's Killer Bees One. See their bee?"

I peered over at them. The women of Killer Bees One seemed to be snacking on something.

"I don't know what it is about Killer Bees One," Angela said. "They always bring their own potato chips. Us, we use the vending machines provided by the lanes."

Next to us, the team that was bowling against Killer Bees Two—Willoughby's Two bar—had undertaken a new routine. Every time one of their members bowled, she would tie a blue plastic rain bonnet over her head. When she had finished her frame, she would give the rain bonnet to the next woman in the lineup. The rain bonnet kept passing from head to head. Apparently this was some sort of good-luck ritual.

"Where'd you get the hat?" Angela called to one of the women.

"She found it in her purse," the woman answered, pointing to a teammate.

I paced on the carpeting behind the alleys. The Greenettes were into their third game; they were far enough ahead that they were assured of being victors for the night. I was due back downtown. Things seemed to be in secure enough shape for me to leave.

I was down by the Lustre King ball-conditioning machine when I heard my women cheer. Jo-Ann had just rolled a strike; they were giving each other the high five. I hurried back so that I could join them.

I told them that I had to take off. We waved goodbye. As I was on my way out a buzzer went off back in the direction of the Greenettes' lane. I looked back; Corky, carrying a Stroh's, had walked past the foul line, setting off an alarm. Her ball was stuck in the gutter, and she was going out to retrieve it. I don't know how Steinbrenner feels when he's walking out of Yankee Stadium, but there's no way that it could be any better.

Bexley

WASHINGTON—I was supposed to deliver this year's commencement address at the high school from which I graduated in 1965. I got sick and didn't make it to the ceremony, so the speech never got made, but I've been giving some thought to what I might have said had I arrived on schedule, and I'm finding that I'm surprising myself.

Bexley, Ohio, is a town of 14,000. It is quiet and sedate, a suburb of Columbus; the cliché "Middle America" probably fits. When I was going to Bexley High School, most of us talked about getting out. It was our obsession. Bexley was too small, too confined, too safe; we wanted the Real World.

Eight hundred students attend Bexley High School; in Chicago, the town where I now make my living, we kill more than that many people every year. In Bexley, there has not been a murder recorded since the town hired its first marshal in 1917. Bexley has five marked police cars; in Chicago, there are more than 11,000 men and women employed by the Police Department. I guess I found the Real World.

And yet as I sit here in Washington, where I'm making my temporary headquarters, my mind is on Bexley, and all of the other Bexleys across America. Chicago may be the Real World, and Washington may be the Power Center, whatever that means, but it seems to me that the Real Worlds and the Power Centers are mainly made up of those of us who decided to leave the Bexleys, and I'm trying to think what I might have told those students at that graduation ceremony.

Because more and more, as I learn of the realities of life in the so-called important locales of the United States, I find myself wondering about Bexley, and whether it was so smart to leave it in the first place. I see the cruelties and the horrors and the outrages that have become the norm in the supposedly sophisticated centers of my Real World, and suddenly Bexley seems pretty good. All of those high school hours spent dreaming of escape . . . and now the dreams are of Bexley.

I know that I'll probably never go back. All of us, the ones who made the decisions to leave the Bexleys and seek out the Chicagos and the Washingtons and the New Yorks, we may dream about it, but it will somehow never get done. The decisions and impulses of your youth have a way of hardening up on you.

But still, I would never have given up my years of boyhood in Bexley, not for anything. The very things we found so maddening as teenagers—the small-town atmosphere that seemed to hem us in and keep us from everything exciting that was happening Out There—are the things that I now treasure most. I think that the most important part of me was formed in Bexley, and it's something that men and women who grew up in the big cities of the land will never know.

For there is something to be said for being allowed to grow up in a world without real problems, something to be said for being allowed to learn about life in a world without crime and without strife and without open hatred on the streets.

I know that there is another side of this to be argued; to grow up in a Bexley is to be made vulnerable and innocent and open to a lot of hurts and truths that you never even suspected exist. Bexley was, and is, white; there aren't even enough blacks living in Bexley to be statistically measurable on a census scale. The families of Bexley are financially comfortable. When a major part of the human spectrum is kept away from you as a child, you grow up ignorant about what much of life is about.

And yet the privilege of being allowed to grow up in such a peaceful world, a world where you are not always looking over your shoulder in the darkness or listening for footsteps in the night—that is a privilege that is becoming more and more priceless in the new world I am seeing. In the Bexley where I grew up, trouble meant getting caught painting our initials on the Penn Central bridge, or tearing the hands off the clock on top of the elementary school. I've learned since then, but I don't know how far I've come.

The irony, of course, is that even now the students of Bexley High School are dreaming of getting out, of finding that same Real World that seemed so elusive to us back in central Ohio. Some of the students in this year's graduating class will make it out, and some of them won't; they will stay in Bexley, and raise the next generation to grow up in Bexley.

And I guess, had I made that speech, it's the getting-out students I would have been talking to—the ones who will leave, and who will make Bexley only a part of their memories. I couldn't have told them not to do it; when you want to get out, there is nothing that can stop you, and I suppose I know that as well as anyone else. But to those who leave Bexley, please at least believe this: you will miss it. Jesus, how you will miss it.

King of the Campus

This curious thing happened. Last summer I wrote a column about a career woman in her thirties who had a good job, a nice apartment, fine friends—but who was miserable because she had no husband. She said that, even with the rest of her life in precise order, she was unhappy every day because she had no one to come home to.

She was afraid that people would think her attitudes were outmoded and behind the times, but that's not how readers reacted. Many business and professional people—men and women—wrote and called to say they felt the same way.

Among the responses were a number of letters from men who said they wanted to meet the woman in question. I had not printed her name; the men sent me long letters directed to her, and asked me to pass the letters along.

As I was reading the letters from the men, I couldn't help but wonder what kind of fellows would express such longing toward a woman they knew almost nothing about. I suppose I was envisioning sad, lonely men who had never been part of the so-called good life.

And then one of the letters stopped me cold. I read it—it was as lonely and poignant as any of the others—and I got to the signature, and I couldn't believe it.

I knew the man.

I knew him from college. Back at Northwestern, he had been one of the freewheeling, good-looking fraternity studs who ruled the campus. He had been in one of the best houses; he was well known as an ace intramural athlete; he ran with the most desirable crowd at the university.

And here was his letter. He wrote to the woman:

"I come home at night to my small studio apartment and fix

myself a tuna sandwich with melted cheese, and I sit down to eat it and I look across the table and there's no one there."

I must have read the letter a dozen times. More than any of the others, it affected me. I read the words, and I thought of his happy-go-lucky face as he jauntily strode across the Northwestern campus in the late Sixties.

I sent the letter on to the woman, but I kept thinking about it. Finally I sought him out; we talked. He is thirty-six now. After college he tried to become a part of the business world, but didn't fit in. He does manual labor for a living.

I told him what my impression of him had been back at college.

"I know what people thought of me," he said. "But that image really wasn't true. I never even dated that much in college."

I said I had remembered seeing him and his friends at fraternity-sorority exchanges; they had always been surrounded by the most attractive co-eds from the best sororities.

"I was fairly shy," he said. "I suppose you could say I was kind of afraid of women. You talk about the exchanges; do you remember . . ." [Here he named some of the best-known fraternity men and athletes at Northwestern.] I said that I did, indeed, remember them.

"They were my roommates," he said. "If there was going to be an exchange at a downtown hotel with the Kappas or the Thetas, we would go down there early in the afternoon before anyone else got there, and start drinking beer. That's how we got through the exchanges. At six o'clock, when everyone else was heading back to campus to get ready for their dates, we'd go to the Toddle House and that would be our evening. I remember one Homecoming when I spent the evening doing my laundry."

He said he sometimes worries about the way things have turned out. "Everyone around me, all my closest friends from college and high school, have successful careers in corporate America," he said. "They have families and everything you're supposed to have. They must be pulling down $100,000 plus.

"I don't know anyone who, like myself, has failed to make any money. All my old friends have nice homes; I live in this crummy little studio apartment. That's a hard notion to live with. You wonder, why haven't you grabbed the brass ring?"

I asked him what had prompted him to write the letter to the woman.

"I was just feeling pretty miserable that night," he said. "I was sitting here in the apartment, having dinner with myself. I guess I thought that by writing the letter, by letting one other person in this world know that I was hurting, maybe I'd feel a little better."

I asked him what he wanted out of life.

"Well, I'm thirty-six and I've never been married, and I love children, and I would love to have some of my own someday," he said. "There was this article in *Newsweek* a couple of years ago about how women are afraid of hearing their biological clock ticking—how they get afraid they'll never have children. Men can feel that fear, too. It's not the same thing with the biological clock, but I feel afraid about it.

"The image of men in their thirties, I think, comes pretty much from beer commercials. You know, the men leave their downtown office to go play rugby, and then they get together for beer and good fellowship. The message is that life is lived from one peak experience to another, every day. But I know my life isn't like that."

We talked about a lot of other things; there isn't space to go into them here. But I kept envisioning him back on campus, in those final years of the Sixties; I kept seeing him coming out of his north campus fraternity house on a crisp fall day, ready to go to class. I asked him if he ever wished he could be back there again.

"No," he said. "I know I can't change places with anyone else. There's no point in wishing. Things work out the way they were intended to work out. There's a plan for all of us, and here I am."

Never Travel For Food

Some people told me they wanted me to try the "best pizza in the world."

In a weak moment, I said I'd go with them. They made me promise not to mention the name of the pizzeria in the newspaper; they did not want to ruin the place by having people from all over creation coming to check it out. I said I'd go anyway; I like pizza.

We drove for an hour and ten minutes. Finally we arrived at the pizzeria. It was a nondescript, low-slung building.

We walked inside. There were a limited number of tables; customers were expected to place their orders as soon as they entered the place, then wait for a table to open up. With luck, their pizza and their table would be ready at about the same time.

I was asked what kind of pizza I wanted.

"Oh, I don't know," I said. As long as I was at the place that cooked the best pizza in the world, I was ready to try anything.

"Go ahead," I was told. "What kind do you want?"

"Double cheese with pepperoni," I said.

"We don't have pepperoni here," I was told.

I stood there dumbstruck. This was no joke; the place with the "best pizza in the world" was telling me that pepperoni was not a feature of its menu.

I could have screamed. I could have cried. I could have kicked the wall.

I did none of those things. What I did do is this: I made myself repeat in my head, twenty straight times, one of the most valuable rules of life—a rule I had no business violating:

Never Travel For Food.

It's basic; it's simple; it's essential. The fault was all mine, for I had willingly violated the rule. No one should ever travel for an hour and ten minutes for a meal. It doesn't matter how good the meal is alleged to be; if a person is foolish enough to travel for an hour and ten minutes, then that person deserves to end up at a pizzeria that does not serve pepperoni.

Never Travel For Food. The rule seems almost quaint in a society that treats restaurants the same way it used to treat ornate and majestic movie theaters, that offers vast fortunes for entrepreneurs who open the right restaurant at the right time, that has *restaurant critics*. It's apparent that Americans have learned to honor and kneel before restaurants, and to travel any distance for a chance at the Right Meal.

Some of us, though, have an attitude that is slightly different. We find nothing magical about food. We are cars, and food is gasoline. When we are empty, we go to the nearest station and fill up. Then we cruise along until we are empty again, at which time we look for a convenient station at which to fill up again. We would no sooner travel an hour and ten minutes to go to a particular restaurant than travel an hour and ten minutes to go to a particular gas station. Give us five bucks' worth of regular and get us on our way.

Food, it seems to us, can do only several things. It can make us feel bloated. It can make us feel sick. It can get us by for a number of hours at a time.

Don't get us wrong; food can taste good. But it's no big deal; whatever the effects of a certain meal are, they are sure to disappear by morning. Spend time traveling for food? How nonsensical.

Our rule of thumb is: If it's close, eat there. What restaurant do we recommend? Almost everyone has at least one restaurant or coffee shop within a few blocks of home. That's the one we recommend; eat there.

On the road, things get a little more complicated. When one checks into a hotel, the first choice for a meal should be room service. It's the closest of all; you don't have to move. If room service is not practical, then the next best thing is to eat in the hotel dining room. That way you don't have to go outside. If for some reason you must go outside, the best place to eat is the first restaurant you run into after walking out of the hotel. Forget the guidebooks that tell you which restaurants in town rate however many stars. The first restaurant you enter will be fine.

Never Travel For Food. Such an obvious and wise concept; yet millions flout it routinely. There are even people who get on airplanes and fly to foreign countries—mainly France—just to eat. They don't eat as a *part* of their trip; the whole purpose of the trip is to eat.

"Why don't you try sausage on your pizza?" the people who had driven me for an hour and ten minutes said.

"I hate sausage on pizza," I said.

"Then what will you have?" they said.

"Double cheese, sausage, and onion," I said.

"We thought you said you hated sausage," they said.

"I do," I said. "The onion will hide the taste."

I made myself eat it. It was punishment, and I deserved it. Never Travel For Food. This wasn't a case of being ignorant—I knew the rule and I paid no attention to it. There was no reason to hurry; the only thing waiting for me at the other end of the meal was an hour-and-ten-minute drive back home. Which is where I should have stayed in the first place; I already had in my refrigerator the same thing they were offering at the best pizzeria in the world: no pepperoni.

Nixon on Nixon

NEW YORK—"I was walking along the street the other day," said Richard Nixon. "I was going over to the Regency Hotel to get a haircut. A couple of young fellows were standing on the corner. And a Secret Service agent said to me, 'Smell that. It's a joint.' Marijuana. Actually, I hadn't smelled it before."

Nixon broke into a small grin.

"I suppose I'm a bit square on that," he said. "I realize that's old hat."

We were in a long conversation, which was nearing the end of its second hour. Nixon, dressed in a blue suit, sat in a corner of his office in a federal government building. The office is not listed on the building's directory board; its telephone number is unlisted, and it is behind a plain, unmarked door.

The idea had been—in this era during which political men somehow all seem somewhat dull and smaller than life—to seek out the one man who had stirred the passions of the nation like no other.

I did not want to talk to Nixon about Watergate, or about the current political season. Rather, I just wanted to see if he would spend time with me. I was not seeking to hear Nixon talk about government or to make him judge office seekers. I wanted to hear Nixon talk about Nixon.

He was wary at first. "I have never been one to do a very effective job of psychoanalysis," he told me. "I don't try to psychoanalyze others, and so I'm not that good at psychoanalyzing myself. I think, frankly, that those who engage in that activity—much of it is superficial and contrived, and most of it is useless."

But as the hours went by, he loosened up. He moved away from his desk—the one with two flags behind it, the American flag and a dark blue flag bearing the seal of the President of the United States—and he sat in a red patterned chair. And he began to talk freely—about his days in the White House, about his relationships with the news media, about his views on television, about his new life in New York, about his feelings on the "drug generation," about the public's perception of him.

"Walter Cronkite," Nixon said.

We had been talking about the fact that public opinion polls often had showed Cronkite to be the most trusted man in America—while the same polls just as often listed politicians among the least-trustworthy categories.

"Yeah," Nixon said. "I think it's probably just a reflection on the fact that television is so powerful. And I would say that whoever is President—if he's so concerned to please everybody, not to ruffle feathers, to be a kind and gentle Walter Cronkite—then God help the country."

The question of public personality seemed to be very much on Nixon's mind. He was aware that Cronkite had attained the status of a beloved and warm American figure—and just as aware that he, Richard Nixon, was destined to go down in history with a reputation as a stiff, cold, bloodless man. He said he realized that many people think that of him; he wondered why they did not think the same of other Presidents.

"Truman was considered to be a very down-to-earth fellow," Nixon said. "But believe me, he didn't want any familiarity with him, except from his close friends.

"Eisenhower with that famous grin and so forth—but he didn't like to be touched. That's right. What I mean by that is that, of course, he would shake hands and all the rest. But he didn't want people to come up and throw their arms around him and say, 'Hi, Ike.'

"Kennedy was the same way. Despite the fact that he had the reputation of being, you know, very glamorous and the rest, he had a certain privacy about him, a certain sense of dignity. Now, Johnson was . . . Johnson was one who believed in touching the flesh, and the rest.

"I, of course, was more like Kennedy."

Nixon seemed aware that, because of his formality, many people found him to be a distant figure, not to be embraced or thought of with warmth. He said that was a product of the way he grew up thinking of the Presidency.

"A President must not be one of the crowd," he said. "He must maintain a certain figure. People want him to be that way. They don't want him to be down there saying, 'Look, I'm the same as you.'

"The White House is a very formal place. One doesn't feel that he can really kick up his heels there. Now T.R. [Theodore Roosevelt], of course, was able to accomplish that very well. His family romped around the White House and the rest. Ours never romped.

"We found one of the reasons we liked Camp David and our place in Florida was that you could sort of put on a sport shirt and the rest and relax. For example—and may I say that this is not intended to say that others should not do it differently—but in all the years I was in the White House, I never recall running around in a sport shirt, let alone a T-shirt. Or sneakers and the rest. Others do it, but I just didn't feel that way.

"And Mrs. Nixon never wore jeans. Maybe they weren't that much in style at that point. But it wasn't because we were stuffy. It was just that we would not feel comfortable in that house unless we were somewhat formal.

"Now, I wear a coat and a tie all the time. It isn't a case of trying to be formal, but I'm more comfortable that way. I've done it all my life.

"I don't mind people around here in the office, particularly younger people—they usually take their coats off. But I just never have. It's just the way I am. I work in a coat and tie—and believe me, believe it or not, it's hard for people to realize, but when I'm writing a speech or working on a book or dictating or so forth, I'm always wearing a coat and tie. Even when I'm alone. If I were to take it off, probably I would catch cold. That's the way it is."

Of all the things that Nixon might ponder concerning the

Presidency, surprisingly the one he chose to bring up is an astonishingly small one—the fact that some newspapers capitalize the word "President" in second reference, while other papers use the lower-case "president."

"Well, yes," he said. "You have what I think is a rather juvenile practice which has occurred in the last four or five years. You do not capitalize the word 'president' when you say 'the President.' Now, I've noted the very significant change. We still follow the British. The British started to capitalize about three years ago. Then the *Wall Street Journal* in this country. Now the *New York Times* does it. *Washington Post,* no. Now that, to me, is a little petty."

Nixon appeared to be puzzled by what he perceives as a growing lack of respect for the institution of the Presidency—as exemplified by newspapers that refuse to capitalize the word "President," and by First Families who dress casually inside the official residence.

"Again, it goes back to the way we were raised," he said. "I recall the first time Mrs. Nixon and I went to the White House. I was a new congressman. And they had, as every President does at the beginning of every new Congress, a reception for all the members of Congress.

"And we had very little then. A congressman, incidentally—when I entered Congress, his salary was $12,500 a year. Which we thought then was not bad. But Mrs. Nixon, she scrimped and she bought a new dress to wear to the White House. A formal.

"And she said to me, 'Well, this is going to be a little hard on the budget, but this may be the only time we'll ever be there.'"

"If I had feelings," Nixon said, "I probably wouldn't have even survived."

We were talking about the traumas of his years in the White House—the public disenchantment with him that intensified

during the Vietnam War, and culminated with his forced resignation from office after the Watergate affair.

"I don't allow my feelings to be hurt," Nixon said. "I learned
very early on that you must not allow it to get to you. And as
the years have gone on—and this used to infuriate my critics
during the White House years—I made the decision not to
respond, no matter how rough the attacks were."

We were at a highly intriguing point in our visit. I had told
Nixon that when I had been in college, and then in my early
twenties in the years immediately following college, I had run
with a crowd that, in the main, despised the very mention of
his name.

"Yeah, most of them were like that," Nixon said.

I said that there were several phrases that people liked to
fling about when talking of Nixon. I wondered if he had ever
heard them: "Tricky Dick," and "Would you buy a used car
from this man?"

"Oh my, yes," he said. "Yeah."

I asked him if, when he heard those things being said about
him, his feelings became hurt. And he immediately said that
he was immune to such hurt.

"What was difficult for me," he said, "was that I was trying
to end the war and end it in an honorable way. And to go
around and have the students yell . . . you know, they didn't
say, 'One, two, three, four, how many . . .' no, it was 'LBJ,
how many boys did you kill today?' And all that sort of thing.
And at the end of it, looking at the period, the treatment of
me was much rougher than what they gave Johnson.

"I remember very clearly something. I was speaking down
in Williamsburg, Virginia, and this was right after I had become President. And I think we had made the first announcement about our first withdrawal of twenty-five thousand. And
this very pretty girl, she was I guess sixteen, seventeen—came
up and spit full in my face and said: 'You murderer.'

"I borrowed a handkerchief from a Secret Service man and
wiped it off and then I went in and made my speech. It was
tough.

"The point is, if I had not been schooled in defeat, then probably it would have gotten to me so deeply that I would not have done a good job. You move from one battle to another. And in order to do the job well, my best advice to someone sitting in this office is, don't be too sensitive to the criticism. I think President Johnson died of a broken heart. I really do.

"Here's Johnson, this big, strong, intelligent, tough guy, practically getting so emotional that he'd almost cry, because his critics didn't appreciate him. He, 'til the very last, thought that he might be able to win them. And the point was, rather than win them, rather than have them love him, he should have tried to do what he could have done very well—have them respect him. And in the end he lost. He neither gained the love nor retained the respect."

There was a momentary silence, as if Nixon might be pondering how those words applied to his own life. He seemed a bit uncomfortable talking about it, and became much more at ease when the conversation turned to his moment of triumph— the day when, after all the years of trying, he first walked into the White House as President.

"In the biographies of Presidents that I read and so forth, they say, 'Well, from the time he was in his mother's arms she looked down and said, "You're going to be President some day,"' and so forth and so on. But I never set my cap for it, so to speak. To say 'I'm going to be Vice-President and then President' and so forth and so on. Oh, my no, no way.

"When I was a kid, of course, I grew up in the Depression. We had it rough. There was a lot of illness in the family. We didn't have much time to dream about the future. We were just trying to keep our heads above water and survive. I would have thought being Justice of the Peace would have been a big deal.

"But what happened was, at a very early age in my career I became involved in a very big story, the so-called Hiss investigation. I was thirty-four years of age. And so I became a national celebrity very early, and I was a fairly good speaker,

and I went around the country and people even at that time
started to come up and say, 'You know, you could be President. You ought to be President.'"

We talked some more, and the subject of his very first night
in the White House came up—the night after his inauguration,
when he moved in as the official resident.

"I had never been in the President's bedroom," Nixon said.
"Except on one occasion—not when Eisenhower was there, but
when Johnson was there. I came to a Gridiron Dinner, and
after the dinner Johnson invited me to come up and have
breakfast with him. He had stayed up late after the dinner.
He had developed a terrible sore throat, laryngitis, and was in
bed. So that was really the first time I was ever in that bedroom. Here was Johnson propped up on one of these big king-
sized beds, and I sat there and had a cup of coffee with him."

For all the times he had been in the White House itself
during the Eisenhower years, Nixon said that on his first night
as President, he found himself wandering around, just looking at things and taking it all in.

"It was a new adventure," he said. "I explored it. When
you're in there as a guest—it's presumptuous to sort of examine
things. And when you're there on your own, you sort of look
at it through different eyes.

"I never tired of walking around late at night. Sleep was a
problem for me. Because you're moving in high tension all day
long. In a period of war, it is tough, because no matter how
you try to put it out of your mind, you're thinking about what
is happening on the battlefield. Anybody in that job is going
to get very charged up. And at night sometimes it's difficult to
sleep. Eisenhower used to take sleeping pills. I used to take
them. I didn't take them much—I liked to take just as little as
possible, because I didn't want to have a hangover the next
day.

"So I never tired of walking around late at night and looking at the paintings and so forth. Coming into the Oval Office,
one has a feeling of the dignity of it and the history of it and
the rest. You cannot walk in those old rooms without feeling
or hearing the footsteps of those who have gone before you."

Imagining Nixon walking alone through the White House late at night, my mind immediately shifted to that famous picture: August 9, 1974, standing in the doorway of the military helicopter on the back lawn, waving his arms as he left the White House for the last time. He had obviously felt such love for living in that house; I asked him what thoughts were filling him as he waved farewell from the helicopter.

Nixon's eyes glazed over.

"I don't know," he said softly. "It's hard to recapture it all. At the time I was frankly so physically and mentally and emotionally exhausted that I really didn't have any profound thoughts. I mean, I knew I was leaving, and that was that."

"I never wanted to be buddy-buddy," Nixon said. "Not only with the press. Even with close friends. I don't believe in letting your hair down, confiding this and that and the other thing—saying, 'Gee, I couldn't sleep, because I was worrying about this or that and so forth and so on.'

"I believe you should keep your troubles to yourself."

We were talking about Nixon's public image. I had told him that many people considered him to be an icy, forbidding figure—not only because of his political policies, which they may have disagreed with, but because of his seeming inability to try to relate to others on human terms.

Nixon nodded his head affirmatively.

"That's just the way I am," he said. "Some people are different. Some people think it's good therapy to sit with a close friend and, you know, just spill your guts.

"I think of this nice gal—apparently, I don't know her, but she appears to be this very intelligent gal—who had to resign from Bendix. [Mary Cunningham.]

"Yeah, and obviously she had met with some press people and has gone into all of her private life. Now, to me, that would be a very embarrassing thing to do, but I know that's what's taught in schools today, so perhaps the younger generation should go in every time that they are asked by the press how they feel about this or that, and they should reveal their inner psyche—whether they were breast-fed, or bottle-fed.

"Not me. No way."

I asked him if that didn't bother him. Here he is, a man who has had more inches in the American press, more time on television, more covers of *Time* magazine, than probably any other political figure in history—and people still feel they don't know him. They have seen him for years, and yet in many ways he remains a mystery man.

"Yeah. It's true," Nixon said. "And it's not necessary for them to know.

"Not to make ambiguous comparisons, but who knew De Gaulle? Who knew Adenauer? People think they knew Eisenhower. Not really. There isn't a good biography on Eisenhower. They are either puff pieces or pieces that are totally frivolous. And he was a very complex fellow. People, when they talk about him as this nice, good man, who sort of presided in a genteel way—they forget that the guy who ordered the landing in Normandy when everything was on the line was no softhead."

I asked Nixon if he relaxed his attitude even around his closest associates—if, for example, during the White House years he had ever, in a personal moment, invited his top-echelon aides to call him by his first name.

"Never," he said. "And none did."

I asked him if it wouldn't have made him feel more comfortable to have someone close to him who could call him "Dick" or "Richard."

"None did," he said. "That was just the way I did it. And Eisenhower was exactly the same way. I perhaps learned a lot from Eisenhower. With President Eisenhower, it was always 'Mr. President' from me. I, of course, was younger than Eisenhower. I never called him 'Ike,' and I never referred to him in my conversations with others as 'Ike.' He was 'the President' or 'the General.' "

I said that surely Nixon's close friends—not his advisers, but his personal buddies—must have been allowed to call him by his first name.

"No," he said. "They didn't. Even my close friends like [Bebe] Rebozo, for example, did not refer to me that way."

I said I found that hard to believe. When Nixon and Rebozo were out on a fishing boat, in casual clothes, and Rebozo wanted to offer Nixon a beer—did he actually say, "Would you like a beer, Mr. President?"

"Yep," Nixon said. "That's right. That's the way."

He began to speak of his ambition—the driving force that took him to the top office in the land, and which, in the end, led to his downfall.

"We all can't be President of the United States, and we all can't be president of General Motors," he said. "Okay. How does it happen? Some of it is luck. Although I can say more of it is a case of taking advantage of opportunities presented.

"Above all, in political life, you must be willing to take great risks. You must risk greatly—I know, looking back on my own political career, of a number of very able people, very intelligent, a lot of mystique, a lot of charisma, etc., who stopped at Congress. Who never went to the Senate. Never went on to become governor. Who stopped at that level.

"Because they didn't want to risk a safe seat. The moment people begin to think of how they can be secure, they are never going to make it clear to the top.

"You've got to take great risks and lose if necessary. And maybe lose twice or three times and keep coming back. That's the secret.

"My public life has not been easy. For reasons that we don't need to go into. And it's very rough on the family, etc. I would say, however, that if I had known what was going to happen, that I would not have refused or declined to get into it.

"I think what you have—what is essential—let me put it this way. When you think of high office, there are two kinds of people: There are the men and the boys. The boys are those who want to be in high office to be somebody. The men are those who want to be in high office in order to do something.

Now you have both. And again, not to put it solely in personal terms, I always felt that I wanted to do something."

I asked Nixon if he thought his personal style had hurt him—if he thought that had he presented himself as a looser, more accessible individual, some of the political criticism of him would have been muted.

"No, the problem in my case was not style," he said. "I mean, I could have had the press in for dinners. I could do those things. I never drank with the press, of course—I don't mind that others do, understand. But I don't think it's a good idea. And I don't think it's a good idea to drink with the Secret Service and that sort of thing.

"You've got to retain a certain . . . be that as it may, I could have had all sorts of little chatty dinners and the rest, and you might get a nice warm piece the next day. But deep down, the problems I had with the press—you're referring to what happened before the resignation period—the problems had to do with what I believed in. I believed in different things than what they did."

"I have never seen myself on television," Nixon said.

At first I thought he was kidding me. Nixon was probably the most televised public figure in the history of the country. But he said it was true.

"No, I don't engage in some of the practices of others," he said. "I've never watched a tape of myself. Oh, a flash on the news or something, if I'm looking at it. But during the White House years I deliberately read the news summaries, which had of course total coverage of what was on the evening news and that sort of thing.

"But I don't—I've never had a tape of myself, and then studied the tape and then gone out and practiced.

"Oh, never. I remember that many years ago, Tom Dewey— whom I greatly admired and I think would have been a great President, secretary of state, chief justice, anything, if the time would have been right—but Dewey was known as somewhat of a mechanical man. And I have heard that he sometimes would practice his speech before a mirror.

"I know that others of course will do that. I noticed, for example, at the last convention, a number of the people apparently went down to the convention hall and practiced their speeches. I've never practiced a speech in my life."

I said that surely, before delivering those famous televised addresses, he must have done a few run-throughs.

"No sir, never," Nixon said. "On TV, I do it live. I don't like to make a tape. I like to do it live, and maybe you flub a little but on the other hand it has more believability.

"I do a lot of the writing myself. When I've been through about twelve drafts, I've got a lot of it up here. But I never read it out loud. No, sir, never out loud. And I don't time it.

"I think if you read the thing out loud, or if you watch yourself on television, you become self-conscious and say, 'Gee, I should have this kind of a gesture rather than that,' and so forth.

"Now you will probably learn things, but on the other hand, your critics—family, close staff, and the rest—they will say, 'Look, I think you were speaking too fast, or you were speaking too slow, or you were looking too much here, there, or you were looking down too much, you should look up more, you should sit straighter'—all these things.

"You should listen. You should take that sort of criticism. But I think when the individual himself gets into that business where he practices it . . . it's very difficult, at least in my case, to retain spontaneity."

I said that it was difficult for me to believe that, before addressing the nation on momentous issues, he had not studied tapes of his previous performances.

"Let me put it in other terms," Nixon said. "I quit playing golf over a year ago—you know, I got so busy with my last book, now I probably won't play again. I've broken eighty, and that is as far as I'll ever go anyway. But I know that the golfers say that they have videotapes made of their golf swing, or they have pictures taken of their golf swing, and they go out and watch the pictures and they try to swing and so forth.

"I could no more do that and play a good game—I'd become so self-conscious, I'd miss the ball. So my point is, don't look at yourself."

For all his protestations about not watching himself on television, however, Nixon seemed to have almost an obsession with the institution of TV. Again and again during our conversation, he kept coming back to it.

"In your colleges and universities and in your speech courses," he said, "they believe that you should listen to your voice. The network people, they all—some are men and some are women—they all have the same lilt at the end, or the drop, and so forth. The same cadence—and to me it's as boring as the dickens. They would be much more interesting if they would talk in different terms.

"CBS, for example, which is a network I listen to a great deal—I also listen to NBC and ABC—but I notice each has a certain cadence, where they must say to some of these people, 'You're going to talk this way.' I think they lose something."

He began to talk about Lyndon Johnson, and suddenly television came up again.

"The trouble with Lyndon," Nixon said, "he had three television sets in the office, and he would look at them, the critics on television, and then call the heads of the networks. Those people were not elected—he was. Well, I took that to heart. One of the first things I did when I came to the Oval Office was to remove all the television sets.

"He even had them in his bathroom. And in the little room there, he had little television sets in the bathroom and he had one in the sitting room, the anteroom off the Oval Office, and three in his bedroom. I took all of them out.

"Yeah. Absolutely. Oh, I didn't have one in the bedroom. I don't have one there now. When I do look at television I usually go to look at sports, and I of course see the evening news. Although I generally get my news from reading—but these days, since eighty percent or ninety percent of the people do see the evening news, you'd better look at it to see what people are doing."

I said that with all the social problems in modern America—teenage pregnancies, widespread drug use, soaring divorce rate, open marital infidelity—I wondered what Nixon thought was the biggest potential problem.

"I would say I am concerned the most about the enormous power of television," he said. "When I read polls to the effect that the average American spends four hours in front of the tube, it to me is a very discouraging thing to see.

"I think the younger generation will come out less well educated than would be the case if they could read more. To be responsible in the world, you can't be looking at the tube and getting these pictures and flashbacks and pontifical comments and so forth and so on.

"I remember, for example, you take a presidential press conference. You're supposed to answer twenty-five questions in thirty minutes. So they ask you the question, What are you going to do about Iran? And you're supposed to answer it in a minute and a half.

"No way. And yet that's the way it's done. So people get a superficial answer. Television commentators, of course—if you get a half a minute on the evening news, it's a big deal. How can you discuss inflation, how can you discuss a new program for drugs? How can you discuss anything intelligently in one-half a minute, and yet that is what the poor politicians have to do every night in order to get on the evening news."

He said that his great concern for his grandchildren's generation is that the legacy of books may be lost on them, replaced by the new legacy of television.

"There are so many good books out there to read. There are so many good articles that are thoughtful to read. It is something people have lost if they sit in front of the tube and turn off their minds.

"And the people who are leading them in television—not that they are bad people, but they may not know. They may not be that profound. And like an Eric Sevareid can sound profound, but it can be very superficial. That's an act with him.

"It's a question of discipline and parental leadership. I understand that parents park their kids in front of the television. They scream and holler until you put them in front of the television. I don't mind it, perhaps, when they're very young—but when they get in school, don't let them be before that tube.

"My best advice to any young person moving up is: Read more, look at television less."

"Somebody who has served as President," Nixon said, "there is nothing else that he can do."

We were nearing the end of our conversation. The talk had turned to Nixon's life today. I was getting the impression that some of his days were emptier than he would like.

"There is not the challenge and not the stimulation of being in office," he said. "And I'm sure there are people retired from any position, no matter what it is, low or high—I think we talked earlier about the problems of youth. I think probably just as great these days is the problems of age.

"We have early retirement. We now have people retiring at sixty and so forth. They may be in the prime of life then. They think they want to play golf and fish the rest of their life, and after about a month they get bored with it."

His days, as he described them, do not vary much. He rises each morning at 5:30, while his wife is still asleep. He eats breakfast alone. He goes out for a walk—usually a mile.

"I come down here [his office], arriving at 7:00 or 7:15," he said. "And then I'm here until about 11:30. Then I go back and have lunch with Mrs. Nixon. I spend the rest of the day there. That way I avoid the traffic both times. The traffic is murderous at 8:00 in the morning, and thereafter it's murderous at noon. So you'd better go at 11:30.

"I don't go to bed as late as I used to—unless the ball game is on, I'll stay up and listen to that, but I go to bed early, around 10:30."

He said that he and Mrs. Nixon have virtually no night life, by their own choice.

"We never go to a cocktail party," he said. "I'll never go to another cocktail party. Just don't like it. A cocktail party is an invention of the devil. The talk—it's so loud, and people drink too much, and talk too much, and think too little."

I said that Richard Nixon, in a room full of drinking, socializing people, must be like a lightning rod. Everyone must want their one scene with him.

"It's a bore," he said. "I just don't go. We say sorry, got another engagement."

Most of his evenings, he said, are devoted to solitary reading.

"I have books around that I can read," he said. "Newspapers. I don't read novels. The only one I read recently, but it's really somewhat true to life although a little too much sex, I thought, not because I'm prudish but because it got in the way of the plot—was *The Spike*.

"If I wake up at night, I don't read anymore. Reading does not put me to sleep, it stimulates me. And I cannot go to sleep if I have music on, because I concentrate on the music. I've never gone to sleep in a movie, nor a play. Even as dull as they can be at times."

The reason Nixon's walks come so early in the morning is that he is likely to be mobbed if he goes out while the streets are filled with people. He is still probably the most famous man in America, and when people see him they press toward him and it soon gets out of hand.

"If you walk and you stop, then you sign the autographs. . . . I've never turned down an autograph in my life. My name is not long, anyway. But I went down to Julie's for the new baby, and I must have had about three hundred at that little hospital. Which is fine, they're awful nice people.

"But New York is a city where you can either take it or leave it, and they leave you alone. Everyone is just pounding away at his own thing, and they have a deep sense of privacy themselves. They're sort of suckers for celebrities in a way. On the other hand, they will leave a celebrity alone.

"It's a cold town in that respect. It can be very cold here, or very warm. But it's up to the individual. You can come here and get lost, if you want. This can be the place where you can be . . . you can find more privacy here than you can in the deserts of California."

Nixon said that he spends a lot of time thinking about the moral decay of much of society. Something that bothers him especially is the widespread and casual use of drugs in America.

"There isn't any question that you'll find the breakdown of morality in terms of the use of drugs and excesses in any way," he said. "In the breaking up of marriages and so forth. That is a danger sign of decadence.

"I think the drug culture, of course, is widespread. It isn't something that is just a so-called low-class thing—that isn't who can afford it. It is in with the beautiful set of people in Hollywood.

"The further this goes, the less strong society is. You see our competitors in the world, and God knows when you look at the Soviets and you look at the Chinese—the Communist system in general—the system doesn't work. Doesn't work economically, the idea has lost its appeal. They stay in power only because of power.

"But it's interesting to note that these societies . . . taking the Chinese, particularly, it's a highly moral society. Even this nuthead Qaddafi in Libya, he runs a highly moral show. Looking at the Chinese—drugs are out. As I look at history, any society that is on the way down moves into the drug culture. The societies that are to survive and be vital move away from it.

"It's a very tough time to raise kids. Right across the street from us, for example, there is a fine Catholic school. Now they do a good job in one respect. Every day at noon they close the street off. For an hour. They don't let any cars in there, and the kids run around, you know, in the street. And this is a school that is grade school and high school. It's mixed, boys and girls. They wear uniforms and so forth. And it's totally integrated. It's really a delight to see the young black kids and white kids playing their games and squealing and so forth and so on.

"On the other side of the coin, on their side of the street, where the school is, no smoking is allowed. On our side of the street—I was walking up the other day at noon, and here were some girls, I am sure they were no more than thirteen. They were smoking, and they smoked cigarettes, and some of them were smoking marijuana. On our side of the street. Yeah, the kids from the school, and there is nothing the teachers can do about it.

"Well, I guess this is quite common, but we saw it firsthand. They were smoking cigarettes and they were smoking marijuana. These are girls. That's what surprised me. Boys you'd expect to engage in all sorts of shenanigans, but little girls—I don't know. But I suppose that's part of the whole women's lib movement. The girls are supposed to be as immoral or decadent as the boys. I hope not."

It was almost time for me to leave. As I sat there looking at Nixon, it struck me that one of these days this fascinating, complex, contradictory man who has been at the center of American life for more than thirty years will be gone. It almost happened once—when he was hospitalized shortly after he left office, and went into shock.

"Frankly, the sense of your mortality grows as you get older," Nixon said. "I mean, after all, you read the obituary page, and you read of people sixty-five, sixty-nine, seventy, seventy-three, seventy-four, seventy-five—all of my generation. They cut off. They die. Heart attacks, cancer, what have you.

"But I never get morbid about it. I never worry about it.

"I just figure that every day may be the last."

Top Dogs

A manufacturer of dog food, in conjunction with the 100th anniversary of the American Kennel Club, has sponsored a survey of the most popular names among American dogs.

The winner is Rover. Spot is second.

Somehow that is reassuring. If I had been asked to guess, I would have predicted that the most popular names for American dogs in the Eighties were probably Lance, Barry, Cyndi, Zoom-Zoom, Crawdaddy, Crochet . . . names like that.

I would have guessed, in other words, that the era of the good, solid, generic dog name was over.

It's nice to be wrong. I like the idea that of all the dogs scampering across the American landscape, Rover is the most popular name.

But I'm so surprised that I have a nagging suspicion that the competition was fixed. When was the last time that you met a dog named Rover? I don't think that Kal Kan, the dog-food manufacturer that sponsored the contest, wanted to tell the American people that it had combed the countryside and had found that the most popular name among dogs was Springsteen.

No, I can envision the folks at Kal Kan sitting around, looking at the legitimate list of favorite Eighties dog names—Taos, Spock, Trendola—and the chairman of the board of the company slamming his fist down on the conference table and saying:

"Gentlemen, we must take a stand! We owe it to our country to protect the citizens from this distressing information! Put out a press release! Damn the real results! We will tell the American public that the favorite dog name is . . ."

A silence. The chairman thinks back across the years, to the nostalgic memory of his happy boyhood.

". . . Rover!"

More silence at the table.

"And the second-favorite name is . . ."

More silence. More warm thoughts of boyhood.

". . . Spot!"

And so the press release was drafted, and the nation was informed that Rover and Spot were the favorite names for American dogs in the Eighties. At which point the Kal Kan board of directors went home and were greeted at their front doors by their own dogs: Jermaine, Ferraro, Tuna Melt, and Sid.

I know from my own experience that Rover, while perhaps the favorite dog name of the Thirties, Forties, and Fifties, is not really the favorite dog name of the Eighties. When we were growing up, we all lived next door to people whose dogs were named Rover; now, more often than not, our neighbors' dogs are named Guccione or Tennis.

When I was a boy, my first dog was a little white mutt named Fido. In the middle of Ohio in the middle of the 1950s, that was the perfect name for a dog. You would almost expect the summer fill-in mailman to stroll up the front walk for the first time, smile as he put the *Saturday Evening Post* in the mailbox, and say, "Hi, son! What's that dog's name? Bet it's Fido!"

But the era of Rovers and Spots and Fidos is long gone; now it is unlikely that a contemporary mail carrier ever would venture a guess that a homeowner's dog was named Fido, although it is not inconceivable that a large number of today's mail carriers are named Fido.

Today when a youngster goes to school and stands up during show-and-tell time to inform his classmates about his adventures with his dog, it is likely that he will be talking about the adventures of Taco or Spielberg or Sin.

And when he dreams of heroic dogs—dogs that belong in the movies, up there on the silver screen—he undoubtedly does not dream of Lassie or Lad or Rin Tin Tin. The super-dogs that dance across his dreams at night probably are named Salad or Nautilus or Fern.

It's probably good for America, though, that the dog-food company is saying that the favorite dog names are Rover and Spot. We are supposed to be in an era of a return to traditional values, and maybe if people read enough stories saying that the favorite dog names are Rover and Spot, they will go home at night and say, "Cappuccino, you are now Rover!" or "Nike, you are now Spot!"

But even if people start doing that, there's no way it can last. We may go through a few new years of Rovers and Spots and Fidos, but then the trend will reverse itself again and you will start seeing dogs named Beach and Psychiatrist and Terrence.

So don't be too hard on that dog-food company for putting out the word that Rover and Spot are the most popular names for American dogs. The company is just doing its bit to raise the nation's morale, and that seems like a harmless enough thing to do. If the company wants us to believe that most people have dogs named Rover and Spot, then let's all tell the company that we believe it.

I would comment further on this subject, but right now I have to go home and feed my dog, Stir-Fry.

Lights, Camera, Clara

The most talked-about actress in America sat silently while her director determined whether the camera angle was right. Even though there was a flurry of activity all around her, she appeared to be so calm she might have been getting ready to go to sleep.

"We'll be set in just a minute," the director said to her.

The actress nodded her assent.

This was not Meryl Streep, Debra Winger, or Goldie Hawn. Who talks about them?

This was Clara Peller, eighty-two, who has rocketed to fame on the strength of one line of dialogue:

"Where's the beef?"

Mrs. Peller—a widow who used to work as a manicurist—is the star of the Wendy's Hamburgers commercial in which she uttered her now immortal line. In that commercial, Mrs. Peller—paired with two other elderly women—stood at a counter that was designed to look like part of one of Wendy's competitors' restaurants. When a tiny hamburger arrived on a huge bun, Mrs. Peller looked at it and said . . . well, you know what she said.

"Where's the beef?" quickly became a national catchphrase. Political cartoonists used it with their drawings. Bar patrons said it to one another as they wait for drinks. Crowds at college basketball games chanted it during timeouts. Ministers based their Sunday sermons on it.

And now Wendy's was preparing to shoot a sequel to the commercial. The cast had been reassembled; along with Mrs. Peller there were Elizabeth Shaw and Mildred Lane, the two women who had appeared with her in the first commercial. All eyes in the room were on Clara Peller, though; she was the one who had said the magic words in all of those living rooms, and she was the new superstar.

Joe Sedelmaier, the director of the "Where's the beef?" commercials, conferred quietly with his assistants and technicians. Off to the side, William M. Welter, executive vice-president of Wendy's, looked at the scene and marveled.

"This is amazing," Welter said. "Our business has increased dramatically as a direct result of these commercials, and there's no doubt that Clara is the big reason why. People just love her. She's not some thirty-two-year-old sexy broad; she's real. She appeals to everyone from two-year-olds to ninety-year-olds. We know because we see the fan mail."

Wendy's does not like to talk about it, but they almost lost Clara Peller last week. After the success of the first commercial she hired an attorney, and for a few tense days it seemed as if the Wendy's attorneys and Mrs. Peller's attorney might not be able to reach an agreement on a contract for the new commercial.

But things had been worked out. Now, as she waited for Sedelmaier to start shooting, she sat with her two fellow actresses.

"I heard they were going to make posters of us," Elizabeth Shaw said.

"I thought it was place mats," Mildred Lane said.

"Whatever," Elizabeth Shaw said. "I'll just talk to my agent." She turned to Clara Peller. "You're the star," she said. "We're just the background."

Mrs. Peller stared down at the floor, where a tape mark had been placed to show her where to stand when the shooting started. Behind the three women was a sign that said HOME OF THE BIG BURGER.

Sedelmaier was ready. Aides carried a Styrofoam cup of ice water to Mrs. Peller. She took a sip.

"All right," Sedelmaier said. "Let's do it."

The women stood up. The idea was that the three were supposed to be back in the restaurant again—this time trying to complain to the manager. In the commercial they stand at the counter, in front of a huge bun and a tiny burger, and Mildred Lane holds a telephone—ostensibly trying to call the manager.

The camera rolled. Mildred Lane said into the telephone, "We *know* it's a big, fluffy bun."

Elizabeth Shaw stage-whispered to her, "Talk to the manager."

Mildred Lane replied, "It *is* the manager."

Down on the floor, hidden from sight, a production assistant named Dwight Irwin sat with his right hand grasping the hem of Clara Peller's dress. Mrs. Peller is hard of hearing; it is difficult for her to hear her cues. So when it is time for her to speak, Irwin's job is to pull on her dress as a signal.

As soon as Mildred Lane had said, "It *is* the manager," Irwin pulled on Mrs. Peller's dress.

And Clara Peller blurted out, like an angry foghorn:

"Where's the beef?"

"Really let 'em have it," Joe Sedelmaier said. "*Where's the beef?*"

"*Where's the beef?*" Clara Peller bellowed again.

"Wait until he tugs on your dress," Sedelmaier said.

Wendy's is spending $11 million on the "Where's the beef?" campaign. Clara Peller, the most valuable part of that $11 million expenditure, readied herself for another take. America, America.

Words of Love

Traveling through Texas, I listened to local radio stations. In San Antonio I found myself listening to KISS-FM, a rock 'n' roll outlet.

On the air, one of the station's disc jockeys mentioned a promotion. "What would you do to meet the Crüe?" he said. He explained that a heavy-metal rock band called Mötley Crüe was coming to San Antonio. Listeners were invited to mail entries to the station. The winners would get free tickets to the concert; some would get to go backstage and meet the band.

I called the station. I said I would be interested in seeing the entries. I asked if there were any ground rules. I was told that the only rule was that listeners had to answer the one basic question: "What would you do to meet the Crüe?"

A week later, I read the entries.

We seem to have come quite a distance from Herman's Hermits fan clubs and "I Want to Hold Your Hand."

From a sixteen-year-old girl:
"What I Would Do To See Mötley Crüe:
"First, I would tie you up, spreadeagle and naked, with leather straps. Then I'd shave all the hair off of your chest, and if I should nick you I'll suck up all the blood as it slowly trickles over your body. Next I'll cover your body with motion lotion to get things really heated up. When it gets *too* hot, I'll cover your body in crushed ice and lay on top of you to melt it down and cool you off.

"Then I'll do things to your body with my tongue that you

never thought humanly possible. Then when you are screaming for mercy and begging for more, telling me how you want it all, I'll slam the spiked heel of my right leather boot into your navel, call you a very naughty boy, and laugh as I slowly walk away, telling you I'm just not that kind of girl."

From a fifteen-year-old girl:
"I want to see Mötley Crüe so bad I'd wear black nail polish and body glitter. . . . When I see them I'd get on my hands & knees & give them my body & even tear my clothes off if I had to. If that didn't work I'd do like Ozzy did and bite a dove's head off & say, 'Okay, let's talk business.'"

From a thirteen-year-old girl:
"I'd do *it* with the Crüe till black and blue is all you can see."

From a fifteen-year-old girl:
"I'm really a big fan of Mötley Crüe's and I would do anything to meet them. Vince Neil and Nikki Sixx are so fine!! I love 'em all. I would even get fucked by the ugliest, fattest, most disgusting guy in the world to meet them. . . .
"My boyfriend gets mad at me because I like them so much, and listen to the radio all the time for their songs to come on! I had to beg him to let me write this letter to you. Hopefully, I will win, because I went through a lot of trouble begging my boyfriend to let me do this.
"That would be just terrific if I won. I would have a chance of meeting Vince Neil! God, he's so fucking fine!!! If it would mean losing my boyfriend, I would fuck his best friend to meet these gorgeous guys. It wouldn't matter, as long as I got to meet Vince Neil and see his fine ass and fine body!! God, I can just see it now! Fucking him would be my biggest fantasy in the world! Well, I hope I win! Thank you!"

From a thirteen-year-old girl:
"I'd leave my tits to Mötley Crüe."

From a seventeen-year-old girl:

"To get backstage to Mötley Crüe I think I'd give them *every* piece of action they wanted. I'd give them my body, money, or whatever they wanted."

From a nineteen-year-old girl:

"I would go down to the local hardware store and buy some chains, leather straps, and nails. I would then put together the most outlandish outfit made of nothing but the leather straps, chains, and nails. I would go to the concert in this Kiss-Ass outfit, because I would do anything to get close to 'Marvelous' Mick Mars, 'Luscious' Tommy Lee, Nikki 'Sexx,' and Vince 'Can't Say No' Neil. P.S. I would take a hammer so the guys (the Crüe) can loosen the nails off my outfit."

From a thirteen-year-old girl:

"What's up? Well, you asked what I would do to be a Mötley Crüe, so here it is. First, I'd spread whipped cream all *over* my body. Then, I'd let Vince Neil *lick* it all off! I sure hope you enjoyed this cause I would love for it to happen."

From a fourteen-year-old boy:

"This is what I would do to join the KISS Mötley Crüe: I would give them my mother, who is very beautiful. She has red hair and brown eyes. She loves heavy metal and especially Mötley Crüe. My mother definitely has *the looks that kill*."

I spoke with the sixteen-year-old girl who said she would tie the band members up with leather straps and shave their chests.

"I didn't let my boyfriend read it before I sent it in," she said. "It would make him wonder what he didn't know about me.

"Why did I write those things? I don't know. I just sat down and wrote what I thought. It took me about half an hour. I don't know where the ideas came from. They just came out."

I spoke with the girl's mother.

"Yes, I read the letter," the mother said. "Actually, I took it down to the radio station for her. I guess I was shocked in a way, but I'm sure she didn't mean anything by it. She's a very Christian girl.

"Did I think about not turning it in to the radio station? Well, it really wouldn't have been fair for me not to turn it in. I promised my daughter I would do it. It wouldn't have been fair for me to put it in the garbage."

I spoke with the fifteen-year-old girl who said she would get on her hands and knees for the band and give them her body.

"I was one of the winners of the contest, but I didn't get to go to the concert because I didn't have a ride," she said. "My father was supposed to take me, but he had to work late. I didn't speak to him for two days.

"I meant what I said. I'd get on my hands and knees and give them my body. I know that they're grown men and I'm fifteen, but so what? It would be worth giving them my body just to meet them. I think it would be neat.

"I heard that in ancient times women used to get on their hands and knees and not even be allowed to look at men. I think rock groups should be treated like that. They're like God, but they're even better. The reason I would take my clothes off and crawl to them is that I would hope that they liked that."

I spoke with the thirteen-year-old girl who said she would do "it" with the band until she was black and blue.

"I just love the group," she said. "I wrote what I wrote because they look like the type who would like that. They look like women-lovers."

I spoke with the fifteen-year-old girl who said she would go to bed with "the ugliest, fattest, most disgusting guy in the world" in order to meet the band.

"I like their hair," she said. "I just like them a lot. It's pretty

boring in this town. I don't like school very much, I get C's
and D's. I wrote those things because I thought it might help
me win. I meant every word of it.

"I really like Vince Neil's body. When he's onstage he wears
a bunch of spikes and leather pants. I'd do whatever I had to
do to meet him. I told my mother's boyfriend about it, and he
said, 'Whatever turns you on.' "

I spoke with the thirteen-year-old girl who said she would
"leave my tits" to the band.

"I really like the way their faces look," she said. "It makes
me excited to see them onstage.

"I wrote what I did because I thought they might like it,
and then I'd get to meet them. You can tell that they're like
that. All rock groups know that they can have any girls' bodies
that they want. That's one of the reasons they join a band."

I spoke with the seventeen-year-old girl who said she would
give the band "*every* piece of action they wanted," and give
the band money.

"They seem like a wild, outgoing bunch of guys to me," she
said. "They seem like they'd do just about anything and not
care about it.

"I'd give them whatever they wanted. They can do whatever they want with my body. They look wild and mean and
evil. What I meant about giving them money is that first I'd
try to convince them in other ways to take my body. I'd follow them where they went and tell them to do with me whatever they wanted to. I think I could convince them.

"But if they wanted money for it, I'd pay them to take me.
It would be worth the money to me. I have some money saved
from baby-sitting; plus my father is a truck driver, and I could
borrow the money from him if I needed more.

"I'd do it with all four of them at once if that's what they
wanted. If they said, 'Be with all four of us or get out,' I'd say,
'Okay, come on.' I'd be crazy not to if that was my only chance
to be with them."

I spoke with the nineteen-year-old girl who said she would dress in chains, leather straps, and nails for the band.

"I think they're all gorgeous," she said. "When I see them, I just naturally think of leather and whips and chains. I think that means that they're aggressive. I happen to love that image; it's a neat image.

"I think it's that kind of aggressiveness that a woman is always looking for. Why did I put that thing in about bringing a hammer with me? Just like I said—they could use it to loosen the nails on my clothes."

I spoke with the thirteen-year-old girl who said she would let one of the band members lick whipped cream off her body.

"They're really good-looking," she said. "Good and mean. They just look like guys who are out to party and have a good time.

"I saw the band in a magazine and I thought they were pretty neat. I like Vince Neil the best of them. He's got the blondest hair; it's kind of long. He's not fat and he's not thin; he's just right.

"I wouldn't make the same offer to my boyfriend that I made to the band. It just wouldn't be the same with him. With the band, you think more of being wild and having a good time. My boyfriend is fifteen. We don't car-date yet; our mothers mostly drop us off at the movies and pick us up afterward."

I spoke with the fourteen-year-old boy who said he would give his mother to the band.

"I wrote that letter because I really wanted to get to go backstage and meet Mötley Crüe," he said. "My mom likes the band, too, and I thought if I offered her to them, I might have a good chance of winning.

"If the band told me that they really wanted my mother? I'd say, 'Take her.' I'd say, 'Here.' I really love my mom; I know she'd go with them."

I spoke with the boy's mother, who is thirty-four.

"Yes, I am a fan of the band," she said. "I sure am. I approved of his letter.

"We keep listening to the radio to hear their music. They're kind of wild; just a little wild.

"Billy and I have a good mother-and-son relationship. He's crazy about me and I'm crazy about him. When Billy said that he had offered me to the band, I said, 'Oh, Billy!' But I really do like them, and I would like to help Billy win the contest."

I was done with the interviews, and I knew it was time to sit down and write this story. First I went outside and took a long walk. Usually that helps to clear my head. For some reason this time it didn't seem to work.

Mother and Child

At thirty-six she is a high school teacher, living in the Chicago suburbs; she has never been married. She had driven to the southern part of the state to visit her parents; her mother, who had been suffering from cancer for three years, was not doing well.

It was a Friday night. Her mother was in bed; she was hooked up to an oxygen tank by a long cord. The daughter climbed onto the bed next to her mother, just as she had as a little girl. The two of them watched "Dallas" and "Falcon Crest." The daughter sensed that her mother was thinking something but not saying it.

The mother looked over. She said the words:

"I just don't want to leave yet."

The two women both started to cry. They held each other, and the daughter could not tell who was rocking whom: the mother rocking the daughter, as in days long ago, or the daughter rocking the mother? They spoke of death; the daughter said that she was afraid she would never get over missing this woman who had been there for her for a lifetime.

The mother said that in time, it happens; the hurt begins to let up. She said that she had been forty when her own mother died; all these years since, she had missed her. They kept rocking each other, the mother and the daughter, and they said all the words that needed to be said.

At the end of the weekend the daughter drove back to Chicago, to work. Within days the news came from downstate: the mother had taken a bad turn. She was in the hospital.

So the daughter made the drive again. A nurse stopped her in the hallway; the nurse warned that the mother looked much worse than she had even four days before. In the hospital room the daughter saw her mother propped up in bed, her eyes seeming to focus on someplace beyond the four walls.

The daughter's father and brother were there, too, as they had been all day. They said they were going to go away for a few hours; the daughter said she would stay with her mother. The mother drifted into a drugged sleep; once she woke up, apparently startled to find the daughter there. She asked: "How much longer will it be?" She didn't wait for an answer. Another time she opened her eyes and said that she was "ready."

"Dallas" was on the television set. The daughter thought: Had it really been a week since they had sat together and watched the show? She stroked her mother's hand and talked softly to her; her mother said that the daughter looked tired and should go home. The daughter said she would rather stay. A nurse came in and gave the mother a shot; it hurt, and she turned onto her side because her back was sore, and the daughter massaged her. Once the mother opened her eyes and the daughter smiled and said the mother was missing "Dallas."

At 11:00 P.M. the daughter's brother came back. The mother

was having trouble breathing; the daughter let the mother rest her head on her shoulder, and the daughter held her up like a baby. Several hours later—about 2:00 A.M.—the mother sat upright and let her legs dangle over the side of the bed. She wouldn't lie back down.

The nurse who was present asked the mother if she knew her daughter and son were there. She nodded yes. She was awake, but this was clearly the end.

The daughter thought: So this is what death is like.

The two children embraced their mother for thirty or forty minutes. They could hear that she was having great difficulty breathing. No one really spoke; they just held on. Finally, with her tired back resting against her daughter's chest and her head leaning against her daughter's shoulder, she closed her eyes and died.

The daughter thought: This wasn't frightening and it wasn't awful and it wasn't terrible. A woman had died in the arms of her children, knowing that she was loved.

The daughter thought: I don't know how I will get over this. I have called this woman on the telephone every night of my life since I was in college. This woman has told me I am all right all of my life, even during times when I wasn't so sure myself. I always hoped that if I ever got married, this woman would be there. But she never bothered me about it. She always said, "You're doing fine; your life is great."

It was twenty-five minutes before the daughter's father arrived back at the hospital. For that whole time, the daughter continued to hold her mother in her arms.

Now that it is over, the daughter lies in bed in her apartment, and she feels as if her mother is still alive. She feels as if her mother is watching her life. "It's like my mother is still in on it," the daughter will think. "It's as if she's in me. She's a part of me."

Of course there are days when the daughter will think of her mother constantly. She will be watching television and suddenly she will start crying. She will see mothers and daughters on the street and again the tears will come.

But there are also days—more and more of them recently—when she will realize that she has not thought about her mother. This surprises her; she had assumed such a time would never come.

"It's the life-and-death of it," she says. "It's the life-and-death of it that spooks me. Life goes on. Oh, my, my."

Doing the Eastern Shuttle

I have just returned from being away for several weeks. I spent most of the time traveling, and as is usual when I am on the road, I discovered many new, amazing, and exotic things.

Nothing I saw, though, was quite so amazing and exotic as the Eastern Shuttle.

"The Eastern Shuttle." It is a phrase that has lurked somewhere near the back of my consciousness for years. I vaguely realized that the Eastern Shuttle was a form of air transportation available to people on the East Coast; I knew that the rules of the Eastern Shuttle were somehow different from the rules of regular airplane travel, but I didn't know precisely how.

I was secretly intimidated by the very idea of the Eastern Shuttle. About six months ago I had to get to Washington from New York at an early evening hour; a colleague in New York said, "That's no problem. Just go out to LaGuardia and catch the Eastern Shuttle." It turned out that the Eastern Shuttle was the only plane leaving from LaGuardia that would get me to Washington that night. Coward that I am, I took a cab to the more distant Kennedy Airport and took a more expensive Pan Am flight to Washington. At the time, I just didn't have the guts to deal with the Eastern Shuttle.

This time, though, I had no choice. I needed to get from New York to Boston in a hurry, and then get back in a hurry. My only option, I learned, was the Eastern Shuttle.

I did a little quick research. The Eastern Shuttle, it turned out, is an economical air service run by Eastern Airlines. It goes between New York and Washington, and New York and Boston. You don't need a reservation to get a seat on the Eastern Shuttle; as a matter of fact, you can't *make* a reservation on the Eastern Shuttle. The Eastern Shuttle operates on the hour, all day and all evening. You just show up at the gate. If the plane is already full, they'll bring another plane for you. Even if there are only five or six of you left over—theoretically, even if you're the *only* passenger left over—they'll bring a plane. You're guaranteed a seat.

Airplanes in the rest of the country, of course, don't operate this way. In the rest of the country, you phone for a reservation. If there are no seats available, you don't get to go on the flight. The Eastern Shuttle is unique; it is pure East Coast, which is probably why Midwesterners like myself are so suspicious of it.

Anyway . . . my cab pulled up to the Eastern Shuttle terminal at LaGuardia. [The Eastern Shuttle has its own building; if you are taking an Eastern Airlines flight to, say, Miami, you go to the regular Eastern building. If you are taking the shuttle, you go to the Eastern Shuttle building.]

I walked into the terminal. I asked a uniformed man where I should go to buy my ticket. He looked at me as if I had dropped my trousers.

"You write your own ticket on the Eastern Shuttle," the man said with great disdain.

I looked all around me. Indeed, men and women were scribbling away on blank ticket forms that they had retrieved from a table, like deposit slips at a bank. I stood next to one of the people and, like a school kid cribbing on a chemistry exam, copied what he was doing.

I followed him down a hallway and on board the plane. It was a huge, wide-bodied plane, and people were sitting anywhere they wanted, just like on a bus. I knew that I hadn't paid for my ticket, but nobody stopped me.

A few minutes after the hour, the plane taxied away from the gate. I looked around me. The passengers on the Eastern Shuttle were clearly business people; clearly *East Coast* business people. I hate to stereotype folks, but if I hadn't known where I was I would have assumed that I had been dropped into the middle of a George Bush look-alike contest.

We took off. A plurality of the passengers began to work on pocket calculators.

I looked at the man next to me. On his wrist he was wearing a watch with two faces: one set to New York time, one set to Los Angeles time.

The captain of the plane came onto the public address system. He seemed to share the East Coast business mind-set of his passengers. He did not wish us a nice day. He said:

"I hope all of you have had a real successful week."

And then he said:

"We'll be flying over to Boston at 22,000."

Not 22,000 *feet;* it was clear that the captain assumed that all of the passengers on the Eastern Shuttle were such world-weary, seasoned travelers that there was no need to waste words.

I looked for someone to talk to, but the people who weren't buried in their *Wall Street Journals* were buried in their "Business Day" sections of the *New York Times.*

I saw a small army of flight attendants heading down the aisles pushing carts. I assumed they were going to offer us refreshments. Boy, was I wrong.

On top of the carts were credit-card imprinting machines. The flight attendants on the Eastern Shuttle were collecting fares from the passengers four miles up in the air, as we hurtled toward Boston. They would grab a passenger's American Express Gold Card, run it through the machine, hand it back, and push the cart to the next row of seats.

The flight attendants finished collecting the fares just as we were descending into Boston. The passengers, looking just as bored and jaded as they had throughout the flight, filed off the plane. I followed them.

I got to my hotel. The person I was supposed to meet called my room.

"When did you get in?" he said.

"About half an hour ago," I said with an exaggerated yawn. "Caught the Eastern Shuttle."

The Woman
in the Photograph

The smartest person I know is my mother. During the years between my birth and the time my brother and sister and I left home, she never had a paying job; although she did voluminous amounts of volunteer work for various charitable organizations, if she had been asked to compile a resumé it would have been blank under the category marked "Employment."

Her job, as she saw it, was to be our mother—full-time. She did this by choice. I had never really thought about what this must have meant to her life; when the editors of *Esquire* told me that the magazine was devoting an entire issue to the American woman and asked me if there was a woman I would like to write about in that month's column, I said yes, there was.

. . .

There is a photograph of my mother and my father, taken in 1942, while they were on their honeymoon. They are seated at a table in a restaurant, my father wearing his Army uniform; in the picture my mother, I think, looks beautiful. She was twenty-three at the time.

Looking at that picture, I see a woman who had she been twenty-three in the 1980s would have had limitless options available to her. She is more than pretty; she is visibly bright and vibrant and interesting. I look at the picture, and I know that had she decided to pursue personal pleasure or professional accomplishment, doors would have been open to her. In the picture she is a person whom, had I been a young man in 1942, I would have wanted to know.

Her history bears this out; although she, like me, was born in Columbus, Ohio, she was educated at Wellesley College and graduated Phi Beta Kappa. When I said in the opening sentence that she is the smartest person I know, that was no exaggeration. Most of us secretly feel that we are innately sharper than the rest of the world; I accept for a fact that, even on my best days, my mother is brighter and more capable than I. I am thirty-seven years old and I have never heard her utter a stupid sentence; I have never seen her make a judgment that seemed wrong.

And yet we come back to a basic fact: she always defined herself as a wife and mother. She was honored in our hometown for her volunteer civic work, but if she was asked what she did, she unhesitatingly answered that she was Robert Greene's wife, and Bobby, Debby, and Timmy Greene's mother. You could see it in her signature: "Mrs. Robert (Phyllis H.) Greene."

Coming home for lunch from school; somehow, that is what I remember most clearly. We didn't live all that far from the school building, and I would come home most days rather than eat in the lunchroom. Invariably she was there; just after eleven o'clock she had started preparing our meal, and when the three of us would walk through the back door she would be putting it on the table.

I suppose today many women would find that to be a demeaning waste of their potential. Why should an intelligent, ambitious woman be satisfied making egg salad sandwiches and heating up cans of soup?

I can't answer that, at least not from a woman's point of view. But it must have counted for something if, all these years later, I can still literally feel what it was like to rush through that back door and see her there putting the lunch on the table. If I recall correctly, we children didn't even talk much to her during those hurried meals between our last class of the morning and our first class of the afternoon; mainly, I think, we talked to one another about things that were going on at school.

I don't know what she thought on all of those afternoons when we jumped up from the table and ran out the same door we had run in. I assume that even back then a woman must have thought—her husband at work, her children at school— that something was missing. But if she felt that way, she never let us know; it never occurred to us that she was supposed to be anywhere but at home, waiting for us.

Today she might be an executive or an entrepreneur or an author. If she ever considered those things in the Fifties and Sixties, she never said them out loud; the world had yet to change its assumptions about women, and we instinctively knew that because she was a woman, she was right where she belonged.

Of my best friends from my high school days—there were five of us—three have already been divorced. Of my parents' best friends—a dozen couples or more—none were divorced. It just didn't happen.

Did men and women love each other more strongly back then? Doubtful. Did they feel a sense of obligation to stay together, a sense of obligation that is missing in today's marriages? Probably. Were they cheating themselves back then? Were they missing out on opportunities for richer lives?

Maybe I'm not qualified to answer. But I am of a generation that, by and large, was brought up in families that stayed together, by mothers who stayed home all day. And I wouldn't trade it for anything. If my mother deprived herself by the way she spent those years, I suppose I am sorry, but I know that she did not deprive Debby or Timmy or me. Whatever good there is about us, much of it came because we had a mother who defined her job as being our mother.

I once knew a homicide detective in Chicago, a man who saw the absolute grisliest, meanest parts of humanity every day. You would expect a man like that to be tough beyond redemption, but I always sensed a soft center to him; a part of him that didn't jibe with his job. One day I sat down with him and asked him about it, and he told me that no matter where he went in his life, part of him remained a small boy—and that inside the small boy there was the memory of his mother.

He told me, "Even when I was in the service, when I'd be out on a pass at four in the morning, I could hear my mother's voice saying, 'Joe, get home,' and I'd go back to the barracks."

I knew exactly what he meant. I am not the best person in the world; there are things about me that I would change if I could, and that I would not particularly respect if I found them in other people. But I know this: whenever I am doing something I sense might be wrong, I can check myself out by asking myself whether I would be ashamed if my mother knew about it.

I'm not saying I ask that question all the time. But this is an age in which the concept of "conscience" sometimes becomes muddied; we are all supposed to be so sophisticated about the nuances and tangents of a full life that sometimes it seems we can explain away anything, make ourselves believe that anything is all right. So it is reassuring to know that a simple rule of thumb is always there: How would I feel if my mother were to see me right this instant?

In a way I think we are a whole generation of men who are

living with that question; men who at times are able to fool ourselves into thinking that we can reinvent the world and change the rules on a daily basis, but who know, in the end, that we really haven't changed at all from the days when our mothers could look into our faces and tell what we had been up to without our uttering a word.

Curiously, sometimes it seems that most men spend much of their lives trying to symbolically deny the fact that their mothers' voices still sound in their heads.

In my business, there is an almost laughable premium put on the concept of hardness and grittiness. About the most flattering thing you can say about a reporter is that he is "street smart"; we love to tell stories in which we see dead bodies and do not flinch; in which we consort with criminals and think it only colorful. I am sure it is the same in other businesses, whether they be medicine or accounting or the law; if we can place enough distance between the men we are now and the little boys we used to be—if we can convince strangers that when we saw the dead bodies we did not cry—then maybe we can also convince them that no one can ever touch us, in any way.

There was a time, though, when we were not so afraid of being afraid. My mother tells me, and I vaguely remember, that as a small child I thought there were monsters in my closet. Before I could go to sleep, I would need for her to make the monsters leave my room. So every night she would say the words—she remembers them even now—"Ruley and duck and goose and wolf, car, airplane, hoo-hoo, and the one who burps—get out of here!" And I would sleep.

I cringe a little, typing that. But it seems that only by recounting the specific can I say what I mean: that in many ways there is nothing that affects a man so strongly as those childhood years spent with his mother; and that I doubt that children have changed so much by now that they are less needful of what their mothers can give them. For most of our lives it is our own responsibility to chase the monsters away; for a few brief years at the beginning, our mothers are there to do it for us.

But what of the woman in the photograph, sitting next to the man in the Army uniform? What of the choices she made, and the choices she might have made had the fates allowed her to be born half a century or so later?

Had she been a 1984 woman, she would have been a success; of that I am sure. I see them every day: women of achievement striding purposefully down the avenue, briefcases in hand, on their way to appointments and meetings. Had she been a young woman today, had she elected to go out into the world of commerce and ambition, I have little doubt that she would have fit right in.

So her salary would have risen, and her resumé would have grown, and maybe one day she would have awakened to find that she was one of the people running the company. She might have found herself going to work in a downtown high-rise where dozens—hundreds?—of other men and women labored for her, men and women whose own professional lives revolved around decisions that she would make.

And what about the end of the day? When she went home, would whatever she felt equal the emotions that she felt staying at home all those years with my father and my brother and my sister and me?

There are some who would argue that by never having the opportunity to know the answer to that question, she was robbed of a part of life that women today take for granted. That today's woman can make a decision to live the same life that my mother did—but can also make a decision to reject that life, a decision that was simply not open to my mother.

I don't know. Many women today, I think, would be afraid to live my mother's life. So much has happened, so much has changed, that for a smart and resourceful American woman to do what my mother did—to devote her life totally to her husband and children, and to fit in other things only when those things did not interfere with her home responsibilities—

would seem not only confining, but a little dangerous, a little foolhardy. I think that even a woman who instinctively might want to lead my mother's life would feel pressured to reject it on principle.

Which doesn't matter; my mother is not a young woman any longer, and the choices that she made she will never have to make again. But I know this: Debby and Timmy and I grew up during a time when a life like my mother's was taken for granted, and I feel grateful beyond words for that. I hope that my mother feels contented; I hope that, looking back on her life, she feels she did the right thing.

There are questions and contradictions here; I know that much of this is troubling, and that I have not summed it up very neatly. All of us move through our grown-up worlds, pretending that we were never anyone else but the fully formed adults that our colleagues see at the office every day. We were, though; a lot of us were once little boys who hurried home for lunch knowing that someone was waiting. It mattered then, and it matters now, and I could not be happier that the woman in the photograph was the one who waited for me.

The Twitching of America

BOSTON—There is a restaurant here called Legal Seafoods, with three locations in the metropolitan area. The restaurant has a unique policy about bringing diners their checks.

When you order your dinner or lunch, your waiter writes down what you want. Then, before bringing you your food, he presents you with your check and requests your money.

Legal Seafoods is not some fast-food operation; it is a respected Boston restaurant, and you pay healthy prices for your meal and drinks. So the pay-first policy is surprising to people who are eating there for the first time.

The reason for the policy is a simple one:

"A large part of our clientele consists of businessmen and businesswomen," said Bruce Ota, the restaurant's manager. "They are always in a hurry. They prefer not to wait around at the end of the meal. If they pay before they eat, then they can get up and leave the moment they've finished with their meal."

Ah. It makes sense. It's not that the management of Legal Seafoods doesn't trust the customers to pay at the end of the meal—it's that they know the customers are twitching in their seats in anticipation of getting back to work, or on their way to the next place they're supposed to be. To wait two or three minutes for a check would drive them crazy.

It fits in with something that seems to be happening all over the country. For want of a better term, it might be called The Twitching of America. All of a sudden, people seem to be in an insane hurry to get too much done in too little time. A reluctance to enjoy a meal and then wait a few minutes for the waiter to fetch the check is merely a symptom.

Time magazine recently touched on this phenomenon in a cover story on stress. The magazine said that increasing numbers of people are running themselves so hard that their stress is starting to become a medical problem; indeed, some men and women may even be becoming addicted to the adrenaline that their own twitching bodies are producing.

If you look around you, you can see The Twitching of America everywhere. There are people who will punch a button for an elevator, and if the elevator does not arrive within five seconds they will begin punching the button again repeatedly—or they will begin looking for a staircase. There are people whose faces become ruddy and flushed in traffic if the car in front of them pauses even momentarily before starting up again after the light turns green. There are people whose pulses begin to race if they call Directory Assistance and the operator does not answer before the third ring. There are people whose days are ruined if they have to stand in line at the bank. There are even people who, while using a bank of pay telephones, attempt to carry on conversations on two phones at once—if they are put on hold on the first line, they will pick up a second line to start a new call while they're waiting.

The so-called laid-back days of our society are definitely over. The Twitching of America is claiming more victims every day; no one really enjoys it, but the inroads it is making are undeniable.

This trip of mine to Boston is probably a prime example. I caught the first morning flight here; tonight I will catch one of the last flights back to Chicago. A day trip like this, halfway across the country, is far from uncommon; businessmen who used to routinely stay overnight in a distant city now check airline timetables so they can do their work and be back in their hometown the same day.

This has nothing to do with saving on hotel bills. It has to do with a feeling that waking up in another city on the morning after you have completed your work is wasteful of your time; you could be back in your office taking care of important tasks. So now, instead of relaxing and having an enjoyable dinner after a hard day in the distant city, businessmen rush to airports so they can get back to their own towns late at night.

It is merely a permutation of the Legal Seafoods phenomenon; the people who start tapping their feet and looking at their watches if the waiter does not bring their check right away are the same people who feel guilty if they waste another half-day traveling, when they could be working.

There is undeniably something deeply unhealthy about all of this; a society that has begun to value the clock so highly has got to be missing out on certain other aspects of a normal life. The cliché, of course, is "Stop and smell the roses"; now not only have people ceased stopping to smell the roses—they resent it if someone who *is* smelling the roses happens to block their path on the sidewalk for three seconds.

So they eat at Legal Seafoods, then hurry back to their offices to drum their fingers on their desks as they impatiently wait for their Federal Express packages to be delivered, inside of which are documents that had to reach them overnight. What would have happened if the packages had been sent via regular mail, and had taken three days instead of half a day to get there? Who knows. The important thing is, the phone has already rung twice, and the secretary hasn't picked it up yet. It's enough to drive a modern person right off the edge.

The Real Superman

If you can believe the newspaper ads, the reviews for this summer's *Superman III* movie have been pretty great.

One critic is quoted as saying: "Get in line fast! The funniest and most bracing of the *Superman* movies."

Another says: "*Superman III* is one of the summer's great escapes. Very funny and clever and strong on the old magic of special effects."

And a third weighs in with: "*Superman III* is the best yet. It's a hit. . . . It's a delight. . . . It's Supersequel! The most entertaining and affecting *Superman* yet."

I have no reason to doubt those critics. But I haven't seen any of the three modern-day *Superman* movies, and my reason is a simple one.

It's this: I was hopelessly addicted to the old "Superman" TV show. When I first heard that there were plans to make a big-budget Superman movie a few years ago, I was afraid that regardless of whether the movie was good or bad, it would forever overshadow the original TV series. And of course that is right; when future generations think of Superman, it will be in terms of the spectacularly successful new movies starring Christopher Reeve.

Which, I suppose, is only right. It must be admitted even by those of us who loved it that the old "Superman" TV series was pretty awful stuff, in terms of craftsmanship and production values. But millions upon millions of us, when we were children, would put down anything else we were doing, and stare at the TV screen whenever "Superman" came on—and we find that, as adults, we do the same thing anytime we come across a grainy rerun in syndication.

The main draw, of course, was George Reeves, the actor who played Clark Kent and Superman. It is hard to define the qualities that Reeves brought to the role. You would think that the character of Superman would demand strength, rock-jawed good looks, inner gentleness, a firmness of vocal tone . . . you would think that, but in the case of George Reeves you would be dead wrong.

The amazing thing about Reeves is that he had almost a mincing quality, and it showed through in every episode. I'm not sure whether we noticed it when we were kids—but for adults watching the reruns, it's almost impossible to ignore the fact that the casting of Reeves seems in retrospect like an in-side joke perpetrated by Hollywood producers on the youth of America. All you have to do is watch Reeves put his hand to his chin and say, "Hmmm, Jimmy, you may be right," and you see what I mean. At times Reeves played Superman like a combination of Jack Benny and Gloria Swanson.

But somehow it worked. The character of Superman was so spectacular that it was impossible to dilute its effectiveness. Children wanted to believe in Superman—and if what Holly-wood demanded was that we believe in an arch, coy, purse-lipped fellow who seemed more like a lummoxing great-aunt than like the man of steel, we were willing to give it a go.

Of course, Reeves was not the only draw. There was Noell Neill, who played Lois Lane, the first working woman many of us ever saw; Jack Larson, who played cub reporter Jimmy Olson; and, unforgettably, John Hamilton as Perry White, the dyspeptic editor of the *Daily Planet*, who kept shouting at Ol-son, "Don't call me chief!"

Looking back on it, it seems as if the *Daily Planet* had no other staffers; Clark Kent, Lois Lane, Jimmy Olson, and Perry White managed to put out the paper all by themselves, and the first three were hardly ever in the office.

But if that factor was designed to stretch our credulity, then what passed for "special effects" tested us even further. Any five-year-old could watch George Reeves flex his legs and get ready to leap from a window or off the sidewalk, and predict the exact point at which the director would snip the film so we didn't see Reeves fall back to the ground. We didn't care. We wanted to believe; we were on his side.

And when the "Superman" theme music swelled up, and George Reeves cradled a crippled girl in leg braces in the crook of his arms to give her a flying tour of the world, our eyes misted and our throats got tight. All the bad acting and lousy special effects in the world couldn't reduce the impact of that kind of scene.

George Reeves committed suicide in 1959; the rest of the cast of the "Superman" TV series occasionally turn up as answers to trivia quizzes. The new multi-million-dollar *Superman* movies have been both critical and financial successes; it is almost a sure thing that when future Americans think of Superman, it will be in terms of Christopher Reeve, not George Reeves.

So I'm glad I have protected myself from that. Never having seen the new *Superman* films, my eternal image of the greatest hero the world has ever known is guaranteed to be the unlikely, hilarious, but ultimately lovable one I first saw on a black-and-white TV screen in the 1950s. Hmmm, Jimmy, you may be right.

Confessions of a Middle-Aged Man

I woke up in a hotel room on the road the other morning, and when the room-service waiter brought my breakfast he also dropped off a copy of the local newspaper. I glanced at Page One, and I noticed something interesting about the date: It was my thirty-sixth birthday.

That struck me as pretty weird. For the last year I had been living fairly comfortably with the notion that I was thirty-five; thirty-five never seemed all that far removed from thirty. But thirty-six was a different matter entirely. Being thirty-six means only one thing; being thirty-six means you are middle-aged.

So I had my breakfast and got dressed and went out to conduct my business. It was the first day of my life that I had ventured out into the world as a middle-aged man. It felt . . . different.

The problem is, the last time I noticed, I was seventeen. My most vivid and cherished memories are of the time I was seventeen; my closest friends are still the people who were closest to me when I was seventeen; the events of the years 1964 and 1965—when I was seventeen—still seem important and meaningful to me. There's nothing wrong with that; I think it's probably pretty healthy to feel good about the early years of your life.

But it's sort of jarring for a person like that to realize he is now thirty-six. Being thirty-six is much more than one year older than thirty-five. A person who is thirty-five is one year older than a person who is thirty-four, but a person who is thirty-six has entered a whole new ball game.

Fortunately, I have been getting ready for this for several years. The first time I started thinking about it was during one of my twice-a-year visits to the dentist. He got done looking at my mouth, and—as I had been doing for years—I asked him if I had any new cavities. He said no.

I was gleeful. The dentist very gently said, "You know, you really shouldn't be worrying about cavities. You're not going to get a whole lot more cavities in your life. Middle-aged people shouldn't be concerned with cavities. They should be concerned with gum problems."

On the way home from that visit, I tried to figure out how the dentist could have meant that without implying that I was a middle-aged person. I knew I was not a middle-aged person; at the time I was only thirty-four, and as far as I was concerned, that made me in my early thirties, not middle-aged. But clearly the dentist had been trying to tell me something.

The message took hold. From that point on, in stories where I was trying to describe someone, I began to delete two adjectives that once were routine parts of my lexicon: "middle-aged" and "aging." The two phrases had suddenly taken on new and different meanings to me. When I used to write "middle-aged," I now realized, I had done it in a somewhat patronizing way. To write that someone was "middle-aged" had the connotation that the person was somehow bland, tired, not on the cutting edge; I had used the phrase for years, but only now did I realize that it had always had a negative connotation.

And "aging"; it used to be a convenient term to use in giving a sentence a bittersweet tug: an "aging centerfielder," an "aging businessman." Now it struck me that the phrase was meaningless; everyone is aging, even a four-year-old. We are all aging every minute of our lives. The phrase seemed mean-spirited, imprecise, and ultimately unfair.

And now here I was. When I had started this trip, I had been a thirty-five-year-old man. Now the person who would be coming home was a middle-aged man. I wondered if my parents realized I was a middle-aged man? If it made me feel so strange, imagine how it must make them feel. How would you like to be the parent of a middle-aged man?

This is definitely going to take some getting used to. When I hear that a person is thirty-six or thirty-seven, that person seems—in my mind—to be a much older person than I am. If I'm making a telephone call to a man I have learned is thirty-six or thirty-seven, I will call that man "Mr." on the phone. A person who is thirty-six or thirty-seven has always seemed to be a person worthy of deference. Now I am that person.

There are almost certainly some positive aspects to this. I know instinctively that even though I am middle-aged, that does not mean I have had all the experiences in life that a person can have. For example, I have never had an olive; that little fact alone encourages me to keep on going and experience the world to the fullest. Who knows what is waiting?

On the day after I turned thirty-six, I packed my bags and headed to the airport for the trip home. On the airplane, I found myself sitting next to a personable woman I had never met. We began a conversation during the course of the flight.

At one point I said to her, "How old are you?" [I have always been known for the ease, wit, and appropriateness of my small-talk.]

"Twenty-seven," she said. "How old are you?"

"Thirty-six," I said, and I saw something in her eyes.

I knew what it was, even though she probably couldn't have put her finger on it. In that one instant, she had found out whom she was sitting next to; she was sitting next to some middle-aged man.

But hey, that was her problem, not mine. Someday soon she will be middle-aged, too; let's wait and see how she likes it.

Rules of the Road

Three years ago this month, "American Beat" started appearing regularly in *Esquire*. As you know if you stop by this space on occasion, you will not find any particular brand of expertise here. We have no special insights on personal fashion, participatory sports, outdoor living, high life, or ethics. All we do is go out and see things and write about them.

Going out and seeing those things, though, has given us—what the heck, me—an intimate look at one particular area of modern life. I stay in an awful lot of hotel rooms in pursuit of my livelihood, and it has been suggested to me that perhaps I should share some of my hotel theories with you. Chances are you stay in a hotel room or two yourself during the course of a month, and maybe you could use the guidance of a hotel-room pro.

Done. Here, for your edification: American Beat's Rules of the Road.

1. If your telephone and your clock are on a night table by the side of your bed, sleep on that side of the bed. It will help you regain your bearings if you wake up at 3:00 A.M. and have no idea where you are. If the phone is on a table on one side of the bed and the clock is on a table on the other side, sleep on the side with the phone.

2. Stay in hotels that offer twenty-four-hour room service. Even if you never order a meal after midnight—and I never have—you want to stay in a hotel with a kitchen that's open while you're sleeping. The reason is that hotels with twenty-four-hour room service are generally clicking on all cylinders

in other areas, too; if they're willing to keep their staffs on hand all night for the few customers who might need them, then they're thinking about you in other ways you don't see or notice.

3. Do not leave your shoes outside your door when you stay in a hotel that offers complimentary shoeshines. You never know. It is far better to have dirty shoes in the morning than to wake up and discover that you have no shoes at all.

4. When you're making reservations at a hotel that's part of a chain, spend the couple of bucks to call the hotel directly, rather than dialing the chain's toll-free 800 number. This rule may be an example of naiveté on my part; but I have become convinced that you get more personal attention if you deal with the specific hotel rather than with the chain's computer bank. I will confess that this probably has more to do with superstition than with reality.

5. The size of your room is much more important than the view. Often a desk clerk will offer you a "lake view" or a "park view," and you arrive in the room to find that it is the size of a moderate closet. For some reason, travelers are perfectly willing to request a particular view, but are shy about asking how big the room is. Go ahead and ask; the clerks know. Almost always, the bigger the room, the better. Do not be fooled by front-desk euphemisms; there is no such thing as a "cozy" hotel room.

6. A corollary to the above rule: There is one set of hotel rooms in America that combine both amazing size with a beautiful view. This is the 02 tier at the Watergate Hotel in Washington. If you get any room there with a number that ends in 02, you are in luck.

7. The best measure of whether a hotel cares about you or not can be found in your room's lamps. If the hotel cares about you, the button to turn the lamp on and off will be found on the base of the lamp, within easy reach. If the hotel does not care, the button will be found somewhere up beneath the shade, or on a little plastic clicker attached to the cord—where you have to search to locate it.

If you are thinking that this is a ridiculous thing to be concerned about, and that you would not notice something like this at home: of course you wouldn't. Homes are never as nice as hotels. You should always expect more of a hotel room than you would of your home.

8.   The other measure of whether a hotel cares about you or not can be found on your telephone. In some of the most expensive hotels in America, there is no red message light on the phone. Nothing is more important to a business traveler than knowing when he has received a phone call; yet many hotels that charge top dollar will not go to the expense of installing message lights.

The desk clerks in these hotels will invariably tell you that someone will always bring your message up promptly and slip it under your door. But of course "promptly" is a state of mind; if you are waiting for a particular call, and you find out three hours later that the call has come in, all the apologies in the world won't help. No message light on the phone is a perfectly valid reason for choosing another hotel the next time you are in town. More to the point, it is a perfectly valid thing to check into when you are making your reservations.

9.   Some hotels have a feature that gives out a beeping sound when you are on the phone and someone else is trying to get through. This is useless; in almost all cases, the phones do not have the capability to disconnect from one call temporarily while you see who the other caller is.

One hotel—the Ritz-Carlton in New York—has come up with a surprisingly simple, yet ideal, solution to this. In every one of the Ritz's guest rooms the phones have two lines—just like the phones you may have at your office. The phones have buttons running across the bottom of the base; if you're talking to a person and someone else wants to reach you, the desk rings the second caller through to your second line, you put the first caller on hold, and you conduct your business. If this sounds like an unnecessary luxury on a short trip, then you don't realize how many calls you're missing in hotels when you're talking to someone else.

10. When you leave your room in the morning, always call housekeeping to request that a maid come by to make up your room right away. Do not rely on her coming automatically, and do not rely on the PLEASE MAKE UP ROOM EARLY signs you're supposed to leave outside your door. If you use your room for business, it does you no good to get back at 3:00 P.M. and find that they haven't gotten around to you yet. The housekeeping people don't mind hearing from you; it helps them get *their* business done as soon as possible, and they like that.

11. At a Holiday Inn, always request a King Leisure. At worst it's the nicest room in the house, and at best you'll think you're at a Westin or a Hyatt.

12. While traveling through America, do not read the *New York Times;* do not read the *Wall Street Journal;* do not read *USA Today*. Read the local papers. The whole point of being on the road is to feel like you're on the road.

13. If you find yourself booked into the Circus Circus in Las Vegas, bring tranquilizers.

14. A serious note: The first thing you should do after checking into your room is go back out into the hallway and familiarize yourself with the fire-exit route. This will take you thirty seconds. Not to overstate the obvious, but it's worth your time.

15. If you have been up all night and want to sleep all day, don't count on it. If you hang your DO NOT DISTURB sign during daylight hours, one of two things will happen: either the maid will knock on your door at 1:00 P.M., wake you up, and then say, "Just checking"; or your telephone will ring and a cheery voice will say, "Housekeeping. Did you want your room made up today?"

16.   On the other hand, when those maids do wake you up, don't be short with them. On a slow day, they can make good conversation partners, and you can learn some interesting things. A maid at the Hi Ho Best Western Motel in Custer, South Dakota, told me that she had once made Harry Reasoner's bed.

17.   Square foot for square foot, the most important area of your hotel room is the bathroom. If your bathroom is in good shape but your bedroom is mediocre, you can still have a good stay. If your bedroom is superb and your bathroom is horrible, your entire trip can be ruined. Pay special attention to shower heads.

18.   As a modern business traveler, you are the beneficiary of a merchandising battle you may not even be aware of: Shampoo Wars.

For some reason, the general managers of America's hotels have decided to conduct their most intense competition in the area of the free shampoo that is provided in the rooms. This is never promoted or advertised, but if you look closely, you will see that it is so.

The nation's hotels are locked in an ever-escalating, never-ending game of one-upmanship to see who can provide guests with the most exotic, distinctive shampoo. Whether this is a matter of corporate hotel ego or of a secret perversity known only to a few lodging magnates, I have no idea; the only way to notice this is to examine the shampoo packets in your room to see what you're being offered. At the Century Plaza in Los Angeles, for example, you get Max Factor Honey and Almond shampoo; in Hyatt hotels you get shampoo manufactured from mink oil.

The most expert and sophisticated of travelers are well aware of this practice. I was in New York one evening, walking along 66th Street on my way to dinner with Bill Lord, the executive producer of "ABC News Nightline."

"Where are you staying tonight?" he said.

"The Helmsley Palace," I said.

"Ah," he said, not breaking stride. "Coconut shampoo."

19. Hotels are in business to make money, and thus can be excused for charging you for anything they feel like. Except one item. In recent months, freed from federal regulations, many hotels have for the first time added a surcharge on long-distance calls that you bill to your credit card or company number. Some hotels charge up to several dollars extra on each call for this; what it means is that you are now paying for something you got last year for free—and that you are paying a stiff penalty fee on top of a phone-company fee that is already increased significantly over the basic direct-dial fee. There are two ways to beat this: use the pay phone in the lobby, which seems silly when you're spending big bucks for a room; or complain bitterly to the manager. If enough people do, maybe this will stop as quickly as it started.

20. Unless your company gives you a credit card that is billed directly to them—and few companies do—get a cash advance and pay for everything on your trip with it. Put nothing on a credit card that will eventually be billed to you.

Once a business trip is over, it should be over; you don't want personal credit card bills coming in months later reminding you of where you have had dinner and where you have slept. By the time you receive those bills, often you have already been reimbursed by your company and have already spent the money. It ends up costing you out of your pocket.

Carry the cash. If your company balks about giving you that much cash up front, ask them for a credit card that's billed to them instead. You'll get the cash.

21. The nicest things about hotel rooms, expensive or modest, are the Gideon Bibles. It doesn't matter whether you're an especially religious person or not; just the idea that the Gideon International folks, year after year, have placed all those millions of Bibles in all those millions of rooms is sort of warming. I know, I know; you've stopped even noticing they're there. Next time, take a minute and read a verse. It won't kill you.

So there you have it. These particular Rules of the Road have been the standard model, for the average traveler. There is a set of advanced rules, too—one that comes to mind is the Style and Etiquette of Hanging Overnight Breakfast Orders on the Doorknob—but those rules are not for everyone, and should not be bandied about in a place like this. Happy trails; see you on the road.

Stranger at the Table

It's hard to make any sense of this story; but then, it's becoming increasingly hard to make any sense of these times.

On a recent Saturday night a man named David Gambill was returning to his home in Richmond, Virginia. Gambill and his wife, Ayer, had been on a week's vacation to Massachusetts; now they were tired, and were anxious to get back to their own house.

They pulled into the driveway. Gambill opened the back door. It struck him right away that something was amiss.

There was food on the stove, and the food was cooking. Chow mein and six fish sticks. But there was no one in the kitchen.

Gambill told his wife to wait by the back door. He began to walk around his house. In a bathroom, he found that a window had been broken. Now he was sure that someone was in his house.

He went from room to room. Later his friends would tell him that he was crazy to do that; the friends would say that he should have gotten out of the house and called the police. But Gambill was determined to find out who was in his home.

He went into his son's bedroom. The door to his son's closet was closed. Gambill opened the door.

Sitting in the closet, huddled behind Gambill's son's rolled-up sleeping bag, was a bedraggled-looking old fellow.

"He looked awful," Gambill said. "He needed a shave, and he was wearing what I can only describe as thrift-shop clothing. The thing I remember most clearly was his eyes. They were just staring back at me. I knew right away that I wasn't in any danger. In his eyes I saw fear—fear and relief that I wasn't going to hurt him."

Gambill stood there staring at the man. The man started to speak.

"I was hungry," the man said. "I was hungry, so I came on into your house."

Gambill didn't know what to say to the man.

"You can call the police if you want," the man said.

Gambill thought of what he should do: pounce on the man, tie him up, lock him in the closet.

But he realized that what he was feeling wasn't anger. It was sadness.

"You really broke in because you were hungry?" Gambill said.

"Yes," the man said.

Gambill knew that, in looking around the house, nothing had been stolen. The only things that had been disturbed, with the exception of the broken bathroom window, were the chow mein and the fish sticks that had been taken from the Gambills' refrigerator and put on the stove.

"You can go in and finish your supper," Gambill said.

So the man straightened up, walked out of the closet, and went to the kitchen. As Gambill and his wife watched, the man put the chow mein and the fish sticks onto a plate, and sat down at the kitchen table.

Gambill, almost as a second thought, picked up the telephone and called the Henrico County police. He told the dispatcher what had happened; the dispatcher said police officers would be over immediately.

"I couldn't believe how fast he ate that food," Gambill said. "He just kept putting it into his mouth as fast as he could.

"I know I probably shouldn't have let him do it. But when I thought about it—he was risking getting arrested so he could have a meal. He was risking his life, really. He could have got shot breaking into someone's house. If he was that desperate, I couldn't deny him the food."

The man finished his meal. He went over and got a water tumbler from the Gambills' shelf. He drew a glass of water from the kitchen sink. He gulped it down.

Gambill said he still felt no danger, being in the house with the man who had broken in. "He wasn't going to spring at me or anything," Gambill said. "There was no threat to me. He was very docile."

The police arrived. They entered the Gambills' kitchen, and Gambill immediately filled them in on what had happened. The police stared at the man, who was still in the kitchen, with the now-empty plate and glass. The man made no effort to flee.

The police began to read the man his Miranda rights.

"It was the most bizarre scene," Gambill said. "The old guy was standing there, and the police were reading his rights to him, and it was like something off a television show. I kept staring at the old guy, and I kept hearing these phrases the police were reading: 'right to remain silent,' and 'right to an attorney.' The guy was showing no visible reaction."

The police put the man in handcuffs and led him out to the squad cars. As the man left, he said nothing to Gambill or his wife. Later, the police would charge the man—whom they identified as Allen Young, age approximately fifty-seven—with breaking and entering, and petty larceny.

"I've felt terrible ever since that night," Gambill said. "I make a pretty good living; hunger isn't a big issue for me. We read about hunger, and we know it's out there, but it takes something like this to bring it home."

Gambill said that, in the days following the incident, he has gone through all the emotions that people who are burglarized often feel: a sense of violation, a sense of being helpless against outside forces, a sense of his home not being entirely his own any longer.

But the dominant emotion was a different one.

"I don't know how to put this, but I almost felt like crying," he said. "Crying at the thought of what's going on out there for people like that fellow. Can you understand what I'm saying? I haven't been sleeping very well at night."

Copy

The journalistic and literary sin that has always puzzled me the most is plagiarism.

I think I know a little bit about why people write, and I have never understood why a writer would resort to stealing another writer's words. It's not so much a moral issue; after all, the world has plenty of people who murder and burglarize, so we ought to understand that some people have hazy ideas of morality.

But to be a writer, I have always thought, a person must have a healthy ego. If you are presumptuous enough to choose to sit down and put words on paper with the hope that other people will read them, you should have a good amount of self-confidence. To plagiarize—to print someone else's words under your own name—is to admit to yourself that your own words and your own thoughts are deficient. I have always wondered how any writer could do that; if he feels that way about his own abilities, then why is he a writer in the first place?

I bring this up because the other day I received a letter from Lt. Col. Henry C. Rilling, of the Fort Huachuca Army base in Arizona. The letter was quite apologetic; enclosed with it was a story from the Fort Huachuca base newspaper.

I read the story and immediately saw why Lt. Col. Rilling had sent it to me. Although the story ran under the byline of one of the Army base's employees, I had written it; it was virtually the same story as one by me that had appeared in a national magazine. Only a few words had been altered.

Lt. Col. Rilling said in his letter that base personnel had discovered the plagiarism only after the story had appeared in the paper. I read the story over several times; it was on an intensely personal topic, and it was a funny feeling, seeing my emotions, in my own words, expressed under another man's name.

I called Lt. Col. Rilling; I told him that I had no interest in bringing any legal action against the man who had "written" the story. But I said I had one favor to ask. I explained that I had never been able to understand why a person would plagiarize; I asked if he could put me in touch with the man, so that we could talk. I really wanted to know what had gone through his head as he had typed up that story.

So it was that, the other night, I called the man at home and introduced myself.

He said that he was embarrassed and sorry about what had happened. I asked him how it had come about.

"I am fifty years old," he said. "I retired from the Army as a chief warrant officer in 1975. Now I'm a civilian working on the base, doing clerical work.

"I don't have any legitimate excuse for what I did. I've been trying so hard to get recognized and be accepted in my job, and I haven't been doing that well. I thought to have a story published in the base newspaper would be an ego trip. I thought that people would see it, and that they would think well of me.

"I had intended to write something of my own. But then I saw your story, and I liked it, and for some reason I just changed a few things and put my name on top of it. I knew I was doing wrong, but I did it anyway."

I asked him if he had had any misgivings when he turned it in.

"I don't think I've ever felt this guilty in my whole life," he said. "My original intention was that I hoped some of the people in higher ranks would like the story, and would recognize my name if my name came up for a good job in their offices. But then the newspaper came out, and I started to get a good response to the story, and I couldn't sleep at night. I felt that I had taken something from someone else; but by this point I didn't know what to do."

I asked him if he had thought about confessing what he had done.

"I may have thought about it, but I didn't do it—until I got caught, of course," he said. "I wasn't used to the kind of recognition I was getting. People came up to me whom I had not even met, and they were commenting on 'my' story. Part of me felt good at the time because the people were noticing me—but part of me realized what I had done."

I asked him if he had even considered turning in some of his own work, and seeing if it would be accepted for publication.

"I think that was my intention, at first," he said. "But I'd been having some problems—my fiancé and I had just broken up—and what can I say? I turned in your story.

"I truthfully don't think of myself as a generally dishonest person. I know that what I did was wrong. But I was at a point in my life when I wanted some positive attention paid to me; I thought it would be good for my sense of pride, and this seemed to be a good way to do it. I guess I didn't analyze it; I just did it."

He apologized again, and I told him again that I had no

desire to take any action against him. He told me that he was afraid he was going to face disciplinary action on the Army base because of what had happened; he asked me if it would be all right to have his immediate superior call me and talk about the conversation we had just had.

I said sure. The older I get, the less certain I am about what makes this world of ours go around.

A Dying Cub Fan's Last Request

The news we were hearing about Steve Goodman was not happy.

Goodman, thirty-six, was the Chicago-born folk singer and songwriter whose biggest national hit was the railroad ballad "City of New Orleans." In his hometown, though, Goodman was just as well known for some of his less commercially successful but equally wonderful songs: "Daley's Gone," "My Old Man," "Lincoln Park Pirates."

Goodman was known for something else, too: for being a truly lovely person who, despite his talent and his success, never went high-hat on his old acquaintances, and never lost the accessibility that has long been a hallmark of performers who get started in Chicago.

For years there was a barely concealed secret about Goodman: his long battle with leukemia. He never talked about it, and music writers did him the favor of not mentioning it in their stories. Goodman simply felt that it was not a piece of information he wished to trade on.

Several years ago, though, Goodman finally went public with the fact that he had been undergoing chemotherapy for the leukemia. He made it clear that he was telling people about it only because there was no longer any way to hide it; he didn't want any favors from anyone. He just wanted to make his music.

Goodman died on Thursday. For days we had been hearing that it was only a matter of time.

He had been in critical condition in the critical care unit of the University of Washington Hospital in Seattle. Hospital official Wendy Lippman said that Goodman was admitted in August suffering from "rapidly progressing acute leukemia"; later that month, she said, he received a bone marrow transplant from his brother David.

Knowing how bad things were, Goodman's admirers in Chicago were struck by a terrible irony about what was happening. If there was anything that Goodman was known for as well as his love of music, it was his love of the Chicago Cubs. He had been a Cub fan all his life; this year's upbeat Cubs anthem, "Go Cubs Go," was his composition.

But there is another song about the Cubs that Goodman was even more closely identified with. It was his warm, funny, bittersweet song about a longtime Cub fan who is near death. The song is called "A Dying Cub Fan's Last Request."

In the song, the dying Cub fan says to the friends gathered around his bed:

> *Do they still play the blues in Chicago*
> *when baseball season rolls around?*
> *When the snow melts away, do the Cubbies still play*
> *in their ivy-covered burial ground?*
>
> *When I was a boy they were my pride and joy.*
> *But now they only bring fatigue*
> *to the home of the brave, the land of the free*
> *and the doormat of the National League.*

Finally this is the year, of course, when the Cubs are threatening to bring a baseball championship to Chicago. And Goodman's Chicago friends and fans were haunted by the words near the end of his song, in which the Cub fan enunciates his last wish:

> *Now I fear that I might never get to go back there,*
> *and I'd like to go one more time before I come to my*
>   *eternal rest.*
> *So, have your pencil and scorecard ready,*
> *and I'll give you my last request.*

> *I'd like a Dixieland funeral in Wrigley Field*
> *on a double-header Saturday.*
> *And the man at the organ plays the National Anthem*
> *and "Na Na Na Na, Hey, Hey, Hey."*
> *Get six bullpen pitchers to carry my coffin.*
> *Let's get groundskeepers to clear my path.*
> *And the umpires call me out as every base goes by,*
> *and I vent my holy wrath.*

> *Take a few of the Cubs out into the infield,*
> *and have one of them drop an infield fly.*
> *Then let everyone eat a Frosty Malt and a bag of peanuts,*
> *and then I'll be ready to die.*
> *It's a beautiful day for a funeral.*
> *Hey, Ernie, Hey, Ernie, let's play two.*
> *Have Jack Brickhouse call up Leo Durocher*
> *to conduct my final interview.*

> *Then build a fire with Danley Lumber and Louisville*
>   *Sluggers*
> *and toss my coffin in.*
> *And let the ashes blow in a beautiful snow*
> *from a 30-mile-an-hour southwest wind.*
> *And as my last remains go flying over the left field wall,*
> *I'll bid the Bleacher Bums adieu.*
> *And come to my final resting place*
> *out on Waveland Avenue.*

In the midst of a baseball pennant race, there was a race of another sort out in Seattle that weighed heavy on the minds of a lot of us in Chicago.

Louisville Slugger

At the newspaper where I work we have a rule that staff members are not allowed to accept any gift of significant value from an outside source. The rule probably makes sense; its purpose is to prevent potential news sources from trying to influence news coverage through the bestowing of lavish presents.

But I recently received something in the mail from an outside company, and if the newspaper makes me give it back they're going to have to drag me out of here kicking and screaming and holding onto it for dear life.

The package was long and narrow. I opened it. Inside was something that brought tears to my eyes and a funny feeling to my throat:

A Louisville Slugger baseball bat—a Bob Greene autographed model.

For five minutes I sat there looking at it and caressing it and speaking softly to it.

There, in the middle of the barrel, was the Louisville Slugger logo, and the famous copyrighted slogan: "Powerized." There, next to the logo, was the trademark of the Hillerich & Bradsby Co., which manufactures Louisville Sluggers.

And there—right at the end of the barrel—were the words PERSONAL MODEL—LOUISVILLE SLUGGER. And where Mickey

Mantle's or Hank Aaron's autograph ought to be, the script words "Bob Greene."

I suppose there must be some item that an American boy might treasure more fiercely than a Louisville Slugger with his own signature on it, but I can't think of one. For all of us who grew up on sandlots and playgrounds, gripping Louisville Sluggers bearing the autographs of major league stars, the thought of owning one with our own name on the barrel is almost too much to comprehend.

In the box with the Louisville Slugger was a letter from John A. Hillerich III, president of Hillerich & Bradsby. In the letter Hillerich said that this is the centennial year for Louisville Sluggers; the first one was manufactured in the spring of 1884. Thus, the enclosed bat—a memento of the 100th anniversary.

When I started to show my new bat to people, the response I got was interesting. Women seemed not to care too much; generally they said something like, "Oh, a baseball bat." They would inspect it a little more closely, and then say, "What's your name doing on it?"

But men—men were a different story. First they would see the bat. They'd say something like, "A real Louisville Slugger. That's great." Invariably they would lift it up and go into a batting stance—perhaps for the first time in twenty or thirty years. Then they would roll the bat around in their hands— and finally they would see the signature.

That's when they'd get faint in the head. They would look as if they were about to swoon. Their eyes would start to resemble pinwheels. And in reverential whispers, they would say: "That is the most wonderful thing I have ever seen. Your own name on a Louisville Slugger. You are so lucky."

For it is true: a Louisville Slugger, for the American male, is a talisman—a piece of property that carries such symbolic weight and meaning that words of description do not do it justice. I have a friend who has two photographs mounted above his desk at work. One photo shows Elvis Presley kissing a woman. The other shows Ted Williams kissing his Louisville Slugger. No one ever asks my friend the meaning of those pictures; the meaning, of course, is quite clear without any explanation.

Hillerich & Bradsby has a photo in its archives that is similarly moving. In the photo, Babe Ruth and Lou Gehrig are standing in a batting cage. Gehrig, a wide smile on his face, is examining the bat. Perhaps you could find another photo that contains three figures more holy to the American male than those three—Ruth, Gehrig, and a Louisville Slugger—but I don't know where you'd look.

Hillerich & Bradsby has some intriguing figures and facts about Louisville Sluggers. The company manufactures approximately one million of them each year. That requires the use of about two hundred thousand trees each baseball season; the company owns five thousand acres of timberland in Pennsylvania and New York to provide the trees. Ash timber is the wood of choice for Louisville Sluggers. Years ago, the wood of choice was hickory.

According to the company, a professional baseball player uses an average of seventy-two bats each season—which comes as a surprise to those of us who always envisioned a major leaguer using the same special good-luck bat for years on end. The company says that, during World War II, some American sporting goods found their way to a German prison camp in Upper Silesia; the American prisoners of war there reportedly cried at the sight of the Louisville Sluggers. During the Korean War, an American soldier reportedly dashed out of his trench during a firefight to retrieve a Louisville Slugger he had left out in the open before the battle began.

As I sit here typing this, a colleague—a male—has just walked up next to my computer terminal, lifted my Louisville Slugger to his shoulder, and gone into a batter's crouch. In a moment, if I'm right, he'll start examining the bat—and in another moment he'll see the autograph.

I can't wait.

His Honor

We were the unlikeliest of friends. The first major story I ever covered as a newspaperman was the Chicago Seven conspiracy trial; Judge Julius J. Hoffman presided, and I thought he was a villain. I'm sure it showed up in my copy.

When you cover a long-running story, you tend to become attached to all the characters involved with it. About a year after the Chicago Seven trial ended—when everyone had moved on to other things—I got to thinking about Judge Hoffman, and about all the days I had sat in his courtroom, watching that bizarre drama unfold. I wrote him a letter saying that I regretted that, for all the words I had written about him, I had never met him personally; I had merely observed him on the bench.

Two days after I mailed the letter, he called. He invited me to his chambers; our visit lasted for hours. He was fascinating; pure ego, but with an overwhelming sense of what he perceived as the majesty of the federal judiciary. He led me around the office, showing me plaques and awards; although he knew his role in the Chicago Seven trial had made him a symbolic enemy of many, he was clearly pleased that, at least for a brief time, he had become the most famous judge in America.

I was amazed to find that we seemed to like each other. And we started to spend time together occasionally. Sometimes I would visit his chambers; sometimes we would have a drink in one of the barrooms of the Drake Hotel, near his home. I was happy just to serve as an audience for him, and he loved having that audience. Strangely, though, he always refused to go on television; he somehow felt that doing so would reflect badly on a man of his position. Once he told me, almost gloating:

"Wallace of '60 Minutes' called me up four times. Twice from New York, twice from Washington. I told him no four times. He told me, 'What? You're turning down an opportunity to be seen by fifty million people?' I told him that I was a federal judge, that I wasn't running for alderman of the Forty-second Ward."

When Hoffman died at eighty-seven last week, the first thing I thought of was a summer night in 1975, when the Public Broadcasting Service was scheduled to run a dramatization of the Chicago Seven trial, with actors portraying all the principals—the defendants, the attorneys, Judge Hoffman himself. I called him the day before the broadcast to ask if he would be watching; he said no. "That trial was five years ago," he said. "I have put it aside altogether. No, I think I'll let it pass."

But the next day he called me. He had changed his mind. "I don't suppose I can be accused of being excessively modest," he said. "Everyone likes to be noticed. Maybe I would like to see it after all."

He told me that his wife had been ill; he did not want to disturb her by watching the show at home. Did I have any suggestions?

I rented a room at the Drake. I told him I would meet him there just before the show began. He showed up right on time, still dapper and well turned out at eighty. I had pulled two chairs up to the room's television set; we sat down together to watch the show.

"Is the set working?" he asked. I assured him it was.

"I took pains to see what the competition is, by the way," he said. "There's not much on tonight on the other channels. I think we'll have a pretty respectable audience."

For me it was a remarkable evening. The screenplay was taken directly from the trial transcripts; all the heat and anger of the testimony were on the TV screen, and the actor playing Judge Hoffman ruled with all the haughty arrogance that Hoffman had exhibited in the trial itself. Hoffman stared at the screen; occasionally he would pull his chair closer to the set, to be sure he was not missing anything.

He seemed to be getting a kick out of the show. The actor portraying Black Panther leader Bobby Seale came onto the screen, and said: "I think there is a lot of racism involved, myself. . . . Look, old man, if you keep up denying me my constitutional rights, you are being exposed to the public and the world that you do not care about people's constitutional rights to defend themselves." And in the hotel room, the real Julius Hoffman chuckled.

When the TV Abbie Hoffman raged at the TV Julius Hoffman, the real-life judge in the hotel room laughed aloud and said, "He's a funny man, that Abbie. He used to wear his hair in a bun in the back. Tied it in a ribbon. We were very close. He used to call me 'Julie.' Not my Christian name, 'Julius,' but 'Julie.'"

At the end of the evening, as the program concluded, Hoffman said that he should be getting home to his wife. We prepared to leave the room, and he said to me:

"They can call me an old bastard if they want. Some people think I'm the greatest trial judge in the country. Others think I'm a rotten judge. . . . Franklin Delano Roosevelt, he was elected to the highest office in the land, and now you hardly ever hear his name. I like to be talked about. I think I'll get a pretty good obituary, don't you?"

Wanna Party?

There is a new verb form being used among the young and the allegedly young at heart: "to party."

You have probably heard the usage. Someone—usually some-one who is a teenager or in his or her twenties—will say:

"I really want to party tonight."

Or:

"We're going to get together around eleven o'clock and party all night long."

Or:

"She's great. She really knows how to party."

Now, most of us grew up thinking that "party" was nor-mally used as a noun. A "party" was a happy event to which we were invited.

When we were very young, a party usually meant a birth-day party. We would be taken to a friend's house by our par-ents, and there would be cake, ice cream, crepe paper stream-ers, balloons, and—if we were really lucky—a pony.

A little later in our lives, a party usually meant some sort of dance. They were often held at the high school gym; we would take our shoes off so as not to mar the basketball court, and we would do steps such as the Pony or the Jerk to the sound of records or a live band.

Still later in our lives, a party usually meant a gathering at a fraternity house, sorority house, or hotel ballroom that had been rented for the night. At these parties we would meet other college students from the same university. Again, danc-ing was common.

We never used "party" as a verb; we never said, "I'm going to party my [obscenity] off tonight," which is what many cur-rent-day partyers say.

This is all heading somewhere; trust me.

The point is: "to party" seems to mean something totally different from what parties used to mean in the Fifties, Sixties, and early Seventies.

When people today say that they "love to party," they say it with a salacious gleam in their eyes. When they say that they "party with the best of them," it has a lewd ring to it; they seem to be hinting at something a little obscene; a little dirty; a little illicit; a little raunchy.

In short, it can be assumed that when they say a girl "really knows how to party," they are not saying that she is good at going to sorority parties.

I have never known precisely what "to party" means, but in the last few weeks I have made a vow to find out. Anytime I have overheard people say that they plan "to party" that night or that weekend, I have stopped them and asked them to tell me—exactly—what they will be doing while they are "partying." Most of these overheard conversations, by the way, have been in shopping malls.

For weeks, virtually none of the people I asked about "partying" answered me. Instead of explaining, they gave me weird looks, as if I were invading their privacy—which, I suppose, I was.

But last week I heard a teenaged girl say that she was looking forward to "partying" later that night. I excused myself for interrupting, then asked her what "partying" meant.

"You know," she said, not pausing in the chewing of her gum. "Drugs. Sex. Alcohol."

Aha. I had suspected as much. In fact, the first time I had heard "party" used as a verb was back when I was writing stories about rock and roll bands on the road. Outside the dressing rooms after the concerts each night, it was not uncommon to find teenaged girls who would invariably say, "Where are you guys staying? We want to party with you."

Naive as I was, I understood instinctively that these girls were not talking about birthday cake, ice cream, crepe paper streamers, balloons, or ponies. [Well, they might have been talking about ponies; on those rock and roll tours, you never knew.]

What they were talking about—it was true, it was true—were drugs, sex, and alcohol.

Now, midway into the Eighties, the verb those backstage girls used—"to party"—is rapidly becoming part of the language. I suppose I can't blame people for using that term in public; after all, it is far more acceptable to say, "I'm going to party tonight" than to say, "I'm going to take drugs, have sex, and drink alcohol tonight."

But I am concerned that I may be wrong. Perhaps I am judging the party people too harshly. Maybe "to party" does not, indeed, mean to take drugs, have sex, and drink alcohol. Maybe "to party" merely means, as in days of old, to go to the high school gym and kick one's shoes off to the strains of a Lesley Gore record. [The record I have in mind is "It's My Party and I'll Cry If I Want To"; somehow I can't imagine Miss Gore, then or now, singing "It's My Drugs, Sex, and Alcohol and I'll Cry If I Want To."]

So today I have a request for all of you party people:

Please, tell me what you mean. Drop me a line at the newspaper. If you can't bear the thought of writing a whole letter [writing is a very un-partying thing to do], call me. Tell me what you mean when you say you're going "to party tonight." Convince me I'm wrong. If I am, I will write a column explaining the error of my ways. If I'm right, though, I will have to go public with the fact that all of you really are spending all that time in the company of drugs, sex, and alcohol.

When I'm finished with this project, I have another, more specialized question I want to ask you:

What do all of you mean when you say you like to "party hardy"?

I'm not sure I even want to know the answer to that one.

The Party Animals Respond

Some things I've learned about partying since I asked you last week what you meant when you said you "like to party":

• You might not be all that interested in presidential politics, the situation in Lebanon, the nuclear freeze issue, or the state of the national economy, but you sure get enthusiastic about so-called partying. The response to the column was so heavy that there's no way I'm going to be able to write back to all of you individually; I've read all the letters, though, so everything that all of you said got taken into consideration.

• In the column I quoted a teenaged girl as saying that "partying" means drugs, sex, and alcohol. A lot of you disagreed. You said that partying was simply a euphemism for smoking marijuana—period. You said that if someone inquires, "Does she party?" what they mean is, "Does she smoke marijuana?" This definition was especially prevalent among college students who wrote.

• Curiously, a lot of you seem to equate vomiting with having fun. A significant portion of the letters reported that you knew you were having a great time partying if you threw up at some point during the evening; a number of correspondents thoughtfully advised me to "party 'til you puke."

• If your letters are any indication, there is a game called "quarters" being played in hundreds of thousands of suburban basements and college dormitories on any given night. Quarters seems to consist, basically, of trying to bounce a quarter off the surface of a table and into a beer glass; if you make the shot, you can then command someone else to drink a full glass of beer. The glass is continuously refilled. The person who drinks the beer is also supposed to catch the quarter between his or her teeth. Apparently this is supposed to be fun.

• A lot of you seem to have a different definition of drugs and alcohol from the rest of the world's definition. A typical conversation with you went something like this. You: "Partying doesn't mean drugs and alcohol." Me: "Then what does it mean?" You: "You know, you might go out with some friends and have a few beers and dance, and then later you might smoke some pot, which is as far as it usually goes unless someone has some cocaine." Me: "But you don't consider beer and marijuana and cocaine to be alcohol and drugs?" You: "Well, not really . . ."

• About the highest compliment you can give a friend is to say that he or she is a "party animal." You seem to confer this title with great affection and pride; to be a "party animal" appears to be the Eighties version of having a Phi Beta Kappa key.

• Not only do you cling to the traditions of the Sixties, you seem to cling to the paraphernalia of the Sixties, too. A large number of your letters mentioned that you own "bongs," which, fifteen years ago, were popular items designed to pull marijuana smoke through a liquid. More than one high school student reported that he or she enjoyed smoking marijuana through a bong filled with Jack Daniel's whiskey. This is probably as good a place as any to mention that I am simply reporting the facts of the response to the column.

• Close to 100 percent of you said that "partying" has nothing to do with sex. You said that when you partied, sex almost never took place.

• However, a few of you pointed out that "to party" may have originated among prostitutes, who often approach potential customers with the question, "Do you want to party?" So it can be assumed that at least some portion of America's partyers are, indeed, having sex—although they may be paying for it.

• On the subject of "party hardy"—most of you accused me of getting the spelling wrong. You said that the phrase was "party hearty," and that it meant, basically, to party excessively. Correspondent Ben Hollis, however, points out that "party hardy" is, indeed, the correct phrase. He lists a dictionary definition of "hardy": "stalwart and rugged; strong; brazenly daring; audacious; hotheaded; capable of surviving unfavorable conditions such as cold weather or lack of moisture."

• To the teachers who assigned their classes to write essays on what the students thought "partying" meant, and who then forwarded those essays to me: I'm not sure that was the appropriate response to the column.

• To give you some idea of the mind-set we're dealing with here, the following is a verbatim excerpt from one of the responses: "'To party' means fun. Dance till you drop and boogie till you puke! You know—WE AIN'T LEAVIN' TILL WE'RE HEAVIN'! You can't *explain* 'to party'—you just have to *party*."

• Seven young men from the suburbs sent me a booklet they had written, titled "So You Wanna Be a Party Animal." If you are the parent of a teenager and you want to browse through something that is guaranteed to depress you to the point of despair, I highly recommend it.

Memories Are Made of This

My father ran the company that bronzes baby shoes. During the summers of my growing up, while my friends were earning money by caddying at golf courses or mowing lawns or painting center stripes for the Ohio Department of Highways, I toiled in a warm room on the first floor of the Bron-Shoe Company, opening packages. Inside the packages were baby shoes—baby shoes from all over the world. The parents of the babies had sent the shoes to Columbus—to the Bron-Shoe Company—so that the shoes could be bronzed.

I recall that most of the shoes were white. I recall that I was always surrounded by literally thousands of them—tiny shoes everywhere. I recall that I was the youngest person in the receiving department; the other workers were middle-aged men who smoked cigarettes and made funny sounds in their throats in rebellion against the crack-of-dawn mornings and the prospect of encountering all those little shoes before it was time to punch out. Mostly, though, my memory of the Bron-Shoe Company is pretty hazy.

I decided to go back and take a look. My father is retired now, and the Bron-Shoe Company has moved to newer, more modern headquarters than the place where I worked. It's still in Columbus, though, and when I called the two men who are now its top executives—Robert J. Kaynes and William P. Moser—they said to drop on by.

The first thing I did when I arrived was ask to see the receiving room. Kaynes and Moser took me there. Twenty years later, there were still thousands upon thousands of shoes stacked all over the room, waiting to be bronzed. Twenty years later, most of the shoes were still white.

"It never changes," Kaynes said. "We're still in the business of memories."

"People may think that bronzing baby shoes is a corny thing to do," Moser said. "But then they have their first child, and that child outgrows his or her first shoe, and the parents can't bear the thought of throwing it away. And so they end up sending it to us."

There was one obvious difference in the new receiving room: each baby shoe that arrived at the Bron-Shoe Company was now listed in a computer. There were video terminals around the room with screens to display the information.

"We plate more than half a million baby shoes a year," Kaynes said. "The computer has been a great help in keeping track of them. We give every shoe a job number when it comes in, and mark it twice—on the bottom of the shoe, and inside the shoe. Very seldom do we misplace one, but when we do, we can track it down right away."

I asked whether parents, when they received their bronzed shoes, could really tell if they were the wrong ones.

Moser laughed. "Are you kidding?" he said. "They know within two seconds. A mother knows her baby's first shoe."

We walked through the plant. Here, in a nineteen-step process, the shoes are plated. Tanks of bubbling solution were arranged over the length and width of the floor; on the periphery, as far as the eye could see, were racks of plated baby shoes.

"We offer several finishes," Kaynes said. "As you can see, each has a different look. There's bronze. There's antique bronze. There's silver. There's pewter. There's gold. And there's porcelain. People always talk about 'bronzing' their baby's shoes, but when they see all the finishes that are available, sometimes they choose one of the others."

I picked up some of the completed shoes from a rack. The detail was amazing. Every little flower design, every crease, every wrinkle showed up through the metal plating.

"That's the whole point," Kaynes said. "The parents want the shoe exactly as the baby wore it. We get castigated if we take a crease or a scuff out. The imperfections are part of the memories."

The three of us went back to Kaynes's office. I asked what people said to these men when they found out what line of work they were in. "People say, 'You bronze shoes? Do they still do *that?*'" Kaynes said. "When I assure them that we do, indeed, still do that, they say, 'Can you actually make a living doing that?'"

"We have one hundred and forty full-time employees," Moser said. "We'll probably always have the reputation of being a very old-fashioned business. We realize that we're perceived that way. But an awful lot of people apparently still want what we do."

I said that it must be an eerie feeling, walking through that factory and being surrounded by so many thousands of people's tangible memories.

"For me, that really doesn't come up too often," Kaynes said. "I suppose I'm like a surgeon—I realize that each of those shoes means the whole world to some family somewhere, but after a while they just become numbers to me. We don't know the babies. We just bronze the shoes."

Moser said that, for all the market studies and all the advertising strategies, there is one key to selling bronzed baby shoes: If a person has had bronzed shoes in his own house when he was growing up, he is likely to have his baby's shoes bronzed. If he hasn't, he is likely not to.

"They even like the older styles," Moser said. "They like the shoes mounted on the old-fashioned flowery metal base, for example. They don't like the new styles, like the Lucite base. They say, 'I want these shoes done the same way my mother had mine done.'"

In the summer of 1960, my father, sitting at the dinner table, pulled a golf ball from his pocket.

"What do you think this is?" he said.

"A golf ball," I said, a trained observer even then.

He handed it to me. "Look closer," he said. "What is it?"

I looked. "A used golf ball," I said.

"That golf ball," my father said, "is the golf ball Arnold Palmer used to win the Masters."

And indeed it was. In addition to bronzing baby shoes, the Bron-Shoe Company has always been willing to bronze virtually anything anyone might want to preserve in metal. On Kaynes's desk, for example, was a bronzed pretzel. "I just keep it here to make me think of possibilities," he said.

In the Bron-Shoe plant on the day I visited were the following items waiting for bronzing: A railroad spike. A horseshoe. A pacifier. A belt buckle. An electric razor. A first baseman's mitt. A nurse's cap. A drill sergeant's hat. Three chocolate-chip cookies. A set of dental impressions. A dice cup. A set of barber's tools. A dog biscuit.

I asked Kaynes and Moser to recall additional items the company had bronzed. A partial list: Athletic supporters. Stethoscopes. Underwear. Blue jeans. Red Skelton's cigar butt. Turkey feet. A Big Mac. Armadillo skulls. Horse manure.

I asked if there was anything they would not attempt to bronze.

"Teddy bears," Kaynes said.

"Teddy bears are the worst," Moser said. "The fur won't hold the plating solution. The solution seeps into the bear, and the metal slowly turns green for the next two years. And then the plating solution comes oozing out."

"We once had a teddy bear here for a year, trying to get it to dry out," Kaynes said. "It just wouldn't dry."

"Teddy bears are miserable," Moser said.

Teddy bears, cigar butts, and horse manure notwithstanding, it is baby shoes that have made the Bron-Shoe Company prosper. And the woman who started the company in the baby-shoe-bronzing business, Violet Shinbach, still lives in Columbus. She is eighty-one now.

"It was 1933," Mrs. Shinbach said. "When my daughter Ibby was a baby, I had taken one of her shoes to a store to have it bronzed. It seemed like a good idea. So I decided to go into business having other people's shoes bronzed.

"I would go door to door. I would look for children's bicycles, or for swings and playthings, outside the house. Then I would ring the doorbell and say, 'How old is your child? We do something that is very novel.' And then I would show them Ibby's shoes."

Mrs. Shinbach's husband, Sam, was in the pants business; she ran the shoe-bronzing enterprise out of the basement of their home, contracting the work out to a metal plater. Eventually it became so successful that Sam gave up his pants store and joined her in founding the Bron-Shoe Company—which, in addition to taking orders for the shoes, would do the plating itself.

She said that she doubts the business could evolve in the same way if it were starting today: "Everyone treated me so cordially. Today, I don't think they'd let a stranger into their house—especially if the stranger was asking about their children."

But, she said, the same emotions that made people like the idea of bronzed shoes in the first place are still at work now.

"When people heard I could bronze their babies' shoes, there wasn't a doubt in their minds," she said. "People never throw a baby's first shoes away. They just don't do it. They used to keep them in a closet, or hang them from their car's rearview mirror. But once they were able to bronze them, they all wanted to do it. A baby's first pair of shoes is like a baby's first tooth. You want to keep it.

"Actually, that's not quite true. At one point I tried to expand the company into bronzing babies' first teeth. It was a failure. The parents didn't want to preserve the first teeth. But the first shoes—yes."

Before I left the Bron-Shoe Company, I stopped in the receiving department again and went through the bins of arriving baby shoes.

Each shoe was marked with a tag identifying the parents of the babies; I wrote some down, and later I called the parents to see what had been on their minds when they had placed their orders.

"It's the traditional thing in my family," said Patricia Franck, thirty-two, of Roswell, Georgia. "It's a way to freeze a moment in time.

"My son, Ryan, is just about a year old, and you can see his personality in his first shoe. He's *worn* it. He's been *in* it. I want to keep that.

"I suppose some people might think that's a little old-fashioned or a little corny, but I don't care. I've ordered the shoes to be bronzed unmounted; when they come back, I'm going to mount them myself, with a pen set in between. That way every time I reach for my pen I'll think of Ryan."

Debbie Watters, thirty-five, of Cuyahoga Falls, Ohio, said, "We had a lot of trouble having our first child. We tried for ten years. There were tests, and there was surgery involved, and finally we were able to have Patrick. So I think he means something a little extra special to us.

"We were at a store called Miller's Jr. Shoe Port when we saw the display for bronzed shoes. We've ordered the shoes to be mounted on both sides of a picture frame in which we'll put Patrick's picture. I used to go through stores, and I'd see baby shoes and baby clothes, and I'd think about the possibility that we'd never have a baby. So there was never any question that we'd have Patrick's shoes bronzed. What else do you do with your baby's first shoes?"

John Manelski, twenty-two, of Wilmington, Delaware, said, "I work at the General Motors plant. I spray-paint Chevettes. When John Junior was born it was one of the greatest days of my life.

"When I was a baby my parents had my first shoes bronzed. They kept them on display in the china closet in our house. That's what I'm going to do with John Junior's shoes. I'm going to keep them in our china closet, or on top of our TV set, right where everyone can see them.

"And then when he grows up I'm going to give them to him. I'm going to tell him that they're his to do with as he pleases, but that he has to follow two rules: He has to put them somewhere where people can always see them. And he should never disrespect those shoes."

The Tradin' Times
They Are A-Changin'

Maybe you're familiar with a publication known as *Tradin' Times.* It's a folksy, nuts-and-bolts newspaper that is devoted to helping its readers sell their unwanted bedroom furniture, camping equipment, stoves, refrigerators . . . anything a person might have around the house.

Each issue of *Tradin' Times* consists of classified ads inserted by people who want to get rid of those things. The paper is bought by other people who might want to buy them. Most of the readers of *Tradin' Times* are suburban or rural; the newspaper has been likened to "a garage sale on newsprint," and is considered to be one of the staples of Middle America.

However . . . recently, there has been a twist in what is available through *Tradin' Times.* If you peruse the pages of the Chicago-Northwest Indiana edition of *Tradin' Times,* you will soon discover that one can now arrange to sell the old lawn mower and have an extramarital affair at the same time.

Tradin' Times now runs—along with the ads for pool tables, end tables, and sofas—ads from married men and women requesting the company of other women and men for the purpose of romance.

Sexual advertisements in the personals sections of certain publications are not new, of course. The so-called underground press pioneered this practice; now it is fairly common to see single people advertising their desire to meet other single people.

But married people? In *Tradin' Times? Tradin' Times* is purchased right along with the eggs and chewing gum at suburban supermarkets and rural drugstores. And yet here are some of the ads:

> NW Suburbs, wht. married male, affectionate, clean, gentle, sincere, 37, seeking loving married female, 23–39, for discreet, romantic companionship, long term. [The advertiser concluded his ad with a *Tradin' Times* box number to which replies were to be directed.]

> Attractive wht. sophisticated married male, 32, great sense of humor, looking to meet an attractive married female, 25–40, for honest, warm, caring, fun-filled relationship. Letter, phone, picture, discretion assured.

> Attractive, wht., high-class married female, 32, would like to meet a warm, sincere, sensitive, wht. married male, 30–40, for honest & caring long-term friendship. Insensitive or uncaring persons please don't write.

Certainly the *Tradin' Times* ads are nowhere near as salacious as the bizarre offerings seen in some less-than-reputable publications. But still . . . this is *Tradin' Times*, not *Hot Love Weekly*. Finding the ads in there is akin to going to the weekly Rotary Club meeting and being informed that the after-lunch speech has been replaced by a screening of "Debbie Does Dallas."

The suburban housewife who pointed this out to me—*Tradin' Times* reader Barbara Tomasek, of Lockport, Illinois—said that she was not naive enough to think that married people in neighborhoods like hers didn't sometimes fool around.

"But silly me," she said. "I always thought that sort of thing . . . well, just happened. I didn't know that you were supposed to advertise in *Tradin' Times* for it."

I told Mrs. Tomasek that this was news to me, too. I said that I would do my best to contact *Tradin' Times* and find out what the story was.

Getting through to *Tradin' Times*, it turned out, is not the easiest thing in the world; the publication's phone lines are constantly tied up by people placing ads trying to sell slipcovers, adding machines, armchairs, etc. When someone did answer, I asked to talk to the boss—and was transferred to Patricia Fry, the newspaper's sales manager for classified advertising.

I explained why I was calling. Mrs. Fry sighed. "I know what you're talking about," she said. "All I can say is that I have no control over what people want. As long as the ads are not dirty or off-color, we print them."

I asked Mrs. Fry if she was sure the ads were legitimate.

"Oh, yes," she said. "We don't make up ads. We are a very reputable firm. The company's feeling is that if the language in the ads is not pornographic or kooky, then we'll run them. These people are being very honest in their ads. They're saying, 'I'm married, but I'm looking for someone.' "

I asked her if anyone responded to the ads I was inquiring about.

"You would not believe it," she said. "We don't open the replies—we just forward them. But it's not uncommon for a person who placed one of those ads to get ten or fifteen responses a week."

Mrs. Fry—who said that she was "over fifty," and that she has been happily married for thirty-seven years—said she tried not to pass judgment on the morality of the people who place and answer the ads.

"I guess times are changing," she said. "I know that in the last year, these kinds of ads have picked up tremendously in *Tradin' Times*. I suppose it's better for a person to admit he's married in one of these ads than for a young girl to fall for an old duffer she meets who claims he's single."

I asked whether there was some lesson here about the sexual revolution finally hitting mainstream America with full force, but Mrs. Fry said:

"I don't think it's anything new. Remember Cleopatra, back on the Nile? I'm afraid it can't be stopped."

I called Mrs. Tomasek, the lady who had alerted me to the new material in *Tradin' Times*, and told her what I had found out.

She paused to reflect on all this.

"I wonder what happens," she said, "when some fellow in the suburbs places one of those ads, and he gets a response that turns out to be his own wife looking for a little action?"

Grandma at the Playboy Club

I received a letter the other day; the return address on the envelope said it was from Heritage House, in Columbus, Ohio. I knew immediately who had sent me the letter; Heritage House is a senior citizens' residence in Columbus, and my grandmother, who is ninety-six years old, lives there.

So I was ready for a newsy little note from Grandma. I opened the envelope—and what dropped out but a Playboy Club key with my name on it.

There was a letter, too. It began:

Dearest Bobby—

When I went to the Playboy Club and told them who I was, you would have thought I had become Queen for a Day! The managers and the Bunnies couldn't have been nicer. At the end of the meal they gave me a membership key for myself—plus keys for you and your father! So now I am a member of the Playboy Club. . . .

My head swam. Last month I had visited Columbus, my hometown, and had been surprised to find a new Playboy

Club there. When I was growing up in Columbus, we had always assumed that if you were in search of certain things, you
would have to leave central Ohio—and one of those things was
a Playboy Club. Now Columbus and Playboy apparently were
ready for each other.

I visited the Columbus Playboy Club; I wrote a column
about the visit, and I thought that was the end of it.

Now, though . . . this letter from Grandma . . . the Playboy Club key . . .

I called the Playboy Club in Columbus and asked to talk to
Steve Smith, the club's director of entertainment. I had met
him during my visit there.

"Steve," I said, "I don't know how to put this—"

"Hi!" Smith said. "Your grandmother was in the other day!"

"That's what I was afraid of," I said.

"She seemed to be having a great time," Smith said. "She
was with a party of four other women, and we gave them a
table in the VIP Room, and I decided to make her a member."

"Steve, my grandmother is ninety-six years old," I said.
"Why would she want to be a member of the Playboy Club?"

"She said she was thrilled," Smith said. "She told me she
thought the food was delicious; she said it was the first time in
years she had finished her sandwich for lunch. I told her that
we have dancing at night, and she promised she'd be back."

"Steve . . ." I said.

"Here," Smith said. "I'll let you talk to the person who
served her."

A female voice came onto the line. The owner of the voice
identified herself as "Bunny Jill."

"Your grandmother couldn't have been cuter," Bunny Jill
said. "When we gave her the key, she said that now she had
a place she could go when she didn't have anything to do."

This was getting out of hand. I called Heritage House.

"Grandma . . . ," I said.

"Bobby!" she said. "Did you get your Playboy Club key?"

"I did, Grandma, and that's what I have to talk to you
about," I said.

"You should have seen it," she said. "As soon as I came in, all the Bunnies gathered around me. I was basking in glory."

"Grandma, I don't think it's appropriate that you be hanging around the Playboy Club," I said.

"Why not?" she said.

"Well, it's just not the kind of place for a ninety-six-year-old woman," I said.

"Nonsense," she said. "I thought the Bunnies were gorgeous. I had heard about them, but I never thought I would ever see one in person. Grandpa's eyes would have fallen out! The dining room was filled with men—and they were all eating their lunch! I thought, what a bunch of fools! They can eat anytime. They should have been looking!"

"Grandma, have you ever even seen a copy of *Playboy*?" I said.

"Of course I have," she said.

"Where?" I said.

"In your room, when you were a little boy," she said. "You had it hidden."

"Look," I said. "I suppose it's fine that you went once. But you're not planning on going again, are you?"

"Of course I'm going again," she said. "I'm a member, aren't I? I'm going to take your Aunt Violet as my guest."

I was resigned to it then. Grandma was going to be a regular at the Playboy Club. I knew there was one more call I had to make.

I placed the long-distance call to Hugh Hefner in California. Naturally, Hefner was still asleep; I should have known—it was only four o'clock in the afternoon out there.

But a few hours later, Hefner called me back. I gave him a rundown of how my grandmother happened to be the newest Playboy Club member.

"Well, she's certainly welcome," Hefner said. "If she feels comfortable as a member of the club, we feel comfortable having her."

I asked him if he didn't think it was a little odd for a ninety-six-year-old woman to be a member of the Playboy Club.

For Members Only 233

"It's completely up to the individual involved," Hefner said. "It's obvious that you have a very special lady for your grandmother. My own mother is eighty-six, and she often goes to the club in Phoenix for lunch. I hope your grandmother enjoys it as much as my mother does.

"Age should not be a limiting factor in the way you lead your life. This is evidence of that, and I think it's wonderful."

Hefner said that he knew it was unlikely that my grandmother would be making a trip to California—but that if she ever did, he wanted her to know she would be welcome as his guest at the Playboy Mansion West.

"We'll be waiting for her in the Jacuzzi," he said.

For Members Only

In this country there is a certain prestige attached to becoming a member of celebrated organizations. Probably the most desirable of all is the United States Senate; when an American is elected to that body, he or she can take comfort in being part of what has been called the most exclusive club in the world.

Other associations carry their own particular symbolism and weight. Be it a college fraternity, a local Rotary, or a suburban country club, there always seems to be a particular organization with the power to make people strive for entry.

Those sorts of clubs aren't the only ones in America, though. According to Denise Akey—who, as editor of the *Encyclopedia of Associations*, keeps track of such matters—there are at least 18,414 organizations in the United States. That's only the ones she knows about; she thinks there are undoubtedly many more.

So if you haven't filed for a run at the U.S. Senate in next fall's campaign, and if the golf club in your city hasn't responded to your application, you might want to keep some of the following in mind. All of them are more than willing to take new members.

The North American Tiddlywinks Association, with headquarters in Gaithersburg, Maryland, is the only national organization dedicated to that sport. Its secretary-general, Larry Kahn, estimates its membership at approximately one hundred.

"The biggest problem we have is our image," Kahn said. "It's almost impossible to recruit new members. They think of tiddlywinks as a children's game. We think of it as a war game that happens to be played on a six-feet-by-three-feet felt mat."

Most members of the North American Tiddlywinks Association, Kahn said, own standard sets of winks—the little red, blue, green, and yellow disks that are propelled around the mat. Top tournament players, though, own many squidgers—the larger disks that are used to shoot the winks.

"I have eight squidgers," Kahn said. "They're like golf clubs; you use different squidgers to make different shots. Some people have as many as twenty squidgers, but they're just showing off, if you ask me. There's no way you need twenty squidgers."

Although the North American Tiddlywinks Association has never been compared to the National Football League, Kahn maintains that tiddlywinks can keep a person in shape. "During a tournament you can be on your feet for eight hours," he said. "At the end of the day you really feel it in your legs."

"We haven't been able to find all of us," said Emma Bishop, president of the Rockette Alumnae Association. "The Rockettes have been in existence for over fifty years, and there were always thirty-six dancers on stage at any given moment, so I think there are probably hundreds of former Rockettes we don't know about."

As it is, there are 320 members of the organization, which has its headquarters in Maplewood, New Jersey. Any woman who has ever been a member of the famed Radio City Music Hall dance troupe or its early predecessor, the Missouri Rockets, is eligible. Major annual functions are a fall luncheon and a spring charity ball.

"We were never thought of as sex symbols," Mrs. Bishop said. "We weren't like Playboy Bunnies. Our image was the all-American, apple-pie, girl-next-door type. The founder of the Rockettes got very angry if we were referred to as a 'chorus line.' He insisted on the term 'precision dancers.' 'Precision dancers' has a more wholesome connotation."

The first question a Rockette alumna is always asked, Mrs. Bishop said, is, "Did you ever make a mistake?"

"I'm sure we all made mistakes," she said. "I know I did. No one's perfect. But we were known for all making every move in unison, so I guess that's what people think about when they think of us."

"It's just what it sounds like," said James H. Smith, Jr., of Camp Hill, Pennsylvania, president of the Jim Smith Society. "It's an organization of people named Jim Smith."

The purpose of the club, which has 1,218 members, is to give people named Jim Smith pride in their name. "When your name is Jim Smith, the tendency is to feel pretty ordinary," Smith said. "Our goal is to make Jim Smiths stick out their chests and stand tall."

One of the problems about being a Jim Smith, Smith said, is that people often assume you are traveling under an alias. "When my wife and I were first married, we used to get strange looks from hotel desk clerks. Her name is Jane Smith."

Smith feels that Jim Smiths often turn out to be overachievers—perhaps as a means of trying to compensate for their names. "I think there may be a subconscious desire for a person named Jim Smith to show the world he's special in other ways," Smith said. "Although I won't kid you—not all Jim Smiths are great success stories. I have had appeals from two Jim Smiths to help get them out of jail."

Smith said that the members of the organization feel quite comfortable when they all get together for outings. "We have an all-Jim Smith softball game every year," he said. "Jim Smiths travel five hundred miles to play. The only problem is what to call each other. You can't just yell 'Jim' or 'Smith.' We usually call each other by the name of the state or town we're from. They call me 'Camp Hill.'"

The Dogs on Stamps Study Unit, with headquarters in Newark, New Jersey, is dedicated to the study of postage stamps that have dogs on them.

"There are more than two thousand stamps worldwide with dogs on them," said Morris Raskin, secretary-treasurer of the organization. "Whenever a new stamp with a dog on it is issued, or we discover a dog on an old stamp, our one hundred seventy-five members communicate with each other about it."

Although most people might be surprised to learn there are so many stamps with dogs on them, Raskin said that the members of his club are hardened to the phenomenon. "We don't get excited about it," he said. "We kind of expect it. The average person might be shocked to look at a stamp and find a dog, but that's what we're always looking for."

The main challenge for the study group, Raskin said, is to find stamps where dogs may or may not be—and then to document that there is, indeed, a dog on the stamp. "Say there's a stamp with a picture of a famous person in a rocking chair," he said. "There's a dark object under the chair. Now, is that dark object a dog? Is it the hair on the head of a dog? Is the dog curled up there? Or is it just another dark object, and not a dog? Our job is to find out."

The Nineteen Thirty-Two Buick Registry is a club made up of people who own Buick automobiles manufactured in 1932. Its registrar, McClellan G. Blair, of Indiana, Pennsylvania, estimates the membership at "a couple of hundred."

Blair himself said that he owns "quite a few" 1932 Buicks. "I suppose I own a couple of dozen. I've never really counted.

Some are hard to call cars—they're just parts. I can't tell if some of them are cars, or half-a-cars, or pieces of cars."

He said the members of the organization hold no illusions that the 1932 Buick was the finest car ever built. "We just like them. Nothing in particular about them. They're just nice. They look sort of oldish, but they're mechanically modern enough that you can drive them and they won't fall apart."

He said that the concerns of his members are generally the same: "We're all looking for the same kinds of parts." He said that 1932 Buick owners are not fanatics. "I don't think that you could accuse us of having rapturous love affairs with our cars. But we do like them a lot."

"Basically, we just want to make Americans better educated about aardvarks," said Thomas P. Byrne, president of the National Association for the Advancement of Aardvarks in America.

Byrne, of Waukesha, Wisconsin, said that he has never seen an aardvark in person—but that he has long been attracted to photographs and paintings of aardvarks.

"Even in Africa, you can live for years and never see an aardvark," he said. "The most fun our members have is exchanging photographs and drawings of aardvarks. We have more than six hundred card-carrying members, but I have a suspicion that a lot of them aren't that serious about aardvarks. I'd say that the hard-core membership is only a hundred or a hundred-fifty."

Byrne said that he is an admirer of aardvarks for their abilities. "The aardvark is the fastest-burrowing animal alive," he said. "They dig faster than six men with spades. They also have tremendous hearing. There's no way to really know, but it's been said that aardvarks can hear army ants while on the march, and from quite a distance, too."

The long-range goal of the association is to hasten the day when aardvarks are accepted as household pets in the United States, Byrne said. "They have certain qualities that would make them better pets than cats and dogs," he said. "For example, they're pretty incapable of taking offensive action. Instead, they'll just roll over on their backs and stick out their feet, adopting a defensive posture. To a person who is deathly afraid of dogs, this could be a big advantage."

The International Barbed Wire Collectors Historical Society has headquarters in Sunset, Texas. Its secretary-treasurer, Jack Glover, said its six hundred active members are devoted to collecting and passing on barbed wire lore.

"Barbed wire is part of our history, just like guns," Glover said. "Do you know what settled the West? Barbed wire and windmills settled the West."

Although many people probably assume there is only one kind of barbed wire, Glover said that there are 898 different patents for barbed wire, each for a different variety. "We display our barbed wire collections on boards," he said. "The wire is cut in eighteen-inch strips. Anyone who would display a piece of wire less than eighteen inches is not a true collector. The eighteen inches are enough to show you at least two or three barbs."

Glover is rather jingoistic about barbed wire. "People from all over the country call me and ask me what kind of barbed wire to buy," he said. "You can buy cheap barbed wire overseas. But then winter's going to come, and that foreign wire is going to stretch and snap. Or if it doesn't it's going to stretch and then sag. In my opinion foreign barbed wire just doesn't have the tensile strength of domestic barbed wire."

He said that he sees nothing particularly unusual about his dedication to the collection of barbed wire. "But you know what I can't understand?" he said. "I can't understand people who collect buttons. Sometimes I think the biggest collectors in the world are button collectors. Me, I wouldn't have a button."

"I probably own twenty thousand buttons," said Lois Pool, of Akron, Ohio, the president of the National Button Society.

"The typical button you will see on a man's or a woman's

shirt is not a collectible button," Miss Pool said. "It's not unique enough. We look for the button that is remarkable enough to want to preserve."

The National Button Society has more than two thousand members, Miss Pool said. "We publish the *National Button Bulletin*," she said.

"It comes out five times a year, and features full-page photographs of buttons, so that we can examine the buttons in detail. We are just about to go to color photos in one issue a year, so that we can study the true colors of the buttons."

She said that members of the society sometimes can't help themselves from looking a person up and down when they meet. "I work as an office manager in a funeral home," she said. "When my boss walks in and he's wearing a new suit, my eyes go immediately to the buttons. It happened just the other day. The buttons on his suit were plastic, encircled in brass, with initials in the center. I couldn't help myself. I said to him, 'When that suit is worn out, I would like the buttons.'"

Why Fathers Are a Cut Above Their Sons

There is only one major difference between my generation of men and my father's generation of men:

My father's generation knew how to carve a roast.

This occurred to me the other day when a male friend of

mine, in a state of panic, was frantically looking through cookbooks. The reason was that he and his wife were having people over for dinner, and he was going to have to carve the turkey.

My friend had no idea how to carve a turkey, just as he had no idea how to carve a roast. Ever since his wife had casually announced that the dinner menu would consist of turkey, he had been losing sleep and imagining how he would react at the big moment. The guests would be seated at the dinner table, the wife would carry the steaming turkey from the kitchen, everyone would lean expectantly toward their plates . . . and my friend would stand there, carving utensils in his hands, without a clue about where to start cutting.

I sympathized. Like my friend, I haven't the foggiest idea how to carve a turkey. And let's be honest: turkeys are generally eaten only on special occasions. The real test of a man's carving skills is whether he can carve a roast. I can't do that, either.

I have taken an informal survey of men in their late twenties, their thirties, and their early forties. It is almost unanimous: Virtually none of us can carve a roast.

Carving a roast used to be the very definition of manhood. If you were a husband and father, you were the person who was responsible for hacking up the meat. Maybe you never went near the kitchen—but when the meat was carried out to the dining table, it was your turn at bat.

Most of my memories of childhood tend to get a little foggy, but in the meat department the scenes are crystal clear:

We would be at the dinner table. The meat would be hunkered down on a wooden base; it seems to me now that the meat and the base were placed on some sort of separate small table right next to the dining table itself, but I can't be sure about that. In any event, there were little troughs cut into the wooden base, to catch the juices from the roast.

This whole setup was just to my father's left; my father, of course, sat at the head of the table. He had been home from work for about forty-five minutes; he was still wearing his white shirt and tie from the office, although he had taken off his suit jacket, and now he had another duty—he had to carve the roast.

I recall him holding utensils in both hands; this is getting dim, but it seems that there was a long, wooden-handled knife in one hand, and in the other hand an elongated rod used to sharpen the knife. I sense him running the knife back and forth over the sharpener; logically the sharpener should have been replaced by a fork or another knife at some point, but I'm not sure. Not knowing how to carve a roast, I have no idea of what the correct tools were, or are.

My father would ask each of us how much we wanted. Then he would carve. We would each pass our plate to him, he would carve precisely the right amount of meat, then put it on the plates. And then we would eat.

This all sounds simple enough. It's deeply symbolic, though. What happened between generations? One day there was a whole country filled with men who knew how to carve roasts. The next day the same country was filled with men who couldn't carve a roast if a gun was held to their heads. Who taught our fathers? Why didn't our fathers teach us?

Social custom undoubtedly has had a lot to do with this. During our fathers' generation, families did not eat meals that were boiled inside plastic bags in individual portions; families did not eat meals that were heated up under tinfoil coverings. As odd as it sounds now, families shared meat cut from the same slab of beef; there was actually food that didn't come precut and enclosed in cardboard with a colorful picture of itself printed on top.

Also—and I may be wrong here—it seems that people did not eat out as much then as people do now. Today restaurants have become almost an entertainment medium; people have become used to eating in restaurants so often that restaurants are reviewed and rated by critics just like movies and plays. And of course the fast-food places have added a dining alternative that simply didn't exist during our fathers' generation.

Still, those are just weak excuses. When the final score is

tallied up, the men of my generation are going to have to hang their heads and meekly admit it. Our fathers could carve, and we couldn't, and that is the legacy we will pass on to future generations.

I know for a fact that this must cause great glee among the men of my father's generation. For years, the message they got from us was that we knew everything there was to know about politics, education, sex, and virtually every other area of life that mattered. Most of the time we made them feel as if we thought we had invented all of those things.

Now, finally, it is their turn to gloat. Our fathers are getting old now, and we are the ones who are moving into society's mainstream. Finally it really is our turn to take over the world.

But that doesn't matter. Anytime our fathers want to show us who's still boss, they don't have to say a word.

All they have to do is roll a simmering, steaming roast into the room. And then say to us:

"All right, smarty. Let's see who can cut it."

A View from the Bridge of My Nose

Most people, it seems, are entranced by the music video craze. If they're not watching MTV they're watching one of the dozens of spin-offs that have proliferated on networks and local stations; the combination of intricately edited videotape and hot new music is the media phenomenon of the Eighties.

When other men and women mention a specific new video to me, I smile and nod. Undoubtedly I leave them with the impression that I, too, am hooked on videos.

But I have decided to confess. I do not watch music videos, just as I did not play computerized video games when those games were said to be the raging new fad. I get my entertainment elsewhere.

What I do is . . . oh, I might as well just come out and say it. My chosen medium of entertainment is the View-Master.

I spend hours with my View-Master, and I never tell anyone about it. Do you blame me?

You know what View-Masters are; you may have forgotten about them, but you used to use them when you were a kid.

View-Master viewers are those binocularlike devices that you press against your nose and eyes, then turn toward a light source and peer into. Into the View-Masters are inserted little disks (called "reels" in the industry), each approximately the size of a cocktail coaster. Around the circumference of each reel are fourteen tiny color transparencies; when you look into your View-Master the fourteen transparencies become seven 3-D scenes. You advance from scene to scene by depressing a little lever on the right side of the View-Master.

I openly admit that being hooked on View-Masters is not the most sophisticated thing that can happen to a man, especially in this media-wise age. I can't help it, though; somehow, secure in my room, my View-Master smashed up hard against my face until the bridge of my nose hurts, my eyes turned toward a table lamp, I feel contented. Those three-dimensional scenes make me happy; whether I am looking at "The Seven Wonders of the World" or "The Butterflies of North America," there is something peaceful and calm about the View-Master experience—something that shifting, changing images on a television screen can't provide.

Maybe it has something to do with the idea that I can advance the pictures at exactly my own rate; maybe it's simply the fact that I know that twenty million other Americans aren't looking at precisely the same thing at precisely the same moment I am looking at it. Whatever the reason, I spend more time with my View-Master than is probably healthy.

The first View-Masters went on sale just before Christmas in 1938. They were manufactured by a company called Sawyer's Inc. in Portland, Oregon. In the Twenties, Sawyer's was the nation's largest producer of scenic postcards; the introduction of the View-Master was an immediate success, and within a year more than one thousand dealers were selling all of the View-Masters that Sawyer's could produce.

During the Forties and Fifties, View-Masters became an American institution. Virtually every child who grew up during that era can remember using a View-Master. In 1966, at the beginning of the modern media explosion, GAF Corporation of New York City purchased the View-Master business from Sawyer's. With many exotic new forms of entertainment available to the American public, View-Master did not fare well; in the late 1970s, the View-Master division of GAF began posting losses. In 1981, View-Master was purchased by a limited partnership formed by a businessman named Arnold Thaler.

"Some people questioned the wisdom of my buying the company," Thaler, sixty-one, told me. "But I was convinced that not everything revolves around the video tube. When you look at something with your own eyes and you see it in 3-D, that's still special."

Thaler said that he has returned the View-Master business to profitability. "The secret is to make the subject matter of the View-Master reels contemporary," he said. "We have purchased the rights to some of the most popular movies and television series. We have *Close Encounters* on View-Master reels, we have *E.T.*, we have "The A-Team," we have "Knight Rider," we have the Smurfs. And now we are getting into rock groups. We have Menudo on View-Master reels, and we are negotiating with Van Halen and Adam Ant and Culture Club.

"And the View-Master is still one of the world's most economical entertainment buys. The viewer costs four dollars, and a packet of three reels costs three dollars. Where can you beat that?"

Thaler didn't need to convince me; I was already one of the converted.

But as we talked I took silent exception to one of his major points. He seemed to truly believe that the TV and movie characters were the key to View-Master's continued popularity.

Speaking for myself, though, I much prefer the old, traditional reels. View-Master has more than six hundred active titles in its "reel library," as it refers to its catalog, and another six hundred in storage. I get much more pleasure out of the vintage reels than out of the new, pop-culture-oriented ones.

For example, I am a big fan of "Coronation of Queen Elizabeth II." The three View-Master reels in the coronation packet were shot in London on June 2, 1953, and I defy any television documentary to tell the story of an event any better.

Another nice one is "Grand Canyon National Park," which, for my money, is just as good as a visit to the canyon. And for bedtime viewing, nothing can beat "Hans Christian Andersen's Fairy Tales." The three reels in that packet (No. B305) are "The Little Mermaid," "The Steadfast Tin Soldier," and "The Emperor's New Clothes." Tune in to the adult movie channel on your cable setup if you will; when midnight rolls around at my house I'll stick with that flaxen-haired View-Master mermaid.

As a writer, I am in awe of the View-Master wordsmiths. Anyone can do a creditable job when they have a couple of pages in a magazine to fill, or a whole book; the View-Master staff writers face the challenge of getting their whole story into the little opening near the top of the View-Master—the hole in the machine that reveals the text printed on each reel. The writers have only seven short sentences—one per 3-D scene—to tell their tales.

The writers are masters of compression. Here, for example,

is the entire text of "Little Red Riding Hood" (Packet B310):

"Little Red Riding Hood went to her Grandmother's." "She told a friendly wolf where she was going." "The wolf ran on ahead to Grandmother's house." " 'Come in, my dear,' said the wolf in a high voice." " 'Grandmother, what large teeth you have!' " " 'The better to eat you with,' the wolf shouted." "A woodcutter saved Little Red Riding Hood."

Whoever wrote that could make a fine living as an editor of *Reader's Digest,* or at least on the rewrite bank of *USA Today.*

I was skeptical when I heard about a new product called the Talking View-Master. The company announced that each Talking View-Master would contain "a microprocessor-controlled unit with a constant-speed motor, linear tracking tone arm, and self-cleaning sapphire needle." This sounded suspiciously like the media modernism I was trying to get away from. My warning signals grew especially loud when I learned that the premiere title for the Talking View-Master was "Michael Jackson's 'Thriller.' "

But—although personally I plan to stick with the old silent, four-dollar, hand-operated View-Master—I must admit that the Talking View-Masters have promise, if you like that sort of thing. Watching Mr. Jackson's little drama on my Talking View-Master (it is heavier and larger than the standard model and runs on penlight batteries), I was impressed with the sound quality and the overall effect of the whole production. I tried another talking reel—"Popeye in 'Paint Ahoy' "—and the spoken dialogue drew me viscerally into the house-painting contest between Popeye and Brutus.

Sometimes it seems as if there's no way to avoid the future.

The senior photographer for View-Master is Hank Gaylord, sixty-four. He has been shooting pictures for View-Master reels for twenty-one years.

"The business has changed," Gaylord said. "For years we emphasized tabletop models of fairy-tale stories. It was such intricate work—we would make as many as thirteen or fourteen exposures on a single frame of film.

"We had three artists on the staff who did nothing but create sculptures for those tabletops. They built sets, just like in the movies. Sometimes we would use a dozen mirrors during a shot, to focus the lighting exactly right on each figurine on the table. It was a real team effort.

"Now it's different. We're out in the field much more. We're shooting on location, and that's a different feeling. I just got back from a Van Halen concert, for example. I was shooting the band for their reel. I used twin Nikons mounted on a bar; there was a belt drive between the cameras, so that when I focused one of the cameras I was automatically focusing the other one, too. That's how you get your precise 3-D.

"When I was shooting 'Thriller,' Michael Jackson walked up to me and asked if I was the photographer from View-Master. I said that I was. He said, 'You know, this was my idea.' It seems that he started collecting View-Master reels when he was a kid, and for all the fame he has, he really wanted to be photographed in 3-D for View-Master."

Sometimes when he is on assignment, Gaylord said, he feels slightly awkward announcing whom he represents. "We were traveling with the Pope in 1979, for example," he said. "We did a set of reels on his tour. There I was with photographers from UPI, and *Time* magazine, and the Associated Press. And when they asked me who I was with, it sounded a little odd to say, 'View-Master.'

"But when people hear it, they usually react positively. They say something like, 'Oh, I had one of those when I was a kid.' And they're genuinely surprised that we're still out there shooting. I just tell them, 'Yep, we're still here.' "

The View-Master people are quick to provide numbers and statistics designed to make us View-Master addicts feel a little less alone. For example, according to the company, View-Master products are currently sold in more than 116 countries, in seventeen languages. Since the development of the device, the company says, more than one billion View-Master reels and more than one million View-Masters have been sold worldwide.

Still, those of us who repair to our rooms to share a few quiet moments with our View-Masters continue to feel slightly out of synch with the rest of the world. Everyone else is lining up at the local theater to see the latest Steven Spielberg or George Lucas film; we're staring at a light source and flipping through "Williamsburg Colonial Restoration" (Packet 181).

I talked about this with Gary Evans, forty-three, one of View-Master's top executives. I thought that Evans might be sympathetic; when your title is Creative Director for View-Master, you're most likely able to justify the way you spend your life.

"I don't want to be too poetic about this," Evans said. "But View-Masters provide classic entertainment, in that they leave a lot to the imagination. I don't think it's going too far to compare a good View-Master reel to 'Ode on a Grecian Urn.' We're talking about images that are stopped in time; elements of real timelessness."

Perhaps. Regardless of what it all means, though, I'm glad that I've gotten this off my chest. Next time my colleagues see me in the morning with red indentations around my nose and eyes, they'll know what I was doing the night before. When you're hooked on View-Masters, you can spot a fellow user ten yards away.

Alice Doesn't Live There Anymore

There is a delicatessen near where I work; it has a service bar in the back, and sometimes at the end of the day I will stop in there.

One night I did. The bartender said, "A friend of yours was in the restaurant the other day."

"Oh?" I said. "Who's that?"

"Alice Cooper," the bartender said.

That seemed odd. "Are you sure?" I said.

"It was him, all right," the bartender said. "He had his wife and daughter with him."

"What do you suppose he was doing in Chicago?" I said.

"Somebody asked him that," the bartender said. "He said he was living here now."

"Alice Cooper is living in Chicago?" I said.

"That's what he said," the bartender said. "I'm right about him being a friend of yours aren't I?"

Yes, he was right. For a brief period of time—not that long, no more than a month, really—I suppose you could even have said that we were best friends.

In 1973, in an effort to take a look at the world of rock 'n' roll from the inside, I made arrangements to join a band as a performing member. The band I became a part of was Alice Cooper, named after its lead singer, a former high school athlete from Arizona who had changed his name from Vincent Furnier and subsequently became one of the biggest pop stars in the world.

The Seventies were a time when planned outrage was in fashion, and Alice Cooper was taking full advantage of it. He was a forerunner of today's fascination with violence, harsh sexuality, and androgyny; his stage show featured simulated bloodletting, raw, suggestive song lyrics, and leering incitements of his young audiences. Alice appeared onstage every night wearing grotesque facial makeup and outlandish costumes; his show was the epitome of calculated tastelessness.

It was working to perfection. The year I joined up, the band took in more than $17 million; they played before more than eight hundred thousand customers in live performance. There wasn't a week that Alice's name failed to appear in one national publication or another. In Britain a member of Parliament, Leo Abse, attempted to have the Alice Cooper show banned. He based his position on what his teenage children had told him about Alice. "They tell me Alice is absolutely sick," he said, "and I agree with them. I regard his act as an incitement to infanticide for his subteenage audience. He is deliberately trying to involve these kids in sadomasochism. He is peddling the culture of the concentration camp. Pop is one thing; anthems of necrophilia are another."

I joined the band and sang background vocals on one of their albums; I went on a nationwide tour with them and played a role in their violent stage show every night. My purpose was to try to see the rock 'n' roll road from their vantage point—from the stage, from the limousines, from the chartered jets—and to write a book about it.

I can't exactly say that Leo Abse's summation of the Alice Cooper show was wrong; actually, it was a fairly accurate appraisal. But I found something out about Alice: he was one of the brightest, funniest people I had ever met. He realized what the tone of the decade was; he was selling his young audiences what they were eager to buy, but he was full of a sense of irony about it. He was as appalled by their avid acceptance of his show's bloodlust as was the most conservative fundamentalist minister; the difference was, even though he was appalled, he was becoming wealthy from it.

On the tour I joined, his original band was in the process of falling apart. There were rampant jealousies among the members; they resented the individual fame that Alice was attaining. Alice was becoming uneasy about having to go onstage and be Alice every night; he seemed to sense that he had created a monster, and that he was that monster. He was drinking heavily and staying barricaded in his hotel rooms between performances.

He wasn't speaking much with his fellow band members, and he wasn't going out, so he and I became unlikely friends. He was twenty-five; I was twenty-six. We would spend hours every day and night just sitting in his room talking and drinking and watching television while bodyguards kept fans away. We came to genuinely like each other, and our companionship grew to be a welcome one. It was destined not to continue; when the tour ended he went to live in California, and I went back to my home in Chicago. But we had each found someone of whom we were genuinely fond.

I have to say, that tour was one of the most interesting things that ever has happened to me. Standing onstage every night, the Super Trouper spotlights glaring in my eyes, looking out at twenty thousand screaming people—there's no way you can put a price on an experience like that. The tour, as it turned out, was the last ever by the original Alice Cooper band; the divisions I was seeing on the road caused them to break up soon after.

It wasn't long before I stopped hearing the name Alice Cooper altogether. New bands came to the forefront of the young public's attention; new records became number one. I read something about Alice admitting his alcoholism and going to a private clinic to seek help for it; once in a while I would see a story in which the members of a new band, their image based on outrage, would pay tribute to what they had learned from Alice Cooper. But it had been ten years since I had spoken with him or seen him; it had been almost as long since I had thought much about him.

And now the bartender was saying that he was living in Chicago.

.   .   .

On a Saturday night an Alice Cooper called my office and left a local phone number. When I returned the call he said that he had, indeed, moved to town; would I like to join him and his wife for dinner the following week?

We met in front of the maître d's desk at an Italian restaurant called Spiaggia. We were both closer to forty than to thirty; we both wore sport jackets and ties. Alice was accompanied by his wife, Sheryl.

After some initial, awkward banter, we were led to a table by the window. I asked him the obvious question first: What was he doing living in Chicago? If there was ever a person who seemed perfect for the entertainment-industry ambience of southern California, it was Alice Cooper. Why had he left?

"My daughter is three and a half years old now," Alice said. "Sheryl is pregnant again. We were living in Beverly Hills, but we just decided that that's no environment to bring up children. It's crazy in Los Angeles—the drugs, the fast life. There are too many negative temptations. I just couldn't see risking bringing my children up in that kind of atmosphere."

Alice's wife said, "There is something less jaded about the Midwest. And my parents live in the Chicago suburbs—Oak Park. We thought it would be nice to be near them."

"The in-laws make nice free baby-sitters," Alice said.

He said he loved being a father. "It puts your whole life in perspective," he said. "The moment your child is born, you feel a chemical response—you become a person you've never been before. All of a sudden there's someone other than yourself who's important to think about and take care of.

"I spend most of every day with my daughter. I'll put a videotape of one of my old performances on the TV, and she'll know that the person on the TV is Alice, and the person sitting with her is Daddy.

"I take her to Sunday school every week. I think it's important to her that Daddy takes her there. Daddy and Mommy do it together—the family feeling is a big part of Sunday."

I asked him what had happened to him professionally in

the almost twelve years since his last number-one hit. I hadn't heard a thing about him; had he stopped recording?

He shook his head. He talked of a dispute with his record company; he felt that they had torpedoed any chance his albums had of becoming successes. "I made six albums that no one ever heard of," he said. "That started to kill me.

"I started getting pretty depressed. I knew intellectually that in rock 'n' roll there is no such thing as something more than a two-year run. I had had my run. Michael Jackson, Prince—I don't care who you name, nobody ever got more publicity than Alice Cooper did. And I missed it. It got to the point where I couldn't watch a video or listen to the radio. I'll admit it, it was jealousy. You realize everyone gets their own shot, and that you're not the only person on the planet. But it's almost like a fighter knowing that he can knock another guy out, but not being given the chance. That's how I would feel every time I heard a hit record."

He said he had decided to try to become a leading star again. "The worst thing in the world is to be considered an oldie," he said. "To be sitting in a hotel room and hear the radio come on and hear them say that you're an oldie—look, I don't want to be Chuck Berry. It's easy to say, 'Well, I was good back then.' But I feel more like an old gunslinger. If the young guys think they're faster than me—bring 'em on."

He said that he was working on a plan. He was going to write the music for an hour-long video, in which he would costar with some of the top heavy-metal bands of the Eighties—the young musicians who grew up emulating Alice Cooper. "The video will be like *The Magnificent Seven* of rock 'n' roll," he said. "And I'll be playing the Yul Brynner role.

"Then, when the video comes out, I'll go back on the road. Now the challenge is going to be whether I can do it again. You know, the first time around we were in competition with the Rolling Stones, with the Who. Now I'll be going up against bands that I never heard of. The rock 'n' roll road used to be like the National Football League—everybody was a known quantity. It was like, 'Who do we play this Sunday? The

Washington Redskins?' Now, because of videos, a band that has never even been on tour can have a number-one album. A band with no Holiday Inn knowledge at all."

I asked him if people still recognized him when they saw him. He smiled.

"Yeah, sometimes they do," he said. "But the other day, I was shopping at Marshall Field's, and these two young boys were whispering to each other and looking at me. And finally one of them came up to me and said, 'Excuse me, but are you really Boy George?'

"I'm not looking forward that much to going on the road again. I'm not drinking at all now, and if you recall, there was a time when I couldn't be more than eight inches away from a bottle of V.O.

"But I have to try, to see what happens. I don't kid myself, though—the most important thing in the world to me is being a good father. Sheryl will be out of the house, and it will just be my daughter and me at home. And I'll say, 'Who's the best rock star in the world?' And she'll say, 'Daddy!' And I'll say, 'Who makes the best records?' And she'll say, 'Daddy!'

"That's all I want, really—to be her hero. You can be a hero to millions of kids, but what you really want is to be a hero to your own."

We sat in the restaurant for hours. We talked of our time together on the road all those years ago, and of what had become of the former members of his band, and of the nature of gigantic stardom. He said that he had once met Elvis Presley in Las Vegas; Elvis had invited Alice to his hotel suite. Elvis handed Alice a gun and told him to point it at him. Alice did; immediately Elvis threw a karate move on him, and the next thing Alice knew he was flat on his back on the floor, with the gun lying by his head and Elvis's foot on his throat.

"And all I could think was: What a great album cover this would make," Alice said.

We laughed, and the talk got to shopping malls and automobiles, to potty training and cesarean sections. The waiter arrived and placed desserts in front of each of us.

Alice looked down at his.

"I don't know," he said, turning to his wife. "This looks awfully rich."

"Oh, Alice," she said. "Go ahead. Live a little."

The Meaning of Culture

CHARLESTON, W. Va.—I had been spending time in New York, which prides itself, with some justification, as the cultural capital of the nation. New York is the home of the country's most prestigious book publishers, of the Broadway theater, of the three major television networks, of the most influential national magazines.

On the way home, I stopped off here in Charleston. And I can't help it; when I think about culture, and about literary life in its truest meaning, what I saw in this West Virginia town is what will stay in my mind long after this trip is over.

I stopped off in Charleston to attend the annual Library Appreciation Day Dinner sponsored by the West Virginia Library Association. That may sound pretty boring to you, but you ought to know what it means.

West Virginia is one of the poorest states in America. It is one of the first states to feel bad economic times, and one of the last to feel the beginnings of economic recovery. There are 1.9 million people in West Virginia's fifty-five counties—far fewer people in the entire state than in the city of New York or Los Angeles or Chicago. Needless to say, no one has ever mentioned West Virginia in the same breath with New York when talking about culture or literary tradition.

And yet the people of West Virginia have deep feelings

about their libraries. There are 164 public libraries throughout the state, and often the local library is the major source of cultural enrichment for an entire West Virginia county. This is a relatively recent phenomenon in the state; since 1965 there have been 128 library building projects in West Virginia.

"Most of our people are rural," said Frederick Glazer, director of the West Virginia Library Commission. "It is impossible to overestimate the sense of isolation. There is not a single city in West Virginia with a population of one hundred thousand. There are counties without movie houses. There are communities down in the hollows that are so isolated they cannot pick up television broadcast signals."

This is where the libraries come in. "Sometimes a library is the only connection with the outside world for people down in West Virginia coal country," Glazer said. "The library can become the only way for people to experience something other than their own walls."

For the Library Appreciation Day Dinner, more than eight hundred West Virginia citizens came to Charleston. For some it was a seven-hour drive or bus ride each way; people came two hundred miles, two hundred and fifty miles, three hundred miles. They weren't lobbyists; most weren't even library workers. They were just people who wanted the state legislature to know that they cherished the state's libraries.

They had dinner in a big room inside the Charleston Civic Center. Their purpose was to ask the legislature to appropriate three dollars for every person in West Virginia to go to the library system. According to officials here, that would make West Virginia the one state among the fifty with the highest per capita commitment to libraries.

"We can't be Number One in many areas," one man at the dinner said. "But we can try to be Number One in libraries."

The politicians of West Virginia took note of this turnout, and of this seriousness of purpose toward libraries. The three top politicians in the state were at the dinner: Governor John D. Rockefeller IV; Clyde See, speaker of the House of Delegates; and Warren McGraw, president of the Senate. So were more than one hundred other West Virginia legislators.

They all met for a cocktail hour, and then for a dinner catered by a company that used fresh-faced Charleston high school girls among its waitresses. Again, I couldn't help but notice the contrast between the typical Manhattan restaurant dining experience and the experience of the church-supper-type dinner being served in West Virginia. But I also couldn't help wishing that some of the high-powered New York publishing executives could have seen this outpouring in support of books and libraries.

"You just don't see this kind of turnout unless people feel very intensely and very personally about something," Fred Glazer told me. "It sounds corny to say it, but these people are here because they know that their libraries make their lives better.

"We've found that, especially in the most isolated parts of the state, people use the libraries to discover and follow their own pursuits. Maybe it's something as simple as someone deciding to spend his lifetime reading Westerns. Or maybe it's more sophisticated than that; a woman down in the hollows will never be able to see the Royal Ballet, or the New York Opera. But from her library she can borrow films of the ballet, or records of the opera or books about them both.

"What it means, I think, is that a person's life does not have to be dictated by where he or she happens to live. I had one woman tell me that she would prefer the legislature to spend money on libraries rather than highways. She said that the highway projects never seem to make it out to her part of the state. But she said that she sees people taking books home from their local library in shopping bags every day."

There are 3.6 million books in West Virginia's 164 libraries, I was told. Figures like that aren't what I'll remember from this visit, though. What I'll remember are the eight hundred people who traveled for much of the day to say that they appreciated their libraries, and wanted those libraries to prosper. That may not be the dictionary definition of "culture," but it's good enough for me.

Fashion Plate

The men's magazines are beginning to feature fashion stories with titles along the lines of "A Return to Elegant Dressing for the Fall."

Drat. Foiled again.

There's not a whole lot in this life that one can accurately predict, but I think it's safe to say that I will not be dressing elegantly this fall. Winter will probably roll around with me dressing approximately the same way I have dressed since 1965. I can't help it. It's part of me, like having a bad personality.

People who see me on the street probably think I have no idea of how to dress. This is not true. I have eyes. I know how people dress when they want to look nice. I just can't do it.

I have three basic uniforms.

The first is what I wear ninety-nine percent of the time. It is a blue shirt with the tie yanked loose and the sleeves rolled up; a pair of old jeans; and Weejuns.

The second is what I wear if I have to have lunch with a boss, or make a speech, or appear on TV. It is a blue shirt with the tie pulled up to the throat, a pair of brown corduroy pants, a blue blazer, and Weejuns. The sport coat is holding up remarkably well; it doesn't look a day older than when I bought it to cover the Richard Nixon–George McGovern presidential campaign of 1972.

The third is what I wore to Gene Siskel's wedding. It is a dark blue suit with stripes in it. I purchased it for the wedding, and planned to wear it on other special occasions, but there haven't been any.

I take no pride in this, and I'm not trying to prove anything. I will be the first to admit that a man my age should not show up at work every day in a pair of jeans and a blue shirt with the tie yanked loose. It's a stupid way to dress. When I see other people who are dressed the way I am, my immediate instinct is that they are dressed badly.

But I simply can't wear nice clothes. I physically can't do it. If I put on elegant clothes, I can't write. There is no way for me to sit down at a typewriter or a word processor if I have on an expensive, well-pressed pair of pants. I could no more write wearing a suit than I could take a shower wearing a suit.

The best way I can describe this is to say that, for me, wearing nice clothes feels like being in prison. All I want to do is break out of there. At Siskel's wedding, for example, all I could think about was getting home and throwing that suit on the floor, where it belonged.

I wasn't always like this. Before I went away to college for my freshman year, I made a point of buying the back-to-school issue of *Gentlemen's Quarterly* and purchasing everything that the magazine's editors recommended for the well-dressed man on campus. I recall, for example, that I was in a near-panic when the day to leave Ohio for Northwestern rolled around, and it suddenly struck me that I had neglected to buy a yellow shirt. I had never owned a yellow shirt in my life, nor had I known anyone who had owned a yellow shirt; but *Gentlemen's Quarterly* said that a yellow shirt was essential for the college man's wardrobe, and so before I set off for campus the last thing I did before departing my hometown was to buy that yellow shirt.

About six weeks into fall quarter I stored all the *Gentlemen's Quarterly* clothes in my closet in my dormitory, and started to dress the way I dress now. I've never changed.

I may not look good, but you have to grant me consistency. I glance at snapshots from the last two decades; the people who are with me in the pictures reflect the changing fashions and tastes of the Sixties, Seventies, and Eighties, but I always am dressed the same way I am dressed this morning, which is the same way I was dressed my sophomore year in college.

There, in the snapshots, are the others in wide lapels, narrow lapels, fat ties, skinny ties, bell-bottomed trousers, cuffed trousers, button-down shirts, big-collared shirts, scruffy revolutionary clothing, conservative business clothing. And there I am. Blue shirt, tie yanked loose, sleeves rolled up, jeans, Weejuns.

There is one great advantage to this; you never have to spend a moment in the morning deciding what you will wear. It is predetermined; your office is redecorated more frequently than you are. To your colleagues at work, you become like a painting that is hung on the wall. You are going to look the same every day of the year.

You'd think I'd get bored with this, but I'm not yet. On principle, though, I know I should change. During the year I was twenty-six I sat down and had a serious heart-to-heart talk with myself; I told myself that this was no way for a twenty-seven-year-old man to dress, and that on my twenty-seventh birthday I would go out and buy some good clothes and start to change. But time seems to have gotten away from me; ten more years have passed, and I'm wearing the same stuff.

Reading those men's magazines that are predicting the return of elegance for fall makes me a little melancholy. I think those men in the magazines look great; I wish I could wear those clothes. Truly I do. If I could put on those clothes and walk out the door to work wearing them, all of the people in my life would be delirious with joy. But I might as well try to leap into the air and fly.

I wonder what I did with that yellow shirt?

Streep

We walked down West Fifty-seventh Street in Manhattan. We passed beneath the marquee above the main entrance to Carnegie Hall. "The problem with walking a baby in New York City is that the strollers are at exactly the height of the exhausts on the cars," said Meryl Streep.

She did not have either of her two children with her on this afternoon. We made our way through the sidewalk crowds; we saw an ice-cream parlor and stepped inside.

We each ordered a chocolate soda with vanilla ice cream. I fetched them from the man behind the counter; we sat on stools near the store's front window.

Streep's presence was causing more of a stir inside the ice-cream shop than it had on the street. Out there the New Yorkers were all in such self-absorbed hurries, were so reluctant to make eye contact with their fellow pedestrians, that only a few people had noticed Streep among them. In the ice-cream store, though, the patrons had relinquished their customary defenses for long enough to look across the room and realize who was here.

They began to approach her for autographs. She obliged, each time putting down her orange-and-white paper cup so that she could sign another napkin. At one point, as she was picking up the cup again, it tipped over; she spilled part of the soda on her bare left arm.

I got up to get some napkins from the dispenser on the counter. When I came back, there were more people waiting to talk to Streep, her arm still wet. As they spoke to her and stared at her, it struck me that there was quite a bit of deference in the air. The people were not reacting to her as they might to this year's most famous athlete, or most notorious rock star. Mixed with their curiosity was an almost palpable feeling of respect; if these people could bestow honors, what they would be giving Streep at this moment was not an Oscar or an Emmy, but some sort of Lifetime Achievement Award. They reacted to her as they might react to, say, Katharine Hepburn; and as I looked at Streep's face, lit by the sun coming through the window, I found it worth thinking about that she was only thirty-five years old.

"My mother and father always thought I was great," Streep said. We were sitting in an office in midtown Manhattan, a place that belonged to one of Streep's business associates. The business associate had said that Streep could borrow the office for the afternoon; now we were talking.

"My parents thought I was just fine," Streep said. "My Aunt Jane, though . . . Aunt Jane, I think, has only come to like me in my older years. She tells me that I was a terrible-looking little kid, and bossy besides."

Streep laughed. I had read references to her ugly-duckling childhood; she always seemed to make light of it. I said that surely it couldn't have been very funny to her back then. Looking good is important to little girls.

"Yes, it's very important for little girls," she said. "It's very important for grown-up women, too, especially if they're in the movies. There aren't so many roles for a female Spencer Tracy, if you know what I mean."

I had also read that Streep had blossomed during high school; that she had become a cheerleader and, eventually, homecoming queen.

"I think that came from an acting instinct," she said. "My first successful characterization is what I devised for myself in high school. I laid out my clothes for the week every Sunday so that I wouldn't repeat. That sounds pretty sick and obsessive, but that's what I did."

On the wall of the office was a framed cover of *Time* magazine, dated September 7, 1981. On the cover of the magazine was a color photograph of Streep; the article coincided with the release of her movie *The French Lieutenant's Woman*. The cover line was MAGIC MERYL.

I looked over at the cover. "That's really an American icon," I said.

Streep seemed uncomfortable. "It's just a role," she said.

"No," I said, "it really is sort of an important part of America."

Streep was shaking her head. "It's the lighting," she said. "The photograph was very well lit."

"I'm not talking about the picture itself," I said. "I'm talking about being on the cover of *Time* magazine."

Now she was blushing, still shaking her head. "Everybody's on the cover of *Time*," she said.

"Everybody's on the cover of *Time*?" I said.

It was clear that she would rather have been talking about something else. "I didn't mean it that way," she said. "What I meant is that they have fifty-two covers a year that they have to fill, and they've got to have somebody on the cover every week. When it happened to me, I didn't feel anything. But my next-door neighbor had her picture on the cover of the *New York Times Magazine*. It was an article about working women. The cover showed her kissing her child goodbye as she headed for work. That was impressive to me. It made me feel that I knew someone famous. When something like that happens to me . . . I don't know, it has no impact."

Every superlative, of course, has been used to describe Streep's acting skill. Her thumbnail biography is known by virtually every man and woman who wants to become an actor. Born in suburban New Jersey. College at Vassar, where acting coaches began to notice her remarkable giftedness. Membership in a small repertory company in Vermont, then three years at the Yale School of Drama, where the praise for her work grew.

Stage work in New York; more plaudits. Then a string of movie roles that transformed her into the most admired actress of her generation: *The Deer Hunter, Manhattan, The Seduction of Joe Tynan, Kramer vs. Kramer, The French Lieu-*

tenant's Woman, Sophie's Choice, Silkwood. Two Academy Awards, and an Emmy for her performance in the television miniseries "Holocaust." And with every acting assignment, a recognition on the part of the public that she was doing things the hard way; that she was choosing unconventional parts, parts that were not guaranteed to automatically please everyone who had seen her last movie. Streep was developing a reputation for unpredictability in what she was willing to try; it was unpredictability in a positive sense—the unpredictability of a person willing to continually test her limits.

Now, on this afternoon, she had recently completed filming a new movie called *Falling in Love,* in which she starred with Robert De Niro. In a few days she would be leaving for London, where another movie project was waiting.

"The packing is driving me crazy," she said. "Winter shoes, summer shoes, medicine, toys, books . . ."

Her husband, Don Gummer, a sculptor, and her two young children, Henry and Mary Willa, would be accompanying her on the trip to England. "I feel like Coach Landry lately," she said. "The unsmiling statistician."

I asked her if her current success was the culmination of some long-hidden childhood dream. "It never occurred to me that I might be a movie star," she said. "I looked at television, and there were the Mouseketeers getting bosoms, and they were all so pretty. And there was Sandra Dee, and she was what a movie star was supposed to be. I watched all of this . . . but I never wanted to be inside the box. I say 'the box' because what I mainly did was watch TV. I didn't go to movies very much. Still don't.

"As a matter of fact, when I was little I never let myself hope for very much, in general. Never let myself hope for very much of anything. If I didn't hope for much, then I wouldn't be disappointed when I didn't get it.

"I remember in high school, walking into the room where you took the SAT tests. What I remember thinking is that you got three hundred points just for writing your name on the test. I have no idea whether that's true or not, but that was the rumor at our high school. So I thought to myself, 'At least I'll make a three hundred.' It turned out that I did okay on the SATs. But my attitude was 'Who cares. It doesn't matter.' The same with people. 'If they like me, fine. If not, that's fine, too.'"

I said that I had a stupid question. How hard was it to memorize lines? After all the years of watching thousands of actors and actresses in the movies and on television, I still couldn't figure out how they managed to memorize all of those words that someone else had written. Was there a trick to it?

"Two weeks ago, I was in London for a brief visit, and it turned out that my mother was in London, too," Streep said. "She was staying at a sublet. She gave me her phone number, and I wrote it down on the pad at the hotel where I was staying.

"Yesterday I wanted to call my mother. And I thought of that pad in that hotel room . . . and I remembered the number. It's a sort of idiot's memory I have, and it's what got me through college.

"I've always felt a little guilty about being able to do that. I'd read a script two or three times, and I'd have my lines. The others were staying up at night studying their scripts. It's nothing I felt particularly good about, though. It's sort of like when I was at Yale, and they would post the cast lists for all of the plays. I was always worried when the lists went up. Not because I was afraid I wasn't going to be on them. I was worried that I was going to be cast in the lead again. I was worried about how the rest of the class would feel about that."

I said that surely those kinds of emotions must be mixed with a fierce sense of pride in herself.

"You know what makes me proud of myself?" she said. "I'm proud of myself when all of these things are set next to each other. If I make a false step, it's only one step. It's like the string of beads in a necklace. One stone may not be as interesting as the next, but the whole necklace is a good necklace."

She said that her plan is to work in spurts—do two or three movies at a time, then take a year or so off to be with her family, then do some more movies. She said she can never be sure how long she will be valuable to movie producers; one of these days, she said, she may wake up to find that she is too old to command the kinds of roles she is offered now.

"I'm going to be sort of, maybe, relieved at that point," she said. "Making movies is hard work. The theater is something I like better. And it's more welcoming to women.

"There's something about movies that I need, though. Making movies is sort of like exercise for my imagination. I turn slovenly very easily. I like the family kind of interaction that comes when you're working on a movie.

"Being a housewife and a mother is much more difficult, though. To be a good housewife and mother, you have to be more self-generated. You have to create your own playground of the imagination and the mind. To be a really good, creative mother you have to be an extraordinary woman. You have to keep yourself involved with your child during great periods of the day when it's just the two of you and you feel that at any moment you may literally go out of your mind.

"I'm lucky, because I get to go in spurts. I do great chunks of work, and then I can concentrate on being a mother. The spark of electricity is always there when you're making a movie; you sit down at a script conference, and it's easier to feel that you're participating because it's not just you. Other people pick up the slack. It's not like that when you're a mother, and that's what's so impressive about good mothers."

I asked her how the concept of ambition fit into all of that. Did she consider herself to be an ambitious person?

"It's changing, the idea of what you're supposed to be," she said. "You're supposed to have teeth and nails now. In pursuit of what, really? There was a time when I was bewildered that other people perceived me as incredibly ambitious. I resented the fact that I was thought of as being self-effacing or coy because I said that a lot of what had happened to me had happened because of luck.

"I would hear from friends that 'So-and-so has this real thing about you—you're the reason that she didn't get this part or that part.' And I would find it hard to believe that people would spend so much time worrying about the course of someone else's career.

"I think you can only be as good as the task at hand. If Jascha Heifetz plays 'Frère Jacques,' it will be very good. But it will only be as good as 'Frère Jacques' can be. Does that make sense?

"My whole attitude is that whatever the task at hand is, as long as I'm doing it, then I might as well try to do it better. If you're washing the floor, at some point the question is going to come up: Do you go in the corners or not? I'm the kind of person who wants the floor clean. The corners, too. It's not a perfectionist thing."

"Then what is it?" I said.

"I guess it's an impatience with being half-assed," she said.

I asked her about being famous. How much did she like it?

"I have a friend who has a son, and the son wants to be a rock 'n' roll star," she said. "He doesn't want to play well. He doesn't want to compose music. He just wants to be a famous rock star.

"I think there's a lot of that out there. People who have no interest in doing anything well—they just want to be famous. And I think, well, they should just spend two weeks with someone who's famous.

"I like some aspects of it. I like the aspects that make New York seem like a small town. Strangers smile at you.

"But I don't like what it does to someone who is with me, and who is not famous. It's gotten to the point where I prefer being with someone who is famous, because it takes the weight off my shoulders. If I'm walking down the street with someone I know, and I'm stopped five times by people who recognize me, I can't help a little corner of my heart curdling for the other person.

"With my children, they're young enough that they don't realize what my situation is yet. They're growing up thinking that New York is an incredibly friendly place. Everyone says hello and smiles. I don't know what it's going to be like when they're old enough to understand."

I asked her if she ever walked into a movie theater where one of her films was showing, took a seat in the back of the house, and watched the show along with the other paying customers.

"No," she said.

"Never?" I said.

"Never," she said. "The first time I watched one of my movies with any audience at all was *Sophie's Choice,* and that was a benefit arranged by the studio.

"But buy a ticket and walk into a theater? I could never do that. If you do that, you really lay yourself open. What if the people laugh at the serious part? What if they snore during the part that's supposed to be funny? I don't know why you'd want to be there to be wounded by that.

"I'll tell you something, though. We don't have HBO on our TV at home, but the HBO movies show up on the screen all scrambled. One night *Sophie's Choice* came on. I could hear it, but I couldn't see it. And I sat there for twenty minutes, and I looked at it—all scrambled and fuzzy, with little corners of the movie showing up on the screen.

"We had just bought a video camera to record the kids growing up. Home movies. And it occurred to me as I was watching the scrambled-up *Sophie's Choice* . . . you know, I have my own home movies. They're my real movies. When other people see them, they may see the plot and the scenery and the actors. When I see them, though . . . I see something else. I'm watching a different movie. I see them and I think about the place where I lived when we were filming the movie, and where we ate, and the arguments we had about different scenes. . . .

"That's what I was thinking about when I was watching the jumbled-up *Sophie's Choice.* I have my own home movies, but everyone else gets to see them. They're reminders of my life, and they're right out there."

We rode through the late-afternoon crosstown traffic. Streep had an appointment with Sydney Pollack, the director; they were supposed to talk about a future movie project. If Streep agreed to do it, she would begin to work on it immediately after the movie in London was completed.

"Do you ever wish that any of this was any different?" I said.

"Well, I think about my children," she said. "When I was a little kid, I was the star in my household. That's how it should be for all little kids. When you're a little kid, you should be the light of the house."

"And in your house?" I said.

"Sometimes, in my situation, it gets a little difficult," she said.

"Did you ever think about moving to a smaller town?" I said. "Just to get away from the New York City atmosphere?"

"I've thought about it," she said. "But I don't know if I'll ever do it."

"Does it appeal to you?" I said.

"I suppose, but you never know what's going to happen," she said. "I mean, a small town sounds great for children. But then you have idiots racing their cars up and down the streets at 120 miles an hour in those small towns. I know. I was in that car when I was growing up. And I didn't say anything. I could have said, 'Jerome, turn the engine off. I'm scared and I want to go home.' But I didn't say a word.

"I guess that's how it is, isn't it? You're scared to death and you don't say a thing."

Letters from Laura

I don't know why this makes me feel so sad, but it does.

About a year ago I wrote a story about a twenty-six-year-old woman named Laura Thomas, who had come up with a rather original idea. Thomas was a fan of television soap operas, and she started thinking: What if people could receive a continuing soap opera through the mail?

Her plan was to write a continuing series of adventures in the form of letters. People would be able to subscribe to the letters; in each letter would be news of a fictional heroine, one "Laura Alexander."

The fictional Laura Alexander, according to Thomas, would be "in her early twenties. She is very naive, very innocent. She is a virgin. She has moved to Chicago from a small town in Iowa, and now she is trying to make her fortune in the big city."

Actually, the personality of the fictional Laura Alexander reminded me a little of Laura Thomas. Laura Thomas seemed to be a wide-eyed, hopeful, trusting sort herself—and she had great aspirations for her "Letters from Laura" idea.

"Each letter will carry a personal salutation," Laura Thomas told me at the time. "I want the person who receives it to feel that he or she is really receiving a letter from a friend."

She said that she hoped there would be a big market for "Letters from Laura" among senior citizens. "A lot of them really treasure it when they get mail," she said. "And I would hope that 'Letters from Laura' would remind them of what their own wholesome, nice granddaughters might be going through in a similar adventure of moving to the big city. I would hope that they would really begin to care about what happens to Laura Alexander."

Well . . . I talked with Laura Thomas again the other day.

"Letters from Laura," it seems, was a total flop.

She took out advertisements promoting the service, and did all she could to let people know about it. Her grand total of subscribers: fewer than fifty.

"I guess people just weren't interested," she said. "It seemed like a good idea to me, but there doesn't seem to be a market for the adventures of an innocent young woman in the city."

And then Thomas showed me the new project upon which she has embarked.

It is a reincarnation of "Letters from Laura."

Only this time Laura isn't a naive young virgin.

This time Laura is a porno queen.

"Now Laura Alexander is a gorgeous, sexy, experienced, un-inhibited young woman who is the biggest movie porno star of all time," Thomas said. "She loves sex. She will do anything. Her letters are totally X-rated—they are very hot."

She showed me a sample of the new "Letters from Laura."

The letter was one of the filthiest things I had ever read. To say it was hard-core would be to engage in massive under-statement. This new version of "Letters from Laura" was raw pornography, pure and simple. There is no way I can quote any of it here.

"I'm doing this because I was pretty devastated when the original 'Letters from Laura' failed," Thomas said. "I felt that I was a bad businesswoman.

"Actually, it was my own father who helped me come up with the new idea. He told me that people just didn't want to pay good money to read about the adventures of some nice, innocent girl. He said, 'Sex sells.' And I decided he was right."

So Thomas has taken out advertisements for the new "Letters from Laura" in some of the raunchiest men's magazines. She has also begun writing a monthly version of "Letters from Laura" for one of the hardest-core of the porno magazines; the editors are not paying her for it, but are running the "Letters from Laura" post office box number so that she can get sub-scribers.

"I had no idea how to do this," Thomas said. "I'm more like

the old Laura Alexander—I'm naive about a lot of things, and I don't have a lot of experience with men. But I went to an adult bookstore and bought some of the dirtiest porno magazines, and I read them and studied the writing. It wasn't that hard to learn to write like that."

She said that she feels the new "Letters from Laura" will do much better in the marketplace than last year's version. "The original Laura Alexander—the nice young woman in the big city—must have been too boring for people," she said. "I guess if you want people to read something like this, it has to be taboo and nasty."

She said she is writing to her original fifty subscribers to tell them that the old "Letters from Laura" are coming to an end. "I'll miss writing for those people," she said. "Sometimes they'd write to Laura Alexander. They seemed very middle-class and conservative. They seemed like nice, decent, home-oriented, down-to-earth, warm people. But there just weren't enough of them."

And now she will begin writing the hard-core, X-rated "Letters from Laura" to see if more people want them.

I told Laura Thomas that I had a question for her:

Last year, when she had begun "Letters from Laura," she had told me that she hoped people would become interested in what became of Laura Alexander. So I wondered: What did become of Laura?

Laura Thomas paused.

"I guess she sold herself," she said.

Then she said:

"That sounds awful, doesn't it? Let's just say that she decided to become a different person."

Yippie vs. Yuppie

It was a scene that stretched credulity.

Sitting backstage in a warmup room for the "Donahue" television show, Jerry Rubin and Abbie Hoffman marked time.

Fifteen years ago, they were in the midst of the Chicago Seven trial—the conspiracy trial that stemmed from their involvement in the street disruptions during the 1968 Democratic National Convention. The trial made them the most famous radicals in America. With their painted faces and angry outbursts, they became better known than all but a few U.S. senators.

Everything changes. Today Jerry Rubin, forty-six, backstage at "Donahue," was sipping from a bottle of Perrier. He was the picture of a successful young businessman—clean-shaven, tailored sport coat, tie, gray slacks, tasseled loafers.

Across the room Abbie Hoffman, forty-seven, slumped in a leather chair. He was bearded and tieless, in corduroy pants and boots.

The two former compatriots were launching a national tour. They plan to crisscross the United States appearing on college campuses, in town halls, and clubs; their act is being billed as "The Yippie vs. the Yuppie."

Also backstage at "Donahue" was one Don Epstein, the president of a New York firm called Greater Talent Network, Inc. Epstein is the agent for Rubin and Hoffman; his job is to get them as many bookings as he can. The fee for a Rubin-Hoffman appearance is five thousand dollars per night, plus expenses.

"We're just beginning the tour, and already I have sixteen cities booked," Epstein said. "I'm confident that I can book as many cities as Jerry and Abbie are willing to work. If they're willing to do one hundred appearances in the next year, I should have no problem lining one hundred appearances up."

The idea is to market the fact that Rubin and Hoffman have gone their separate ways. Rubin has become an entrepreneur, Hoffman still espouses many of the causes that he believed in as a Sixties radical; thus, the premise for "The Yippie vs. the Yuppie" tour.

"It's a classic confrontation," Jerry Rubin explained. "A passionate set of disagreements between two personalities who are connected in people's minds."

Abbie Hoffman said, "The colleges today are so boring and bland—they remind me of hospital food. I really hold college students' feet to the coals."

"And I disagree," Rubin said. "I tell college students that I promote the entrepreneurial ethic and working within the system. I tell the students that they should become powerful businesspeople and take over the country with the money they earn."

Whatever . . . the point is, Rubin and Hoffman have become business partners themselves. Their joint venture is the lecture tour, and they knew that their success on the road would depend, in large part, on how well they did on "Donahue." The show is perhaps the most powerful in the country in terms of reaching consumers—and Rubin and Hoffman knew that if the sparks flew on TV today, Don Epstein's booking job would be made much easier.

A visitor to the anteroom wondered: Did today's college students even remember Jerry and Abbie?

"They remember, they remember," Hoffman said.

"Of course the kids remember," Don Epstein said. "Jerry and Abbie are a part of history. We should get, at the least, between a thousand and fifteen hundred people everywhere we go."

It was almost time for the show to begin. Out in the studio, a "Donahue" producer was talking to the audience.

"Do you remember the Sixties here in Chicago?" she said. "How many remember what went on in Chicago in the Sixties?" There were some hands raised, and a smatter of applause.

The producer said: "You remember the Chicago Seven trial, right?"

There was silence.

"No?" she said.

Hoffman and Rubin were led to chairs that were placed on a riser. Microphones were pinned to their shirts.

The producer, reading from a card, introduced the two to the audience, and called them "two of the Sixties' wildest radicals and most entertaining activists."

Phil Donahue appeared one minute before air time. A floor manager counted down the final seconds, and the show began. Rubin and Hoffman did their best to disagree vehemently with each other and make the point that they were now on different sides of the political fence; at one point Hoffman said, "If you scratch Jerry Rubin, you're going to find Ronald Reagan."

After some heated exchanges, Donahue broke for a commercial. The houselights dimmed.

Jerry Rubin craned his neck, as if looking for someone. He found who he was looking for: Don Epstein, sitting in the back row.

"Donny, how is it?" he called out.

The agent meshed his fingers together and held them up for Rubin to see.

"Interact more, Jerry," he said. "Interact more."

"I'm trying to," Rubin said. "But Phil moved away."

The commercial ended. The houselights went back up. Donahue began his questions again. Rubin and Hoffman resumed their arguing. Coming soon to an auditorium near you.

Set Point

Along with millions of other Americans, I watched the telecasts of the recently concluded U.S. Open tennis tournament. It struck me how much tennis has changed in such a short time.

When I was a boy, I harbored a dream of becoming a world-class tennis player. I never made it, but I tried hard enough for a number of years; the last paying job I had before becoming a newspaperman was as a teaching pro at some local public courts, and that's as close as I got.

Tennis was the last major sport to change. It was rooted in politeness and tradition; you were not allowed on the courts unless you dressed completely in white, and even on schoolyard courts players obediently wore their "whites." The major tennis tournaments were for amateurs only; professional tennis players had their own circuit, but the prestigious events, including the U.S. national championships, were available only to amateurs. There was no such thing as a "U.S. Open"; if you got paid for playing tennis, then you were disqualified from the U.S. championship.

It was as if the men who ran the tennis establishment believed that there was something holy in amateurism. Frankly, it was kind of nice. Tennis paid for this anachronism, of course; even the loftiest tournaments were seldom televised, and you were lucky if you could find a tennis story on the sports pages. Those of us who dreamed tennis dreams assumed that we could never attain the fame, never mind the money, of the stars in sports like football and baseball. But we didn't care that much. There was something special about tennis.

I was thinking about this as I watched John McEnroe and Ivan Lendl and Jimmy Connors play in this year's U.S. Open.

Some of the players were like walking billboards; they seemed to be selling any available inch of their clothing to sponsors who would pay to paste their logos on a tennis star. Their clothes were colorful and distinctive; the era of "whites" is long past. The U.S. Open was being telecast to live audiences all over the world.

What it got me thinking about was a Davis Cup sectional match back in 1962. The United States was playing another country; I'm not sure, but I think it was Canada. The series was being held at some courts up in Cleveland, and like most tennis events, it was no big national deal. No television; little press coverage.

A friend of mine named Bruce Friedman and I rode the train up to Cleveland to watch the matches. He had the tennis dream, too, and there was no way that we were going to let the country's best amateur players be that close to where we lived, and not see them.

We hung around for the first day of competition. The crowd was small; really no more people than you would get for the end-of-summer finals at a good-sized country club. It was great to see the U.S. team, but that's not what truly excited us. What was really exciting was that Pancho Gonzales—one of the greatest tennis players in American history—was serving as a coach for the U.S. Davis Cup team.

Gonzales was a pro by this time. From our seats in the stands, we watched him watching the team. He was tall and brown and lean; he was everything an athletic hero should be. The day's matches ended, and the players wandered off into a combination locker room area and snack bar.

My friend and I hung around. At dusk, walking out of the locker room, we saw Gonzales. He was in tennis whites now; he carried several racquets in his hand. He was accompanied by a player named Chuck McKinley, and it was clear that the two were going to play; they were going to have an impromptu workout.

My friend and I walked over to the court; there was virtually no one else around. Gonzales and McKinley started hitting back and forth, and one of us got up the nerve to ask Gonzales if they needed ball boys.

Gonzales nodded and motioned the two of us to opposite ends of the court. For the next two hours, as we shagged balls and tossed them back to the players, we got a priceless gift: we got to watch the great Gonzales up close.

You talk about the best tennis lesson a person could ever get. Gonzales was famed for his serves—both the booming flat serve, and an American Twist that leapt skyward as soon as it hit the court. We crouched down and watched how he did it; we studied his ground strokes and took note of how he moved across the court. Who would have guessed, just one day earlier, that we would ever have gotten an opportunity like this?

Gonzales wasn't the sweetest guy in the world; a few times, when we were watching him too intently and not chasing the balls rapidly enough, he cursed at us and reminded us that we were supposed to be ball boys. We didn't mind; we were a couple of suburban teenagers and he was Pancho Gonzales, and if he wanted to chew us out, that was his privilege.

It strikes me that something like that probably couldn't happen today. Somehow, with the publicity and the commercial endorsements and the marketing strategies and the telecasts, I can't imagine, say, John McEnroe walking out onto a solitary court at the end of the day during a big tournament, and allowing the only two kids left in the area to chase balls for him. The crowds would be too big today; the time schedule would be too regimented.

That's what I was thinking about as I watched the U.S. Open. On that day in Cleveland, after Gonzales had finished, he started walking back toward the locker room. Almost as an afterthought he called out in our direction; when we looked back at him, he tossed us the tennis balls with which he had been playing. That's what I was thinking about.

The New Generation Gap

I was talking with an eighteen-year-old girl, a senior in high school. She said she wanted to ask me something.

"Who was Ed Sullivan?" she said.

I said I didn't think I understood the question.

"I mean, who was he?" she said. "Was he, like, your generation's David Letterman?"

Not precisely, I said.

"Well, what did he look like?" she said.

I asked her if she meant that, were Ed Sullivan to walk into the room at that very moment, she would not recognize him?

"No," she said. "I wouldn't."

Then she said:

"Did he look like this?"

She stood up and let her arms hang in front of her like an orangutan.

I said that actually he had, indeed, looked a little like that. Where had she seen him?

"I think I saw him in a Beatles video," she said.

The Beatles hadn't made videos, I said; they had made movies.

"Let me ask you something else," she said.

I said to go ahead.

"Is it true that Elvis Presley and the Beatles made their first appearances on the Ed Sullivan show?" she said.

I said that bascially that was true.

"Well, why did you watch them, then?" she said. "If they hadn't been on TV before, how did you know that you wanted to see them?"

I said that we watched Ed Sullivan every week.

"You mean you watched his show no matter what was on it?" she said.

I said yes.

"I see," she said. "Kind of like MTV."

Alas . . . it has come to pass. My generation, which alienated the rest of America in the Sixties and Seventies by acting as if we had created the concept of youth, is now on the far side of a generation gap that excludes millions of our younger countrymen who have no real memory of Ed Sullivan.

The young woman is not alone; there are millions upon millions of bright, intelligent young people out there who are no more familiar with Iron Butterfly or Dobie Gillis than we were with Rudy Vallee or Jack Armstrong, the All-American Boy. To them Lyndon Johnson is as distant a figure as FDR was to us; to them the idea of watching Jack Paar on television is as unimaginable as our thoughts of listening to Fred Allen on network radio.

This shouldn't be so surprising, of course; it happens to every generation, and it is probably a healthy thing.

But there has never been a generation that seemed so happily, smugly sure that it was inventing the world for the first time than those of us in the so-called Baby Boom. Because we represented a big hump in the country's demographic profile, we always felt comfortably surrounded by others just like us; there were so many members of our generation that often we felt important just by being alive.

Which makes it all the bigger a shock when we now realize that a completely new generation has come along—a generation that frankly regards us as middle-aged and sort of quaint. The fact that they're right doesn't help any.

This phenomenon has even extended to politics. Those of us who grew up during the war in Indochina and were still relatively young when Watergate happened view the universe with a gimlet-eyed perspective that we always considered sort of weatherbeaten and world-weary. We may have assumed that the generations that came along after us would eagerly imitate our political attitudes.

But as my eighteen-year-old acquaintance said to me:

"I'm real sorry about Vietnam and everything, but I don't see why your generation hates the government and hates America so much."

Although she was oversimplifying, I knew exactly what she meant; it is far more likely that a member of her generation will join the Marines than end up marching on a picket line protesting some bit of American foreign policy.

My conversation with her was not the first time I have seen this new set of attitudes come up. A few months ago I was talking to another teenager—this one seventeen years old—and she mentioned that her parents liked to play tapes in their car.

I asked her what kind of music her mom and dad played.

"You know, classical stuff," she said.

Like what? I asked.

"The Grateful Dead," she said.

And my old college roommate called me the other day to ask me if I'd seen the current issue of *Playboy*—the one that features a pictorial about young men being romantically involved with older women.

"The 'older women' in the article are younger than we are!" he said. "The 'older women' are thirty-five years old!"

Oh, well. My eighteen-year-old acquaintance asked me another question about what Ed Sullivan's show had been like.

I was going to tell her about Topo Gigio, but I didn't have the heart.

Book 'em

Friends have asked me to name the most bizarre moment of all. At first I was tempted to say it came in Los Angeles, when I found that there were going to be two of us on a morning talk show—just me and Britt Ekland, who was there to discuss her theory of "sensuous beauty."

Then I was tempted to say it came in Washington, when I stepped into the makeup trailer and found that the person being worked on before me was Little Richard.

Then I was going to say it came in New York, when I reported for a radio interview at which the person who would be answering the questions was me, and the person who would be asking the questions was Howard Cosell.

But I decided that the most bizarre moment probably came early one morning in Aurora, Ohio. "The Morning Exchange"—a Cleveland television program—was broadcasting live on location from Sea World, located in Aurora. It was a chilly, stormy day; thunderclouds covered the sky, and rain was descending in harsh sheets.

The show was being telecast outdoors. I was sitting on a canvas director's chair, between the two hosts of the program, Fred Griffith and Jan Jones. To protect us from the weather, we had been positioned under a stone ledge halfway up the side of a man-made cave. Across the way from us, sitting in a covered grandstand, were several hundred northern Ohio housewives.

And between us was the otter pool. The otters were sticking their noses up through the surface of the water, attempting to leap into the rainy dawn. There we were—Fred, Jan, and me—up on the ledge of the cave. There they were—the audience—beneath the roof of the grandstand. And separating us were the storm and the agitated otters.

I clutched a wireless microphone in my right hand and spoke into it. I heard my voice echoing back from the grandstand and bouncing off the wet walls of our cave. It struck me that, when I had first decided I might like to grow up to be a writer, I had not quite imagined this.

The book tour is a staple of modern literary life. Sadly, the day is long past when you could count on large numbers of people strolling casually into a bookstore, browsing at their leisure until they have spotted a title that intrigues them, then deciding, on an impulse, to give that title a try.

People are in a hurry today. In most cases, they will purchase a book only if they have heard of it. How do they hear of it? Media.

So a little community of sorts has sprung up. The main players—the publicists who work for the publishing companies, and the "bookers" who work for the television and radio shows—change relatively infrequently. They deal with one another on virtually a daily basis. The publishers call and say who will be coming through a particular town in a given week, and the bookers decide if the literary travelers sound interesting enough to put on the air.

The variables—the folks whose names change with the seasons—are the authors. On a given day, there may be scores of authors on tour somewhere in America. Armed with photocopied itineraries, plane tickets, and pocket cash, they have been put on the road for a simple reason. A book will not sell unless people know about it. The way most people know about things in the Eighties is by watching their television sets, listening to their radios, and reading their newspapers. Thus, the book tour.

In a recent twelve-month period it happened that I was sent on three separate national book tours. I visited thirty-six cities. It was unlike any experience I have had before.

First, a disclaimer: I have read stories in which touring authors have moaned and complained about the long hours, the bad hotels, the indifferent interviewers, and the general pain that come with going on a book tour. I can't quite buy that.

Maybe it's just me, but I can't help feeling flattered every time I learn that someone actually has said he or she is willing to interview me. Because I wrote stories for a living, I'm always a little surprised when someone agrees to turn the tables, and do an interview with me. In that sense, a book tour is one continuing ego trip—how often does a writer get to hit the road and talk about himself all over the country?

Having said that, I must quickly add that a book tour is probably the most disorienting thing I have ever been a part of. It lifts you out of your daily life, plops you into a world that you were previously only vaguely aware of, then drops you back into your daily life again. Your job is to retain some sense of equilibrium, which is a challenge you quickly learn you may not be up to.

Sometimes it all happens in a flash. You wake up in your own bed in your own town, have breakfast, then head for the airport to catch a flight to Los Angeles. Upon arriving you take a cab to Vine Street, to a television studio inside which you are scheduled to appear on "The Merv Griffin Show." A makeup artist dabs liquid on your face, you are led to a lounge equipped with a bar and a television monitor, and soon enough the monitor flashes to life and you hear an announcer's voice say that tonight Merv's guests will be Susan Anton, Erica Jong, a stand-up comedian, and you. Before too long you are led onto the set, where Merv Griffin greets you, an audience full of strangers applauds, and you talk to Merv for eight minutes. After you finish, the audience leaves and so do you; the next day you are back in the town where you live again, working at your own desk again.

Sometimes it happens in slow motion, so repeatedly that you begin to feel like a tired old boxer who is being beaten against the ropes by a healthy young stud eager for an early knockout. The schedule for one day in Detroit: 9:00 A.M., "Kelly and Company" talk show, WXYZ television; 10:20 A.M., interview with J. P. McCarthy, "Focus" show, WJR radio; 11:00 A.M., "The

Sonya Show," WDIV television; 11:45 A.M., "Midday" show, WWJ radio; 12:15 P.M., "Metro Magazine" show, WOMC radio; 1:00 P.M., "Mark Scott" show, WXYT radio; 2:30 P.M., taped interview for early evening news, WDIV television; 3:30 P.M., newspaper interview with *Ypsilanti Press,* Detroit Metro Airport. Immediately following interview: flight to next city.

Again: all this attention is gratifying; all this attention is more than any writer has a right ever to ask for. And perhaps that is the thing that makes a book tour so confusing—so exhilarating, yet so exhausting—to be a part of. I know that on each of my three recent tours, I found myself thinking: this is a part of America that everyone should get to experience once. Few people are even aware it's out there, yet it's going on every day.

There is a relatively new phenomenon that has become a part of book tours: the "media escort."

Media escorts are men and women who take visiting authors around to their various interviews. They live in the towns the authors pass through; they charge considerably less money than limousine services, and are more reliable than cabs. Take another look at that Detroit schedule. Without an escort waiting with his car and knowing his way around the city, a schedule like that one would be impossible to book.

Media escorts see a side of the literary world that few others do. They become acquainted with a far greater number of prominent authors than even the most gregarious Manhattan editor or agent. They sometimes escort a different author every day; they spend up to twelve hours a day with "their" authors, and therefore can tell author stories far more intimate and revealing than the stories garnered by the broadcasters who do the quick interviews in the studios while the escorts wait outside.

Often the media escort is the only person whom an author will leave a given town with a real memory of. By the time the author reaches the next town, though—usually late at night, in order to be present for the next morning's first talk show—the next media escort will have left a message at his hotel, giving instructions about where to meet just after dawn. My favorite instruction, delivered on a pink hotel message slip: "Look for an aging blonde in a silver Mercedes."

An author on a book tour learns to look for familiar sights. One of these, he realizes early on, is his book. It is often the only thing that he can recognize as being a part of his real life. So when he arrives at each ensuing television or radio station, his eyes involuntarily begin to search for his book. The sight of it begins to give him a warm feeling, like a letter from home.

The other familiar thing a touring author learns to look for is other touring authors. Over the course of a year there may be hundreds and hundreds of them on the road, but during a given week, in a specific section of the country, you are likely to find the same people. So when I saw Jane and Michael Stern, the authors of *Square Meals,* in the San Francisco airport, it did not seem at all odd that I had seen them only hours before in the lobby of KRLD radio in Dallas. And when I ran into a psychologist named Elliot Weiner, the author of something called *The Love Exam,* no fewer than seven times in two cities during one twenty-four-hour period, I did not question it; it was sort of like in high school, when you used to see the same people in the hallways between classes every day.

In an effort to maintain my sanity, I started keeping notes during my book tours. In the margins of my daily schedule, I would scribble my impressions about the people who were interviewing me.

So while Don Miller of the *Santa Cruz Sentinel* was asking me questions in my hotel room in San Francisco, I was writing on my schedule: "Why is the photographer lying on my bed?" While Marcia Alvar was talking to me on KUOW radio at the University of Washington in Seattle, I was writing: "This woman is really good." While Jim Bohannon, sitting in for host Larry King, was interviewing me on Mutual Radio's syndicated "The Larry King Show," I was writing: "Why are all of these obviously intelligent, apparently well-read people up at three o'clock in the morning making phone calls to a person they have never met?"

Sometimes something would happen that required me to turn the schedule over and write on the back. After a live interview on "Midday L.A." at KTTV television in Los Angeles, I wrote: "A producer came up to me on the set and said, 'You'll have to clue me in on who you are.' I said, 'I'm a writer.' She said, 'Like an author?' I said, 'Yes.' Her eyes glazed over and she said, 'Oh, interesting.' I could tell she was expecting someone else. I asked her who she had thought I was. She said, 'A water commissioner.'"

Between 9:00 A.M. and 10:00 A.M. Eastern Time every Thursday morning, there is a telephone number—it is in the 556 exchange in Manhattan—that constantly rings busy. That is because virtually every author on the road—and representatives of virtually every publishing house back home—is trying to get through.

This is the telephone line on which the editors of the *New York Times Book Review* place a tape recording of their best-seller lists, both hardback and paperback. On Thursday mornings a new tape is put on the machine; on it a voice announces the fresh best-seller list that will appear in the Sunday *Times* ten days hence.

In Seattle, it's 6:00 A.M. In Denver, it's 7:00 A.M. In St. Louis, it's 8:00 A.M. In Boston, it's 9:00 A.M.

In hotel rooms everywhere, groggy authors punch the New York telephone number, get a busy signal, hang up, and punch the number again. Soon they will be out in a new city, for a new day. Right now, though, they can't face the morning without hearing the tape. If book touring is a game, the tape is the scoreboard.

.   .   .

When my third tour of the year was over, I went back to my newspaper office in Chicago. One of the first telephone callers was a woman from the publicity department of a publishing house in New York.

"We've got a very interesting author who will be in your town next week," she said. "He's written an important new book, and I think it would make a great story for you. . . ."

I closed my eyes and thought of airports. And otters.

Wedding Story

Olive Johnson, who went through the first seventy-seven years of her life as a single woman, got married the other afternoon. After a lifetime of hearing people call her Miss Johnson, now she is being called Mrs. Lange. That may not be front-page headline news, but it is making her very happy.

"Mr. Lange . . . Harold . . . and I both live here in the retirement community," the new Mrs. Lange said. She was explaining how she had met her husband, who is seventy-five. The retirement community is called the Holmstad, and is located in Batavia, Illinois.

"One day about four years ago I was working in the garden," she said. "I was breaking up some sticks to mark off the garden, and Mr. Lange . . . Harold . . . was in the next garden. He started bawling me out; he said, 'If you do it that way, you're going to get slivers in your hand.' He went and got me some other sticks to use."

Olive Johnson had accepted the fact that she would never marry. "I suppose I thought about it when I was a young girl," she said. "I felt bad when all my girl friends were getting married, and I wasn't. I missed the companionship. But my mother was ill, and so I lived with my parents to take care of her. Then my father became ill, and I took care of him, and after a while I didn't think about getting married anymore."

Harold Lange and Olive Johnson began to become good friends. He was married before, but his wife died; Olive Johnson did not let herself think about the possibility that, so late in her life, she might finally wed. But as the two of them began participating in more activities together at the retirement community, she realized she was beginning to feel emotions she had never felt before.

"I didn't know what it was like to be in love," she said. "But other people began to say to me, 'You're in love.' They said that they could tell by looking at my eyes."

At seventy-seven, her days and nights had developed a pattern.

"In the morning I would get up, and I would go to the breakfast table," she said. "I have a studio apartment; I would fix myself some cereal and some fruit or orange juice. I'd sit there by myself and listen to Wally Phillips on the radio.

"The days would be spent with the other people here in the community. I would have good company, but I never lost sight of the basic fact that I was alone. At night, before bed, sometimes I'd fix a snack for myself. I'd listen to the radio again, and I'd get into bed and read. When my eyes closed and my book dropped out of my hands, I'd know it was time to sleep."

More and more, she found that she was looking forward to the hours she spent with Harold Lange. "We have so much in common," she said. "We love our gardens, we enjoy classical and religious music, we both enjoy church. Mostly, though, we simply enjoy each other's company."

When it finally happened, it caught her by surprise. "He had driven me to an appointment I had with my doctor," she said. "He waited for me, and as we left we were driving through the parking lot, and he stopped the car. He pulled a ring out of his pocket, and he said it: 'Will you marry me?'

"I looked at him and I handed him my hand, and that was how I said yes."

So the other afternoon, in front of almost five hundred guests, including more than three hundred fellow residents from the Holmstad retirement community, Olive Johnson became the bride of Harold Lange.

"I feel like a young kid," she said. "I feel like years have dropped away. I feel like I'm on Cloud Nine."

She said she is realistic about the future: "I know there's no guarantee of how long we'll have each other. But we'll love each other and enjoy each other as long as we can. I hope that we can give each other some years of happiness. I'm so grateful that there will be no more lonely nights."

As I said it, it's not headline news. The new Mr. and Mrs. Lange will be living in his apartment; she is moving out of her studio and into his home. That will happen in a few weeks, though; right now they are on their honeymoon. They are driving through Wisconsin and Canada to see the leaves turn colors.

"That's something I always wanted to do," the new Mrs. Lange said. "I always wanted to get a chance to go north and see the colors of autumn, to see the leaves turn.

"But I never did it, because I didn't want to take a trip like that by myself. I never felt that I cared to do it alone. Well, I'm not alone now, and I'm going to see the colors."

Platinum Card

He had an embarrassed, furtive sound to his voice. He said he had a confession to make.

"I got the American Express Platinum Card," he said. He was referring to the new credit cards that are sold for $250 a year to the top echelon of American Express's charge-card customers.

"You really have one?" I said.

"You can't use my name," he hurriedly said. "I'm a funeral director, and it wouldn't look good for the families around here to think that I'm spending their hard-earned money on something like the Platinum Card."

I asked him to tell me the whole story. Start at the beginning, I said.

"Well, first I just had the regular American Express green card," he said. "I thought that was a pretty good card to have. Then we were at lunch at Kon-Tiki Ports, and the bill came. I gave the waiter my card. He came back and said, 'I'm sorry, but it's going to be a while. There's a problem with the phone lines, and we have to wait to get verification on your card.'

"My friend who was with me whipped out his Gold Card. He said, 'Will we have to wait with this?' The waiter said, 'No, sir! Right away!'

"They said sir to him. They never said sir to me. I thought, 'Phooey on this. I need a Gold Card!'"

So he applied for one and he got it. American Express's regular green cards cost $35 a year; the Gold Cards cost $65 a year. But he figured it was worth it.

Then, earlier this year, he looked at an American Express imprinting machine in a restaurant. There were decals on it showing the regular green card and the Gold Card. But there was a new decal, too: the Platinum Card.

"I asked the person at the restaurant about it," he said. "He told me that the Platinum Card costs $250 a year, and only the very elite of American Express's customers could get one.

"I had to do it. I called American Express and asked how I could get a Platinum Card. The person on the phone was very snotty about it. The person said, '*We* will determine who receives a Platinum Card. You cannot *apply* for it. You must be *invited.*' Very aloof.

"Part of me realized that there is something very warped about a society that tells you that you can pay $250 for a charge card that has a different color to it than your regular charge card—and you actually want the $250 card anyway.

"But each day I looked in my mail for an invitation. It didn't come and it didn't come. I felt brokenhearted. I wasn't good enough for the Platinum Card. I wondered what I had done to get American Express mad at me.

"Each day I woke up and thought, 'Maybe this is the day.' Each day passed, and I wasn't one of the chosen people.

"But then it happened. In October, it came. The envelope was like parchment. There were platinum lines all over it. It made me feel like someone was asking me to marry their daughter.

"I opened it up. It was an invitation to obtain a Platinum Card. Not an application—an invitation.

"I sent my check for $250 in. When the card came, it was in an envelope from Fort Lauderdale. This is no kidding—I took it in the bathroom to open it up. I didn't want anyone else around.

"Inside me, a little voice was saying: 'You're living a double standard.' I told the little voice to shut up.

"I had to use it right away. So I went down to a Toys-R-Us store to buy a video game cartridge for one of my kids. Very casually, I handed my new Platinum Card to the girl behind the counter.

"All she said is, 'I'm new here, I've never done an American Express card before. I have to get the manager.' The manager came up and he just processed the card. No big reaction. No bells ringing. People were standing behind me in line—no reaction from them, either. I felt like I wanted to cry. I had just laid a Platinum Card on them—and nothing.

"I went home and walked in the house with a big smile on my face. I said to my wife, 'Guess what I got?' I whipped out my Platinum Card. She said, 'That's nice, dear.' I said, 'No, honey, you don't understand. This is a *Platinum Card.*' She said, 'Yes, honey. An American Express Card.'"

He said it was all downhill from there. So far, there has been virtually no reaction to the Platinum Card he spent $250 for. Once he took a friend to lunch, and when he paid for it with his Platinum Card, he thought he noticed the two men at the next table looking over and smiling.

"But after lunch I kept asking myself: Were they smiling or were they smirking? Did they think I was one of life's special few for having a Platinum Card? Or did they think I was a jerk for putting out $250 for a credit card?"

In his dark moments, he has had a troubling thought: "I see them sitting around in the American Express boardroom, and suddenly one of the big corporate bosses says: 'I need a new pool in my back yard. Let's color some of our cards platinum and see if we can get some suckers to pay $250 for them.'"

He said that every time he pulls out his Platinum Card now, he's not sure how he should feel. "It doesn't exactly give you a warm feeling, like sex or a hot toddy," he said. "But there's a definite twinge you feel in your ego."

So what was the final answer, I asked. Did his Platinum Card make him feel like a special person or like a sucker?

"I feel like a special type of sucker," he said.

Where Have You Gone, Dick and Jane?

There are dozens of theories about why children today don't read with the same fervor as earlier generations of children. Television gets the blame, and family structure gets the blame, and a lack of discipline throughout society gets the blame.

There's another possibility, though. When you look at the way we learned to read in the Thirties, Forties, Fifties, and Sixties, and you compare it with the way children are learning to read today, one glaring difference makes itself evident:

The Dick and Jane books have gone out of print.

The Dick and Jane books were published by Scott, Foresman and Company; they were a series of preprimers and primers, used in the lower grades of elementary school. For millions upon millions of us, the first words we ever read by ourselves were contained in the Dick and Jane books.

The scene repeated itself in classrooms all over America. The first-grade teacher would call us to the front of the room, where she had gathered a semicircle of chairs around a huge stand-up version of the first preprimer: *We Look and See*. She would open the book; there, beneath a brightly colored picture, was the first word we were to be taught: "Look."

There were only seventeen words in the version of *We Look and See* that was used in schools in the Fifties: *look, oh, Jane, see, Dick, funny, Sally, Puff, jump, run, Spot, come, Tim, up, and, go,* and *down*. Those seventeen words, though, were enough to start us on a lifetime of reading pleasure.

Even back then, every time we would read a new story in *We Look and See* and a brand-new word would be introduced, it would feel like a minor electrical jolt. We had never seen the word "jump" before; we turned a page, and it entered our lives, and by the end of the day it would be a part of our reading vocabulary forever. At the time we might not have realized how important that was—but we knew it was essential enough to talk about excitedly at the dinner table that night.

In addition to *We Look and See,* the other preprimers were *We Work and Play* and *We Come and Go.* When we had mastered those, we were ready for our first genuine reader: *Fun with Dick and Jane.*

None are available for use in schools in the Eighties.

Of the authors whose bylines appeared in the Dick and Jane books that were in use in the Fifties, only one is alive today. He is A. Sterl Artley, seventy-seven; he lives in Columbia, Missouri.

When asked if he realized that, in a way, he was the most influential author in the lives of uncounted millions of American men and women—being, as he was, the first author in their lives—Artley laughed it off.

"I've never really thought of myself as being influential in any way," he said. "We tried to do an honorable job of devising a reading program that would teach children the first words they would ever know. We were very serious about our work, but influential? We didn't think in those terms."

Artley was part of a team of educators who worked on the Dick and Jane books. "The method was solid," he said. "That's what you should remember. The method was built around word identification and word perception. The vocabulary was carefully controlled in the stories. Only one new word was allowed to be introduced per page. And once a word had been introduced, it had to be repeated a certain number of times. There was never a word introduced that was 'lost'; once it was a part of the text, it remained a part of the text.

"With Dick, Jane, and Sally, we knew we had something

very, very special. We knew that, as simple as the books seemed, what we were doing would reflect on how generations of American children would learn to read. And I can't imagine too many things that are more basic to a culture than that."

Artley said that, in his mind, Dick, Jane, and Sally had distinctive personalities, each clearly defined:

"Dick was sort of the hero of the family. He was the one whom the children followed. He set the pace for all of their activities. The leader of the gang.

"Jane was the typical American girl. She never got dirty—but then, I guess none of the children in the books ever got dirty. Jane was very school oriented. She wasn't quite so much a leader as Dick. I guess you'd say she was a mother in miniature.

"Sally was sort of the tagalong. She was the baby of the group. She was a lovable little youngster; in today's terms, you would say that she was very sensitive. She tended to emulate Dick."

Although the very mention of the Dick and Jane books brings a rush of warm nostalgia to today's older generations of Americans, Artley said that there was some vocal criticism of the books' methods back when they were being used.

"We were attacked for using so much repetition," he said. "Some educators said that children just didn't talk that way in real life—'Run, Sally, run,' and 'Jump, Dick, jump.' We tried to explain: the teachers were instructed to 'read' the pictures first—they were supposed to explain to the class what was going on in the pictures. Then they were supposed to read the words aloud—the words were the words of Dick, Jane, and Sally, going along with what they were doing in the pictures. It was very natural."

Artley said that, by design of the team of authors, the behavior of Dick, Jane, and Sally was always exemplary. "They never fought. They never got into real trouble of any kind; they were models of good behavior. This was a conscious decision on our part. We knew that the books were going to be a part of the curricula of so many millions of children; we wanted to portray a behavior pattern that would deserve the approval of the parents.

"Because of that, Dick, Jane, and Sally became role models for American children. Teachers and parents would say to children: 'Would Dick have done that? Would Jane have done that? Let's do what Dick and Jane would have done.'

"So in a way, I suppose, we did more than teach children how to read. We helped set a cultural pattern for the times. You could probably say that we helped create several American generations of Dicks, Janes, and Sallys."

The last surviving editor who was in charge of the Dick and Jane books is Lee Horton, eighty-two, who now lives in Wilmette, Illinois.

"The popularity of the Dick and Jane books peaked in the mid-Fifties," Miss Horton said. "I think we had eighty-five percent of the market then.

"People wondered what our secret was. It wasn't really that complicated. First, the Dick and Jane books told a real story. Every story, no matter how short, had a beginning, a middle, and an end. The story may have been as simple as Dick and Jane playing, and Sally gets hold of a wagon, and the wagon rolls down the sidewalk. But even in a story that elementary, the children who are reading it retain interest because there is some suspense; they know that something is going to happen, and they want to find out what it is.

"The second thing was that we took a position on the educational argument over phonics. The big question was, do you teach children sounds—phonics—or do you start with meaningful language? The Dick and Jane books started with meaningful language, and I think time has shown that we made the right decision."

Miss Horton said that the first Dick and Jane books were published in the Thirties; the last revised editions were published in 1965, and by the early Seventies virtually all of the books were out of print.

"With all the revisions, some things never changed," she said. " 'Look' was always the first word the children learned, for example. People may laugh at that, but I'll tell you something: studies used to be taken among college English students, in which they were asked to name the characters they best remembered from all the literature to which they had been exposed. And Dick, Jane, and Sally ended up on every list.

"You should have seen the response from children back in the heyday. I would get literally thousands of letters a year from children writing to Dick, Jane, and Sally. The letters were piled up in my office in boxes. I must have had a thousand letters just asking one question: What was Dick and Jane's last name? We never answered that. What would you choose? An Irish name? A Polish name? An Italian name? We didn't want to say.

"Why did the books go out of print? By the Seventies our culture had changed. Dick and Jane were based on the structure of the family as it existed in the Twenties. There was a father, and a mother, and two or more children, and pets. The mother kept house and the father worked.

"That was fine, but then the American family began to break up. There was a lot of divorce. We had pressure groups telling us that we had to show the mother going to work, and the father staying home to take care of Dick and Jane. We were told that the other way was a bad stereotype and we had to get rid of it.

"Then there were the other pressure groups demanding that we make the Dick and Jane stories multiethnic. They had a good point; near the end of the series we had a character named Mike and his twin sisters move in next door to Dick and Jane. The new family was black. I was told by our Southern office that we'd never sell another copy south of the Mason-Dixon line, although we did, of course.

"But things were getting so complicated . . . even I had to admit that Dick and Jane no longer really represented the culture. People just did not all live in houses with white picket fences and two children and the mother staying home and the father going to work anymore.

"I suppose everything has to change. But I see these poor little youngsters today, stretching their necks so they can see a computer screen that gives them no human response. . . . I have to say, I miss Dick and Jane."

It is not widely recalled, but Dick and Jane had competition.

"Some school systems used books other than the Dick and Jane books," said Darrel Peterson, now seventy-three, who used to be a top Scott, Foresman salesman and rose to become chairman of the board before retiring in 1976.

"I remember one of our competitors had a series of Alice and Jerry books. And when I was out on the road, my job was to persuade the schools that Dick and Jane were superior to Alice and Jerry. Dick and Jane won out; we had more of the reading business than all of our competitors put together."

At Scott, Foresman today, the editorial vice president for reading is Roxane McLean, forty-three.

"Dick and Jane just kind of came to an end," she said. "The sales started falling off in the 1960s. By 1970 we had started a new reading program that contained no mention of Dick and Jane at all.

"The women's groups and civil rights groups that started campaigning against Dick and Jane were pretty fervent. They made the argument that Dick and Jane represented a middle-class white American disposition that just didn't speak for the country anymore. They said that Dick and Jane ought to be replaced because they were no longer effective.

"So we replaced them. We still get requests from school systems, asking us to ship them Dick and Jane books. They can't get them, though, because they don't exist. When they place those orders they get a computerized form saying 'Out of print.'

"Would we ever bring Dick and Jane back as they were? I have to say no. It's just not going to happen.

"But I'll tell you . . . I can still remember sitting in my first-grade classroom and learning to read from the Dick and Jane books. I loved those books. I learned a love for reading back then, and I still have that love for reading today. So when people talk about whether Dick and Jane did their job or not . . . well, I think there are a lot of us out here who are living proof that they did just fine."

The Strange Case of the Beatles' Bedsheets

When the Beatles first came to America twenty years ago, it seemed that everything they touched turned to gold.

But that wasn't quite true. There was the strange case of the Beatles' bedsheets. Now the story can be told.

When the Beatles made their first concert tour of America in 1964, two enterprising young directors at WBKB television in Chicago sat down and tried to figure out a way to cash in on the hysteria the group was causing. The men were Richy Victor and Larry Einhorn.

They hit on what they thought was a perfect scheme. They would contact the managers of several of the hotels where the group was staying, and arrange to purchase the bedsheets and pillowcases slept on by the Beatles. Then they would cut the bed linens up into one-inch-square pieces and sell them for a dollar each.

"We thought it was a magnificent idea," Victor recalls now. "Can you imagine anything more exciting for a young fan than an actual sheet that was slept on by an actual Beatle?"

So when the Beatles arrived in Detroit, and then in Kansas City, for performances, Victor and Einhorn called the managers of Detroit's Whittier Hotel and Kansas City's Muehlebach Hotel. The men made cash offers. They would pay $400 for the Beatles' bed linens at the Whittier, and $750 for the Beatles' bed linens at the Muehlebach. [The group spent two nights at the Muehlebach, Victor said. Hence, two sets of sheets; hence, a bigger price.]

"The managers accepted our offers," Victor said. "We told 'em to plug the rooms up as soon as the Beatles left. Seal 'em up like a murder scene."

Victor and Einhorn went to the hotels with lawyers and witnesses. They procured signed affidavits vowing that the Beatles had, indeed, slept on those very sheets.

Then they cut the sheets up and mounted the one-inch swatches on copies of letters from the managers of the hotels. The letter from the manager of the Whittier began:

> To whom it may concern: This is to certify that the "Beatles" stayed at the Whittier Hotel, arriving at 1:17 A.M. Sept. 6, 1964 [Detroit Time], occupying Executive Suite No. 1566, checking out at 2:05 P.M. Sept. 6, 1964. This is also to certify that the bed linen so designated is authentic and factual as to each of the "Beatles" using same.

And underneath the manager's signature was a small piece of bedsheet or pillowcase. Next to each piece of linen was a notation: either "John Slept Here" or "Paul Slept Here" or "George Slept Here" or "Ringo Slept Here."

"Actually, that part was not quite truthful," Victor said. "We had no idea which of the Beatles slept on which sheets. We were just given bags full of sheets. We had to guess who slept on which sheets. For all we know, all four of them slept in the same bed with four girls."

National news outlets picked up the story of the two entrepreneurs who were selling the Beatles' bedsheets. Victor and Einhorn thought they were going to become rich. They figured out that they could cut 164,000 little squares out of the sheets and pillowcases they had purchased. They could almost feel the $164,000 in their pockets.

Then two things happened.

The first was that no one bought the pieces of the Beatles' sheets.

"Don't ask me why," Victor said. "I've never understood it. I think it was because people thought we were phonies. There was so much Beatle junk being sold those days—the drugstores were full of it. I don't think anyone really believed that we had bought the Beatles' actual bedsheets."

The second thing that happened to Victor and Einhorn was that they received a letter from a New York attorney named Walter Hofer. Hofer's letter said:

Gentlemen: Please be advised that this office represents the interests of Paul McCartney, George Harrison, Ringo Starr, John Lennon, individually and collectively known as the Beatles.

It has come to our clients' attention that you are advertising and offering for sale certain linens allegedly used by the Beatles; and in connection therewith using the name of our clients. We are advised that you have not received authority or permission from the Beatles in connection with same.

Your activities in this connection are causing great damage to our clients, and unless you immediately cease and desist this improper and unauthorized activity, we shall have no alternative but to proceed in accordance with our clients' instructions.

So on the one hand Victor and Einhorn had 164,000 pieces of Beatle bedsheets that no one believed were real, and no one wanted to buy; and on the other hand they had the Beatles' attorney threatening to sue them.

"I think we sold between 700 and 800 of the pieces of sheets," Victor said. "We lost money. We didn't even get back what we paid for the sheets."

And now twenty years have passed. Victor dropped by the other day. He gave me four pieces of Beatle bedsheets.

"Richy," I said to him, "after I write about this, and people start wanting to contact you so they can get pieces of the Beatles' bedsheets, what should I tell them?"

"No one's going to call you," Victor said. "You know how many calls you'll get? Zilch.

"There has been publicity about this over the years. Nobody ever wants the sheets. Walter Cronkite mentioned the sheets when they first came out. The only response we got was from Walter Cronkite himself. He said he wanted a piece of the sheets for his kid."

I asked Victor how many pieces of the Beatles' sheets he had left.

"Bags and bags of them," he said. "I keep them in shopping bags. They're going to be with me for the rest of my life."

Off the Wagon

I dimmed the lights.

I put on my best suit. I placed an album of classical music on the stereo. I lit a candle and set it upon the table.

I brought out a crystal goblet and filled it with ice.

And then I did it—I poured a Coca-Cola into the goblet.

My hands were shaking. I reached for the goblet. For a moment I hesitated; did I have the guts to really do it? Something inside was telling me no, but my heart was telling me yes.

It has been a year. One entire, agonizing year.

One year ago I went on a diet. In a relatively brief time, I lost twenty-two pounds. I did this by drastically reducing the number of calories I consumed each day.

Surveys say that for every hundred pounds that Americans lose, they regain ninety of them within a calendar year. That hasn't happened with me; the twenty-two pounds have stayed off. And one of the most dramatic reasons is that, exactly one year ago, I gave up Cokes.

This may seem like a simple thing to you; logical, even. Coca-Cola is laden with wasteful calories; diet colas contain only one calorie per serving.

But I was a Coke addict. Had been for most of my life.

From the time I was six years old, I drank—on the average—three bottles of Coke a day. Back in 1975, during a slow period, I sat down and figured out how much Coke I had swallowed up to that point in my life. It came out to 4,893 quarts—the equivalent of 9,786 pounds.

Clearly, if I was going to lose weight, I would have to give up Coke. Which was like asking Buddy ("Nature Boy") Rogers to give up wrestling.

But I did it. The major problem was learning how to request a substitute. Every time I asked for "one Tab" I felt like a stewardess. Nevertheless, I persevered; for twelve long months I did without Coke, and the twenty-two pounds stayed off.

And now it was my anniversary: one year from the day I had last tasted a Coke.

As a reward to myself, I vowed that I would have one. Just one; one couldn't do that much damage, and I felt I was entitled. For old times' sake.

So there I was, in a darkened room with a candle glowing and violins playing on the turntable.

I reached for the goblet. I lifted it to my lips. I tilted it toward me. And the Coke coursed down my throat.

My body shivered and shook. It was as if someone had plunged an intravenous tube into my arm and shot me full of some rich medicine. The sensation was almost too much to bear. My teeth even hurt.

I had expected to be disappointed; I had expected that either the Coke would taste exactly like Tab, or—on the other end of the spectrum—that it would taste so syrupy and sugary that I would ask myself what I had ever seen in it in the first place.

Oh, I was so wrong. It was nectar from the gods, that's what it was; it was the most divine liquid that has ever flowed among us.

In that instant—the instant I swallowed my first mouthful of Coke in a year—the entire previous 365 days disappeared. It was as if I had never lived them. Instead, with the taste of the Coke still on my tongue, my mind was filled with memories:

Coming home from elementary school in the Fifties, rushing into the kitchen, ripping open a bag of potato chips, and then going into the refrigerator and pouring a Coke into a jelly glass with Howdy Doody's picture painted on it.

Cruising by the lake at dusk on summer nights in the Sixties, the radio playing, a cold 6½-ounce bottle of Coke in my left hand, the glass of the bottle clinking against the metal of my high school class ring.

Staying up all night to study for college finals, sitting at long tables in the basement of the fraternity house, friends on all sides, the TV playing in the background, a Coke from the vending machine resting on the Formica next to my books.

The feeling was so intense—and I had finished only one gulp of the Coke.

I took a few more tentative sips. I knew I must stop before this went too far. No wonder that addicts instinctively know that they must never, never go back to the fruit of their addiction, no matter how great the temptation; the aftertaste of the Coke in my throat [so much more real than the aftertaste of Tab, never mind Diet Rite!] warned me that if this continued, I might never be the same man again.

I stood up and walked around the room. I held the goblet of Coke in front of me, pausing every few minutes to look down at its undulating surface, the ice cubes protruding like so many miniature glaciers. It was as moving and as beautiful a sight as I have ever experienced.

But I knew what I had to do. Feeling the moisture coming to my eyes, I walked to the kitchen, leaned over the sink and—before I had time to stop myself—poured the remainder of the Coke down the drain. I could hear it gurgling away.

In a moment it was gone. I let out a deep breath. It had been a long year, and the future stretched drearily out ahead. I turned the lights up to full brightness and blew out the candle. Welcome back to the brave new world. One Tab, please.

Farewell to Hef's Pad

You've probably heard: the Playboy Mansion in Chicago is going to be turned into a dormitory for art students. The Playboy Mansion—a seventy-two-room, four-story house on the city's Near North Side—has sat virtually vacant since the mid-1970s, when its principal inhabitant, Hugh Hefner, moved to Holmby Hills, California, and purchased an estate that he began calling the Playboy Mansion West.

Apparently Hefner liked life in California; the West Coast mansion featured outdoor fish ponds and meandering wildlife and tennis courts and hiking paths, providing the owner with a fresh-air atmosphere he had never known before. After settling in at his Playboy Mansion West, he never really returned to the original Playboy Mansion, at least not on a permanent basis. Night after night the huge Chicago house at 1340 North State Parkway would sit with its lights darkened.

And last summer the official announcement was made: Playboy Enterprises Inc. would donate the original Playboy Mansion to the School of the Art Institute of Chicago. Beginning next January, approximately fifty Art Institute students will use the mansion as a dormitory. Playboy will eventually receive tax credits as a result of the donation. From here on in, it was announced, the building will be known as Hefner Hall.

I know I'm not the only one; I know, in fact, that I am merely one man among millions.

I grew up sneaking copies of *Playboy* out of my father's shirt drawer, where each month the magazine was hidden beneath a pile of white shirts with the expectation that the children would not be able to find it. *Playboy,* at the time, was considered racy almost to the point of sinfulness; it was not displayed out on the magazine racks along with *Time* and *Newsweek,* the way it is today, and responsible parents most certainly did not just leave it lying around the house.

There were a lot of fantasies in that magazine every month, starting with the beautiful women. But the fantasy that hit me the hardest was a more basic one. I may have been just a naive, skinny teenager in central Ohio, but I knew what I wanted. All I wanted to do was move to Chicago and be Hugh Hefner's friend so that I could be invited to—as it was called in the magazine—Hef's Pad.

Hef's Pad was the Playboy Mansion, of course, and I do not think any single edifice has ever been more successfully promoted in the pages of a magazine or newspaper. I had never been there, obviously; I was a kid, and I had never even been to Chicago. But I had seen it and read about it so often in the magazine, I knew the Playboy Mansion as well as I knew the homes of some of my closest uncles and aunts.

There was the brass plaque welcoming visitors, inscribed in Latin: SI NON OSCILLAS, NOLI TINTINNARE ("If you don't swing, don't ring"). There was the massive living room, decorated with suits of armor and LeRoy Neiman paintings, where all of Hef's friends were always dancing the Watusi—the men wearing expensive Italian-cut suits, the women wearing cocktail dresses or bikinis. In the magazine, everyone at Hef's Pad was always smiling and having the time of their lives.

A typical article from the magazine in the 1960s summarizes the atmosphere at one of the parties at Hef's Pad; this is the vision we Midwestern lads were being served up:

> No phase of the good life at the Mansion matches in reputation the far-flung fame of Hefner's legendary parties— Gatsbyesque whee-for-alls in the grand manor (and the grand manner) that leave the launching pad at midnight and orbit until dawn, with a passenger list of four hundred or five hundred revelers aboard. No sooner will you enter the main room—arriving at a fashionable three or four, when the revelry has reached its apogee—than you'll find yourself swept up in the heady atmosphere that prevails at these sumptuously swinging galas, and greeted by a phantasmagoria of sight and sound: crimson-liveried housemen threading their way through the throngs bearing trays of hot and cold canapés, mixed drinks, and champagne; the throbbing go-go beat of the combo in the corner, where Sal Mineo's sitting in on drums tonight; June "The Bosom" Wilkinson, in a skintight sheath, frugging up a storm in the middle of the dance floor; Hugh O'Brian chatting over cocktails with an elegantly gowned Chicago socialite just arrived from an evening at the opera; bikinied beauties still dewy from a dip in the pool, checking out the action in the ballroom. . . .

That was just the beginning, though. There was the pool itself, down in the basement, with a hidden cranny where Hefner's lust-crazed pals liked to take their dates. The cranny was called the Woo Grotto, and all of those devilish bachelors thought they were guaranteed total privacy when they swam into it. But were they in for a surprise! Hef and his other gag-loving friends had a secret trapdoor above the Woo Grotto, in the living room, that they could open and spy on the unsuspecting couple below.

There was the game room, stocked with all of the latest pinball machines, pool tables, slot-racing courses, and the like. There was the underwater bar, built in a subbasement level, featuring a window revealing the depths of the pool. To reach this barroom you could either climb down some narrow, winding stairs—or slide down a fire pole that led directly into the midst of all the revelry.

And of course there was Hefner's bedroom, with the circular, motor-driven, rotating, vibrating bed. Here, we were told, Hefner worked as well as played, often never going outside the building for months at a time. The Bunny dormitory— where two dozen Bunnies from the Chicago Playboy Club lived and paid a nominal rent—was only steps away.

Cruising the streets of our hometowns, it seemed to many of us that all the fun in the world was being had at Hef's Pad. In later years many of us would question some of the values that went along with life inside the mansion, and question some of the messages that the magazine had been selling us; but if the truth be told, to a generation of boys whose nighttime horizons extended no further than softball diamonds and Dairy Queens and suburban recreation centers, the image of life at the Playboy Mansion seemed like Christmas morning every day.

It so happened that I did make it to Chicago and, eventually, to Hef's Pad. In 1973, working on a Sunday magazine story for the newspaper where I was employed, I talked Playboy into allowing me to live in the Playboy Mansion for a week.

Arriving for the assignment, I had an eerie feeling. I was giddy over the prospect of finally seeing the place I was so familiar with from the magazine. But once I got there, it struck me that there was nothing I hadn't already seen. There didn't seem to be a square foot of the place that hadn't been photographed and published repeatedly; everywhere I wandered, it felt like a movie set—this seemed like a scale model of the Playboy Mansion, not the real thing.

I was assigned to a bedroom called the Blue Room; it fronted on the mansion's ballroom, and shared a bathroom with the adjoining Red Room. It turned out that the Red Room was occupied by a young woman who had come to town for her Playmate of the Month photo session; we had to work out a series of knocks to let each other know who was using the bathroom, and she seemed as unnerved and daunted by the mansion as I was.

Hefner himself was on the premises. Invariably clad in pajamas and velvet slippers that bore his initials, he would play Monopoly all night with a group of his friends. He had compiled a handwritten list of all the properties on the Monopoly board—which ones were the most potentially profitable, which were a waste of money. There was a stereo nearby; Hefner had a mammoth supply of albums to choose from, but he kept playing the same two over and over: a collection of old ballads by Harry Nilsson and another collection of old ballads by Peggy Lee. The two records would play, they would click off, and Hefner would start them over again. If the repetition was bothering his friends, they didn't say anything. When I turned in for the night, Hefner would be sitting at the Monopoly board and singing along with Nilsson: "Maybe I'm right and maybe I'm wrong . . ." When I would wake up the next morning and leave my room for breakfast, Hefner would still be there, still singing along: "Maybe I'm right and maybe I'm wrong . . ."

But this story isn't supposed to be about the reality of what I found at the Playboy Mansion; this is supposed to be about the fantasy of that mansion held by earlier generations of American teenaged boys, and the fact that the fantasy is now officially past tense.

A few days after it was announced that the Playboy Mansion would be turned into the art students' dorm, I went over to take one last look. Already the transformation into Hefner

Hall had begun; young men wearing green-and-white T-shirts bearing the legend THE ART INSTITUTE OF CHICAGO were trimming the shrubbery in front.

I was met at the front door by Eileen Harakal, a member of the Art Institute's administration, who was going to show me around. Since she really wasn't yet familiar with the building, she had enlisted the help of Marv Meadors, sixty-four, the Playboy Mansion's longtime chief engineer and handyman.

Meadors looked a little sad. We entered the building; the "If you don't swing, don't ring" plaque had already been taken down. The furniture looked pretty much the way it had in all those magazine layouts past, but everything had red or green inventory tags attached in preparation for removal.

We walked past the swimming pool. I asked Eileen Harakal if the Art Institute planned on keeping it.

"We just don't know," she said. "We have to look into the insurance requirements. The safety of the students has to be foremost in our minds."

Marv Meadors had a wistful expression on his face.

We moved on past the famous fire pole that led down to the underwater bar. I could almost close my eyes and see all those color magazine photos with happy men and women hoisting cocktails and sliding down the pole to join their friends.

"This definitely gets taken out," Harakal said. "We'll take the pole out and cover up the opening. What possible function could it serve for the students? There is a real risk of broken legs. It will go."

Marv Meadors looked off in the other direction.

We went to Hefner's bedroom. In the middle of the white carpeting there was a circular impression where the bed had once been. It had been removed. All that remained were some electrical cables that had presumably been used to make it revolve and vibrate.

"This is a nice room," Harakal said. "I like the size of it. I think we will use it as a classroom, for programs that are open to the community."

Marv Meadors and I sneaked a brief glance at each other.

We passed through the mansion's living room.

"Marv," I said, "will you do one thing?"

"What's that?" Meadors said.

"Will you open up the trapdoor so that we can look down into the Woo Grotto?"

A soft smile crossed Meadors's face. He went to the wall, found a hidden button, and pressed it. Slowly, a square piece of the floor began to lift up; as it did so a stereo tape player was automatically activated, and from down below romantic music wafted up.

We peered down. There was the Woo Grotto, all right: a secluded little corner of the pool hidden behind a man-made cave, where no one could see what was going on—save for the people up here in the living room.

"Well," said Eileen Harakal, "this is a surprise. I can guarantee you that this will be sealed up. That's all we need, a student bumping into the button by mistake and falling into that hole in the floor."

I don't know what Marv Meadors was doing right then; I was gazing off somewhere in the distance, and I didn't see him.

So Long, Davies

Nothing is as good as running a college news-. paper. No matter how much luck you have later on, in the real world, it can never top the feeling you have on your college campus when, for the first time, you are part of a daily newspaper, and it belongs to no one but you and your friends, and whatever successes or failures it achieves are yours and yours alone.

Later on the pleasures and the pains will be diluted; when you work for a large organization there are plenty of people to share your triumphs and your mistakes. The process of putting out the paper becomes institutionalized; it is safer, but it is also less personal.

Five of us put out the *Daily Northwestern* in 1968 and 1969. There were many more on the staff, of course, but we were the seniors; it was our year. John Walter was the editor; Steve Sink, Bill Harsh, Tom Davies, and I were the other editors. Davies and I wrote columns.

It was pretty heady stuff for both of us. We would walk around campus and people we had never met before would stop us—they would recognize us from the pictures in our column logos—and they would tell us what they thought of that day's story. The first few times that happens to you you think you are in heaven.

Davies and I had a friendly rivalry; I would try to get fancier in my column than he would in his, and I would come into the newsroom to hear him telling the rest of the staff, "That Greene has no idea how to write a *news* story." Our columns alternated. We were constantly trying to outdo each other.

One day Davies had a pretty good column, and through a mistake at the printing shop, my logo appeared above it. I was upset about it until, that evening, a co-ed stopped me in the library and told me how much she had liked it. I didn't correct her; as I recall, Davies was not amused the next day.

The five of us who put out the *Daily* thought we were all going to be world beaters; we had marvelous plans for ourselves. Davies considered himself to have a leg up on the rest of us because he was a stringer for the *New York Times;* he hoped to convert that into a full-time job.

But something happened. Right after graduation Davies married Betty Jean Peters, a girl he had known since kindergarten. On their honeymoon in Fort Lauderdale he became violently ill. He thought it was the flu, or at worst bronchitis. They went back to their hometown of Toledo, Ohio. The doctors took tests. Davies had a deadly disease—systemic lupus erythematosus.

The doctors told the newlyweds: "You will not have a long life together. You will not grow old together." Gone were the plans to try to be a journalistic whiz kid. Davies and his wife settled down in Toledo, and he went to work for his home-town paper, the *Blade*. The editors of the *Blade* had known Davies since he was in high school. They hired him even knowing that he had the disease. He would often remark, later, that probably no other paper in the country would have been kind enough to offer him a chance at employment know-ing what they knew.

For the next eight years Davies wrote for the *Blade*. He was often in terrible pain; he was in and out of hospitals, and it was not uncommon for him to miss sixty, seventy, eighty days of work a year. He became depressed; he was afraid that the other reporters and editors would think he was taking advantage of the newspaper.

The rest of us from the college paper went out and traveled the country and the world and did the best we could. Davies, meanwhile, eventually went off the full-time staff at the *Blade;* he had to spend more and more time in bed, so he worked on a part-time basis at home. When he would go out to conduct an interview, sometimes the strain would be so great on him that it would put him back in bed for another three or four days after the story was completed.

He never got tired of seeing his name in print, though; when the paper boy delivered the *Blade* to his house, he would rip it open to his stories. It still meant something to him, to see his work in a newspaper.

The rest of us were a little awkward whenever we talked to him; we knew the troubles he was having, and we could never find the right words to express what we were thinking. In 1979 we had our tenth *Daily Northwestern* reunion in Chi-cago. Davies seemed to be in good spirits at dinner, but he was drinking heavily. Near the end of the meal he called me aside.

"Greene, I'm a dead man," he said. "I won't be at the next reunion."

I knew he wasn't kidding, and he wasn't. Tom Davies died the other day; he was only thirty-five years old.

"He loved to follow what the rest of you were doing with your lives," Betty Jean Davies told me. "He knew that it wasn't destined to happen with him, so he took great pride in what the rest of you accomplished.

"You, though, Bob . . ." she said. She laughed. "Sometimes he would see something you had written, and he would hold it up in the air and say, 'That boy *still* can't write a news story.'"

Toward the end, she said, Davies sometimes talked about a fantasy he had. "He would say that he was thinking what it would be like if you guys all bought your own newspaper somewhere," she said. "What it would be like if you got to put out your own paper together again. Those days turned out to be the best of his life."

She did a very nice thing for his funeral. She found an old feature story he had written, and she had the reverend read it aloud during the funeral services. It was a funny story; everyone in the congregation laughed. Ah, Davies, those days were pretty good for the rest of us, too.

Icebreaker

A weary, road-battered traveler—Mr. Greene himself—pulled into Cleveland at the end of a long evening. I decided that it might be a nice idea to have one quick drink before bed.

A bar called the Shalamar looked inviting. I prepared to

enter, when a perky young woman seated at a table next to the front door said, "Which initials would you like?"

"Huh?" I said.

"Which initials?" she repeated.

I decided it was best to ignore her. "I don't want initials," I said. "I just want a drink." I walked into the bar.

It didn't take a genius to see that something unusual was going on. Oh, the bar was typical enough in most respects— tables, muted lighting, music from a live band whose members wore red Vegas-style jackets.

But the customers . . . they all had big initials pinned to their chests.

There was a woman marked "A.N." A man marked "J.B." Another woman marked "L.T." Another man marked "T.Z." All around the room, the people wore the letters.

I selected the last available table in the bar and looked for a waitress. As I peered around the room, I noticed that everyone else's eyes seemed to be focused on an area just above the bandstand, near the ceiling.

What they were looking at was a computerized screen—a long screen that featured messages trailing across it, kind of like the weather bulletins the television stations sometimes feature at the bottom of the TV screen during a show.

I read the messages:

FROM T.G. [MALE] TO B.B. [FEMALE]—LET ME TAKE YOU AWAY FROM THIS AND GET CRAAAAAZY! I'M SITTING UP ON THE LEDGE.

FROM L.L. [FEMALE] TO T.K. [MALE]—I LIKE THE WAY YOU LOOK IN THOSE JEANS. LET ME SEE THEM UP CLOSE ON THE DANCE FLOOR.

FROM T.T. [MALE] TO M.Z. [FEMALE]—ARE YOU ALL TALK AND NO ACTION? I GUESS THERE'S ONLY ONE WAY TO FIND OUT FOR SURE!

The messages moved across the screen, one after another. This was pretty bizarre; apparently all these men and women with the initials pinned to their chests were somehow sending the messages to one another.

I made a reconnaissance cruise around the room. Sure enough, at the different tables men and women were checking each other out through the smoky haze. They were writing down their thoughts about specific members of the opposite sex who wore specific initials.

I kept walking. At the far end of the room, I found a computer operator sitting at a keyboard. In front of the operator was a wooden box; the men and women in the bar were dropping their messages into a slot in the top of the box. Periodically the operator would empty the box, then punch the messages onto the keyboard. Soon, the messages would come flashing across the screen.

This was hard to believe. I had never seen this before. I had heard about the "personals" in newspapers—the classified ads designed to help the people who placed them find romance. And I knew, of course, that this was the computer/ video age.

But could this be happening? Could people really be coming to a bar, sizing up men and women across the room, then trying to seduce those men and women via this computerized, live "personals" setup?

I wandered, fascinated. The people seldom looked away from the screen. They all seemed to be looking for their own initials to come scooting across.

The man in charge of the bar was a fellow named Jim Gauss. He confirmed that this was, indeed, precisely what was going on.

"This is the fourth week we've been using this setup," Gauss said. "We're getting a very positive response from everyone. The word-of-mouth is great. People hear about it and come to try it."

He said that the customers are given the initials when they first arrive at the Shalamar. The initials are not necessarily the person's real initials; one can choose any combination. But once a set of initials is taken, that same set cannot be used by anyone else that night.

I asked Gauss why on earth anyone would do this—send

computerized messages to someone else who might be standing a mere five feet away.

"There are some individuals who are sort of shy," Gauss said. "Maybe they don't have the nerve to say something, or to ask someone to dance. With this system, they can do it on the computer. It makes it easier."

"So there's no fear of rejection?" I said.

"Oh, there's a lot of rejection," Gauss said. "You should see the people who send a message to someone they're attracted to; they wait for their message to be returned, and when it never is, you can see the reaction on their faces."

As the night grew later, the messages grew bolder. Gauss told me that the keyboard operator was instructed not to process messages that were too racy; but there seemed to be a definite correlation between the lateness of the hour, the consumption of alcohol, and the borderline lewdness of the messages that crawled along the screen.

There was probably a lesson here—about human nature, or the depersonalization of society, or the unspoken distance that still exists between men and women. Instead of thinking about that, though, I dropped a message into the wooden box next to the keyboard operator:

B.G. [MALE] IS CONFUSED. SEEKS SYMPATHETIC CHEESEBURGER. GRILLED ONIONS PREFERRED.

We all have our own definition of romance, and the road is long.

BOB GREENE is a syndicated columnist for the *Chicago Tribune;* his column appears in more than two hundred newspapers in the United States. He is a contributing editor of *Esquire* magazine, where his "American Beat" column appears each month. He is a contributing correspondent for "ABC News Nightline." He has written seven previous books.